Congratulations on 25 years of ordained ministry!

with respect,
Steven, Rhonda, Caleigh, and Matthew Huber

The Spirit Divided
Memoirs of Civil War Chaplains

THE UNION

Compiled and Edited by

Benedict R. Maryniak and John Wesley Brinsfield, Jr.

Mercer University Press, 2007

Endowed by
TOM WATSON BROWN
and
THE WATSON-BROWN FOUNDATION, INC.

© 2007 Mercer University Press
1400 Coleman Avenue
Macon, Georgia 31207
All rights reserved
MUP/H715

First Edition.

Books published by Mercer University Press are printed
on acid free paper that meets the requirements of American National Standard
for Information Sciences—Permanence of Paper for Printed Library Materials.

Library of Congress Cataloging-in-Publication Data

The spirit divided : memoirs of Civil War chaplains :the Union/compiled
and edited by Benedict R. Maryniak and John W. Brinsfield. — 1st ed.
p. cm.
Includes bibliographical references and index.
ISBN-13: 978-0-86554-996-8 (hardcover : alk. paper)
ISBN-10: 0-86554-996-6 (hardcover : alk. paper)
1. United States—History—Civil War, 1861–1865—Chaplains.
2. United States—History—Civil War, 1861–1865—Religious aspects.
3. United States. Army—Chaplains—History—19th century.
4. United States—History—Civil War, 1861–1865—Personal narratives.
5. United States. Army—Chaplains—Biography.
6. Military chaplains—United States—Biography.
I. Maryniak, Benedict R. II. Brinsfield, John Wesley.
E635.S685 2007   973.7'78—dc22
2007001906

Contents

Preface — ix
Acknowledgments — xi
Introduction: The Union Forever! — xii

Chapter 1. Reporting for Duty — 1
The Work of an Army Chaplain: Ordination
   of Chaplain Charles Humphreys,
   2nd Massachusetts Cavalry, at
   Harvard University's Divinity Hall.
"God's Honor—Man's Ultimate Success,"
   A Farewell Sermon by Rev. Moses Smith
   upon leaving Plainville, Connecticut, for the Army — 13
"Good-by for a Year," Chaplain George H. Hepworth,
   47th Massachusetts Volunteer Infantry — 26
"Religious Army Chaplains," Suggestions by
   Chaplain John E. Robie, 21st New York
   Volunteer Infantry — 28
"Hardships of a Chaplain's Life," The Massacre
   at Conrad's Ferry by Chaplain Gamaliel Collins,
   72nd Pennsylvania Volunteer Infantry — 34

Chapter 2. Ministry in the Camps — 37
"How a Camp is Arranged," Letter from
   Rev. Henry Rinker, 11th New Jersey Volunteer Infantry — 40
"Our First Camp," Letter from Chaplain
   Levi Norton, 72nd New York Volunteer Infantry — 43
Pocket Diary of Chaplain John Crabbs, 67th
   Ohio Volunteer Infantry in the Shenandoah Valley — 47

"Two Great Wars of America: Fourth of July Address,"
  Chaplain Horace James, 25th Massachusetts
  Volunteer Infantry   59
Letters of Chaplain Thomas K. Beecher,
  141st New York Volunteer Infantry.   75
Letters of Chaplain Peter Paul Cooney,
  Roman Catholic Chaplain of the 35th
  Indiana Volunteer Infantry   86
"Army Chaplains," Benjamin F. Taylor,
  Correspondent for the *Chicago Daily Journal*   93

Chapter 3. Ministry on Campaigns   98
"A Chaplain's Experience in the Union Army,"
  Chaplain Frederic Denison, 1st Rhode Island Cavalry   101
"A Soldier's Funeral," Chaplain Alonzo H. Quint,
  2nd Massachusetts Volunteer Infantry   122
"Fredericksburg," Chaplain John C. Gregg, 127th
  Pennsylvania Volunteer Infantry   126
Gettysburg. A Tribute to Chaplain William Corby,
  88th New York Infantry   134
"Chickamauga," Chaplain William W. Lyle, 11th
  Ohio Volunteer Infantry   138
From Shiloh to Atlanta. Memoirs of
  Chaplain Milton L. Haney, 55th Illinois
  Volunteer Infantry   145
"March of a Day," Letter from Chaplain Randall Ross,
  15th Ohio Volunteer Infantry   172
Petersburg and Appomattox. Letters from
  Rev. Henry Rinker, 11th New Jersey Volunteers, 1865   179

Chapter 4. Ministry in Prisons and Hospitals   182
"The Bright Side of Life in Libby Prison,"
  Chaplain Charles C. McCabe, 122nd Ohio
  Volunteer Infantry   185
"Inside the Stockade," Chaplain John S. McCulloch,
  77th Illinois Volunteer Infantry   204

Ministry at the U.S. Hospital, Hampton, Virginia. Chaplain Amos S. Billingsley, 101st Pennsylvania Volunteer Infantry	211
Chaplain Reports from Field and Hospital Death Notifications	219
"Disclosures of the Soldier's Heart," Chaplain Henry Clay Trumbull, 10th Connecticut Volunteer Infantry	233
Chapter 5. The Measure of Ministry	237
"Chaplains in the Volunteer Army," Chaplain James H. Bradford, 12th Connecticut Volunteer Infantry	240
Appendix: Biographical Anecdotes	251
Bibliography	257
Index	263

Preface

During the last two decades historians have just begun to recognize religion as an important facet of the Civil War. Because neither the Confederate nor the Union war departments had an office governing military chaplains, nearly 4,000 of them in both blue and gray were almost lost to future study. After many years of research, most of their names, assignments, and denominational affiliations have been recovered. This anthology is designed to preserve not only their names, but also their written memoirs.

In an organization created to destroy the enemy, chaplains ate, drank, and slept dissonance! Older than most soldiers and looking at battle with very different eyes, chaplains had their beliefs brutally tested at the same time they instilled a faith in God and country that sustained men through adversities and tragedies. This book is a collection of letters, reports, and recollections in which Army chaplains describe their motives and methods, their failures and achievements. Some threw away their somber black uniforms and became dashing staff officers who rode over battlefields to deliver orders, even capture enemy soldiers. Scorning these "chaplains militant," others were in the words of a battlefield journalist, "bearers of the cup of cold water and the word of good cheer—the strong regiment might be the colonel's, but the wounded brigade is the chaplain's."[1]

Chaplains were also, of course, human in every way. They wondered about God's purposes, and if their ministries—and the deaths of thousands—might be in vain. President Abraham Lincoln summarized some of the issues they pondered in his second Inaugural Address:

> On the occasion corresponding to this four years ago, all thoughts were anxiously directed to an impending civil war. All dreaded it—all sought to avert it. Both parties depreciated war, but one of them would make war rather than let the nation survive; and the other would accept war rather than let it perish. And the war came.

---

[1] Benjamin Franklin Taylor, *Mission Ridge and Lookout Mountain with Pictures of Life in Camp and Field* (New York: D, Appleton & Company, 1872) 123.

Neither party expected for the war, the magnitude, or the duration, which it has already attained. Each looked for an easier triumph, a result less fundamental and astounding. Both read the same Bible, and pray to the same God; each invokes His aid against the other.

The prayers of both could not be answered; that of neither has been answered fully. The Almighty has His own purposes. Fondly do we hope—fervently do we pray—that this mighty scourge of war may speedily pass away. Yet, if God wills that it continue, until all the wealth piled by the bond-man's two hundred and fifty years of unrequited toil shall be sunk, and until every drop of blood drawn with the lash, shall be paid by another drawn with the sword, as was said three thousand years ago, so still it must be said, "the judgments of the Lord, are true and righteous altogether."[2]

The Union chaplains saw God's Spirit powerfully at work in prayer meetings, in worship services, and in hospitals. Yet there were revivals on both sides of the contest. Was the Spirit divided, could God be punishing both North and South for the national sin of slavery as President Lincoln suggested, or was there some other explanation for this seemingly endless war?

The reflections of these men of the cloth, who were drawn from many denominations, have much to teach modern readers. They had to find, above all, the faith and perseverance to sustain the spirit of their people, their soldiers, during the greatest war ever fought on this continent.

These are their stories.

Benedict Maryniak, Lancaster, New York
John W. Brinsfield, Columbia, South Carolina

---

[2] Roy P. Basler, ed. *The Collected Works of Abraham Lincoln* (New Brunswick NJ: Rutgers University Press, 1953) 8: 332–33. The second inaugural occurred on 4 March 1865.

Acknowledgments

For more than a decade numerous organizations and individuals have contributed to the research required for this book. Some, such as the office staff at Forest Hill Cemetery in Chattanooga, Tennessee, helped locate graves of chaplains and the associated birth and death dates on the tombstones. Other organizations, such as the Military History Institute in Carlisle, Pennsylvania, furnished copies of numerous chaplain memoirs for reproduction and several photographic prints that were purchased without copyright restrictions. To all the libraries, archives, colleges, and historical societies listed in the notes and bibliography, I owe a debt of thanks.

Among the many individuals who helped with this effort were researchers and historians Phil Murphy of Mechanicsburg and Roger D. Hunt and Paul Kallina of Gettysburg, Pennsylvania; Sue Greenhagen, technical services librarian, Morrisville State College, New York, and town of Eaton, New York, historian who researched numerous catalogs and necrologies in seminaries and colleges; and National Archives staff members Michael P. Musick and DeAnne Blanton-Wolfe who helped me navigate through mountains of information. Karen L. Bellin, a graduate of Princeton, did excellent work in helping with the editing process.

To all who assisted, including my incredible spouse, Catherine, I am forever grateful.

Benedict R. Maryniak
Lancaster, New York

Introduction

The Union Forever!

"He hath sounded forth His trumpet..."
—Julia Ward Howe

On 18 January 1861, William T. Sherman, superintendent of Louisiana State Seminary of Learning and Military Academy, resigned his position as the chief officer of that institution.[3] In a letter to Louisiana governor Thomas O. Moore, Sherman wrote,

> Recent events foreshadow a great change, and it becomes all men to choose. If Louisiana withdraws from the Federal Union, I prefer to maintain my allegiance to the Constitution as long as a fragment of it survives; and my longer stay here would be wrong in every sense of the word. And furthermore, as President of the Board of Supervisors, I beg you to take immediate steps to relieve me as superintendent, the moment the State determines to secede, for on no earthly account will I do any act or think any thought hostile to or in defiance of the old Government of the United States.[4]

Sherman's reaction to the threat of secession was not based on his opposition to slavery, even though he thought slaves should have the status

---

[3] Now Louisiana State University.
[4] William T. Sherman, *Memoirs of General William T. Sherman* (New York: Da Capo Press, 1984) i, 156.

of human beings and should not be sold except as families.⁵ Sherman's concern was for the preservation of the Union as defined in the Constitution of the United States, the document he had supported for twenty years as a West Point cadet, an Army officer, and a private citizen. By the seizure of the US Arsenal at Baton Rouge on 10 January, the State of Louisiana had signaled a hostile rebellion against Federal authority. The secession of the state two weeks later confirmed it.

The Constitution of the United States, as Sherman knew it, was not ambiguous concerning insurrections. The Preamble stated that the signatory states formed a Union; and Article I, Section 10 further forbad states from entering into "any treaty, alliance, or confederation," from keeping "troops, or ships of war in time of peace," from entering into "any agreement or compact with another state, or with a foreign power," or engaging "in war, unless actually invaded."⁶ Congress, moreover, maintained the sole power to "dispose of and make all needful rules and regulations respecting the territory or other property belonging to the United States."⁷ In Article III, Section 3, treason was defined as levying war against the United States, "or in adhering to their enemies, giving them aid and comfort."⁸

By Federal law, therefore, the politicians of the South who had seized Federal property, armed their militia forces, and formed a rival government were already in rebellion against the Constitution. If this illegal combination of Southern state officials were to commit an act of war, they would also be traitors to the United States.

The theory that the Southerners advocated was the concept that the Union was a voluntary compact, and that states could leave the Union whenever grievances, real or imaginary, could no longer be satisfactorily addressed by Congress or by the other branches of the Federal government. Jefferson Davis, president of the Confederate States, and a former US senator, noted that if the South lost, the epitaph should read "died of a theory."⁹

---

⁵ Ibid., i, 149.

⁶ *The Declaration of Independence and the Constitution of the United States* with an introduction by Pauline Maier (New York: Bantam Books, 1998) 67.

⁷ Ibid., 74 in Article IV, Section 3.

⁸ Ibid., 72 in Article III, Section 3.

⁹ E. Merton Coulter, *The Confederate States of America* (Baton Rouge: Louisiana State University Press, 1950) 43–44.

In March 1861 the newly-inaugurated president, Abraham Lincoln, tried to forestall the outbreak of war while at the same time fulfilling his constitutional obligation to "take care that the Laws be faithfully executed."[10] Yet throughout the South the state governors were seizing US arsenals, arms, and ammunition. Louisiana authorities had obtained more than 47,000 rifles and muskets from the Baton Rouge Arsenal; Georgia nearly 23,000 at Augusta, and South Carolina and Alabama smaller amounts at Charleston and Mount Vernon, a town twenty miles north of Mobile. Southern agents were also traveling north to buy weapons from northern manufacturers, Colonel Samuel Colt among them.[11] President Lincoln could not abandon Federal property to rebellious combinations of citizens without a response. Accordingly he ordered Fort Monroe in Virginia strengthened and Fort Sumter in South Carolina to be resupplied.[12]

During the month of March, as events in Washington and South Carolina were developing, William T. Sherman left Louisiana for his family home in Lancaster, Ohio. "All along the way," Sherman recalled, "I heard warm discussions about politics; to the effect that, if Mr. Lincoln should attempt coercion of the seceded States, the other slave or border states would make common cause, when, it was believed, it would be madness to attempt to reduce them to subjection." Some orators Sherman heard asserted "there would be no war, and that a lady's thimble would hold all the blood to be shed."[13]

The attack on Fort Sumter on 12 April 1861 put an end to such speculation. The Rev. Henry Clay Trumbull of Connecticut wrote that when "the old flag was there hauled down under hostile fire of those who had been trusted as its defenders, and the aroused North was in the white heat of a righteous indignation," he could think of but one relevant Bible verse, Luke 22:36: "let him who has no sword sell his robe and buy one."[14] The Reverend Arthur B. Fuller of Massachusetts viewed the actions of the

---

[10] US Constitution, Article II, Section 3.

[11] Coulter, *The Confederate States of America*, 199, 201.

[12] The state of South Carolina had transferred ownership of the sandy spit on which Fort Sumter stood to the federal government in 1841, twenty years before the Civil War began. In April 1861, Fort Sumter was a federal fort on federal land.

[13] Sherman, *Memoirs*, i, 166–67.

[14] As cited in Warren Bruce Armstrong, "The Organization, Function, and Contribution of the Chaplaincy in the United States Army, 1861–1865" (Ph.D. diss., University of Michigan, 1964) 114.

South as treason, "a despicable act of cowardice."[15] George H. Hepworth, a Unitarian minister in Boston, speculated that the independence of the South could re-open the slave trade, bring the price of Negroes down, and increase the profit for planters who depended on slave labor.[16]

On 15 April, the day after Fort Sumter surrendered, President Lincoln called for 75,000 volunteers to suppress the insurrection. This news swayed four border states to join the Confederacy. Two other states, Kentucky and Missouri, were in sympathy and open support of the Southern cause. Although the maintenance and extension of slavery were the penultimate causes of the war, the attack on Sumter and Lincoln's response provided the igniting points.

Falling In

Lincoln's call for militiamen came because the United States Army was made up of only 16,000 officers and men in 1861, and these were widely scattered across the western frontier. By 3 May, scarcely two weeks after the attack on Fort Sumter, President Lincoln requested an additional 42,000 volunteers as the campfires of Virginia rebels glowed across the Potomac River. That same month, the 7th New York State Regiment arrived in Washington by train to provide security for the government. It was said that Mr. Lincoln greeted them warmly as they marched by the White House.

The response of the governors of Northern states to Lincoln's call was remarkable. By July, Brigadier General Irwin McDowell could count 35,000 troops in the ranks in Virginia, even though many were untrained "civilians in uniform."[17] Within eleven months the US War Department had 676 regiments enrolled, a total of approximately a half-million soldiers stationed from Maryland to Missouri.[18] Serving in the regiments were 437 commissioned chaplains, all volunteers, and almost all without experience.

---

[15] Richard B. Fuller, *Chaplain Fuller: Being a Life Sketch of a New England Clergyman and Army Chaplain* (Boston: Walker, Wise and Company, 1864) 173.

[16] George H. Hepworth, *The Whip, Hoe, and Sword; or the Gulf Department in '63* (Boston: Walker, Wise and Company, 1864) 91–92. Trumbull, Fuller, and Hepworth all eventually served as chaplains in the Union Army.

[17] Roger W. Hicks and Frances E. Schultz, *Battlefields of the Civil War* (Topsfield MA: Salem House, 1989) 26.

[18] *Journal of the U.S. House of Representatives*, 37th Congress, 2nd Session, "Regimental Chaplains. Letter from the Secretary of War, June 19, 1862," copy in the Pentagon Library, Washington DC. Unfortunately, Secretary Edwin Stanton

Even though chaplains had served in the US Army since 1775, during the twenty years before the Civil War their numbers had been few. Since the 1830s approximately thirty post chaplains had been authorized for garrison sites such as Fort Monroe, Fort Moultrie, and Fort Leavenworth. Only nine chaplains—or equivalents—were known to have served in the Mexican War, and three of these were Mormon elders with the Mormon Battalion. The challenge in 1861 was to provide one chaplain for each Union regiment, and by 1862 at least another chaplain for each hospital.

Under the Congressional Act of 3 August 1861, chaplains were to be elected and then appointed to be commissioned officers. The exact wording was that a chaplain is "appointed by the regimental commander on the vote of the field officers and company commanders on duty with the regiment at the time."[19] Once the regimental commander made the appointment, he forwarded the chaplain's name to the War Department for a commission to be issued. Service could be for three months, nine months, or even for three years, depending on the terms of enlistment for the regiment as a whole.

Chaplains were paid $100 a month, allowed two rations per day, and forage for one horse. Their uniforms were black, with a plain black frock coat with standing collar, and one row of nine black buttons, plain black pantaloons; black felt hat or army forage cap, without ornament.[20] Issued during April 1865—too late to have any impact during the war—War Department General Orders No. 247 called for black braid around frock buttonholes and an embroidered silver "US" surrounded by a gold wreath on hat or cap. There was no authorized insignia indicating the men in black were chaplains.

During the four years of the Civil War, 2,398 individuals were commissioned as hospital chaplains of US Volunteers, US Army chaplains, or US Navy chaplains. This amounted to five percent of the available clergy in the North of the appropriate age group. Their average age, based on their muster rolls, was thirty-eight years at the time they volunteered, and they served for an average of thirteen months. Almost 40 percent were Methodists, with Presbyterians and Baptists making up another 17 and 12

---

noted that of the 437 chaplains in the Army in June of 1862, some 13 were absent without leave.

[19] *Journal of the U.S. House of Representatives*, 37th Congress, 2nd Session, "Regimental Chaplains," 2.

[20] War Department, *Revised United States Army Regulations of 1861* (Washington DC: Government Printing Office, 1863) 524.

percent respectively. Seven other denominations, including Roman Catholic, Jewish, and Unitarian clergy were also represented on the chaplain rolls.[21]

In additional to denominational diversity, there was also racial and ethic diversity among the chaplains. Seventeen African-American chaplains were commissioned for the Union Army including Chaplain Henry M. Turner of the 1st US Colored Troops, who was appointed by President Lincoln.[22] There were Irish priests, German Lutheran pastors, and Scottish Congregationalists and Presbyterians. There was even one semi-official female chaplain, Mrs. Ella Hobart of the 1st Wisconsin Heavy Artillery, who was paid $1200 for her services as a chaplain but never commissioned.

During the war some 116 Union chaplains died of wounds or disease, almost 5 percent of those who served.[23] Nine were killed in action, four were mortally wounded, one was killed when his horse fell on him, one died in a train wreck, and 101 died of disease during the war or immediately upon discharge. Four chaplains were awarded the Medal of Honor, three while serving as chaplains and one while serving as a line officer immediately before being commissioned as the chaplain of his unit.[24]

During or after the war, eighty-one Union chaplains wrote their memoirs or their regimental histories. Their stories contain many scenes of valor and cowardice, sacrifice and selfishness. Their faults are obvious but so are their virtues—including their incredible determination to keep the Union intact and strong and its citizens free.

---

[21] John W. Brinsfield et al., *Faith in the Fight: Civil War Chaplains* (Mechanicsburg PA: Stackpole Books, 2003) 43–45.

[22] William A. Gladstone, *United States Colored Troops 1863–1867* (Gettysburg PA: Thomas Publications, 1990) 32.

[23] The second-highest casualty rate for chaplains in American history. Approximately 11 percent of the Revolutionary War chaplains died during that eight-year war. In World War II there were 164 Army chaplains who died during hostilities, less than 2 percent of the 9,111 who served.

[24] Francis B. Hall, 16th New York, at Salem Heights VA; Milton L. Haney, 55th Illinois, at Atlanta GA; John M. Whitehead, 15th Indiana, at Murfreesboro TN; and 1st Lt. James Hill, 21st Iowa, at Champion Hill MS, commissioned a chaplain nineteen days after his act of heroism in capturing three prisoners.

Illustrations & Photographs

The National Archives, the Library of Congress,
and the Civil War Preservation Trust, Washington, DC;
Military History Institute, Carlisle, Pennsylvania;
Benedict Maryniak Personal Photographic Collection, Lancaster, New York

Chaplain Thomas K. Beecher
141st New York Infantry

Chaplain Amos S. Billingsley
101st Pennsylvania Infantry

Chaplain Philos G. Cook
94th New York Infantry

Father Peter Cooney
Chaplain 35th Indiana Infantry

Father William Corby
Chaplain 88th New York Infantry
and the Irish Brigade

Chaplain John C. Gregg
127th Pennsylvania Infantry

Chaplain Milton L. Haney
55th Illinois Infantry [Medal of Honor]

Chaplain George H. Hepworth
47th Massachusetts Infantry

Mrs. Ella Gibson Hobart
Chaplain 1st Wisconsin Heavy Artillery

Chaplain Horace James
25th Massachusetts Infantry

Chaplain Charles C. McCabe
122nd Ohio Infantry

Chaplain John S. McCulloch
77th Illinois Infantry

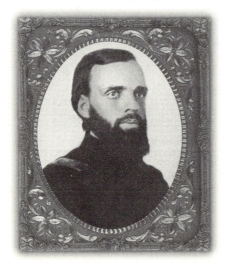 

Chaplain Levi Warren Norton
72nd New York Infantry

Chaplain Alonzo Quint
2nd Massachusetts Infantry

Chaplain Henry Clay Trumbull
10th Connecticut Infantry

 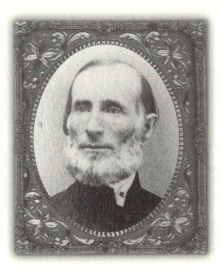

Chaplain Henry M. Turner *Chaplain Edmund B. Tuttle*
1st US Colored Troops *US Hospital Chicago*

Chaplain Sullivan H. Weston
7th New York Infantry

Camp preaching: Chaplain Lemuel Drake addresses the 31st Ohio Infantry at Camp Dick Robinson, Kentucky 1861

Chaplain Sullivan Weston preaching to the 7th New York Infantry at Camp Cameron, Virginia, May 1861. Note drumhead pulpit.

*Chaplain John Robie (hat over his head)
with the 21st New York Volunteers at Fort Runyon, Virginia, 1861*

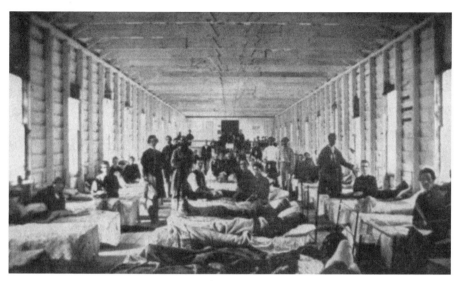

Union Hospital at Alexandria, Virginia

Chaplain Charles A. Humphreys, 2nd Massachusetts Cavalry

Union soldiers playing cards and smoking a pipe in camp

Union soldier with his lean-to and campfire

Father Thomas Scully, Chaplain 9th Massachusetts Infantry, with officers at Catholic Mass

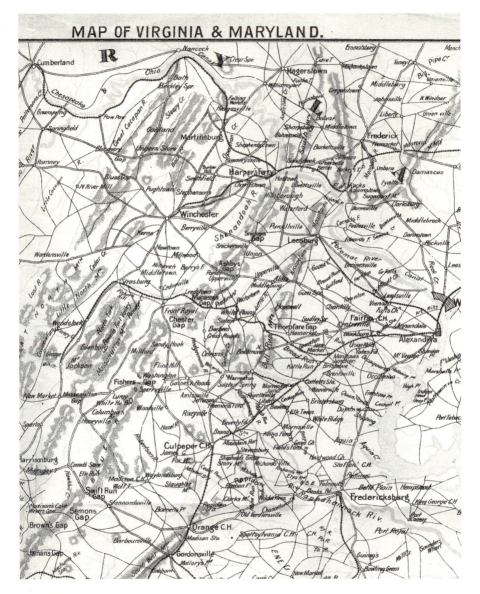

Civil War Map of Virginia and Maryland
Most of the battles in 1861 and 1862 were fought in this area.

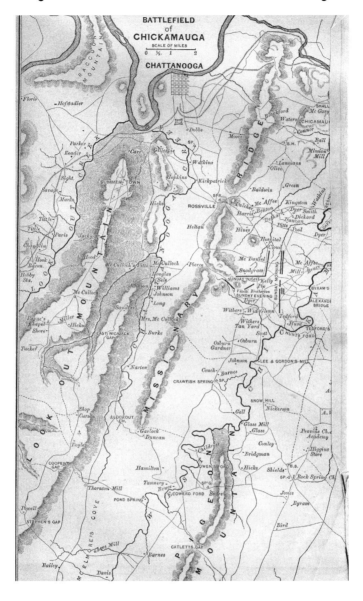

Battlefield Map of Chickamauga, Georgia 1863

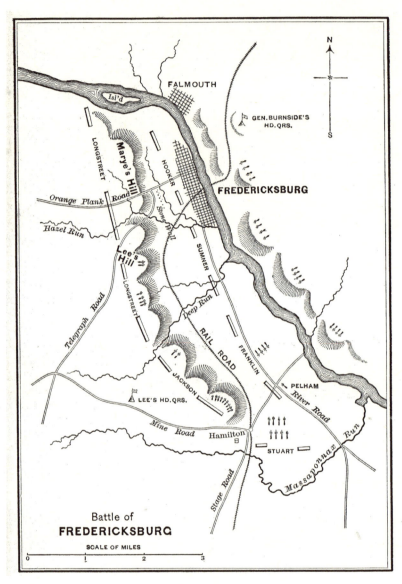

Battlefield Map of Fredericksburg, Virginia 1862

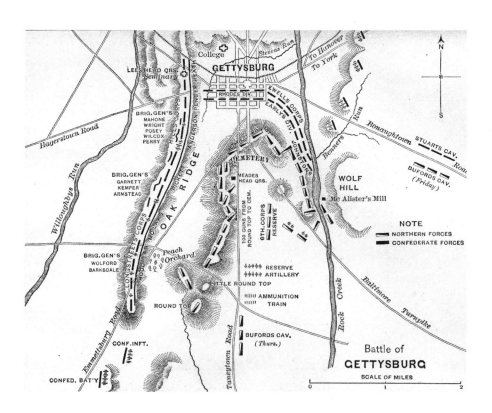

Battlefield Map of Gettysburg, Pennsylvania 1863

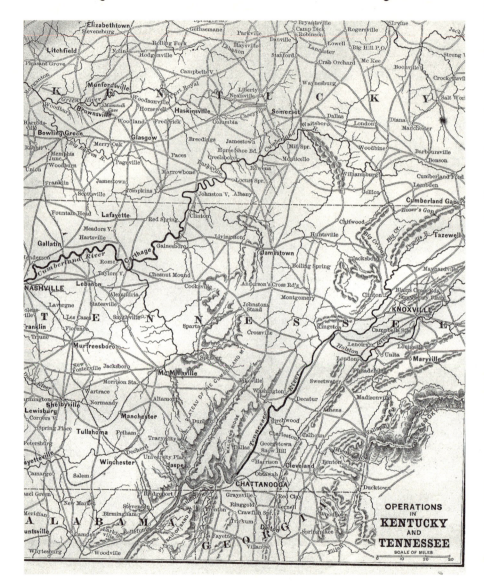

Civil War Map of Kentucky and Tennessee showing Bowling Green, Nashville, Chattanooga, and Knoxville

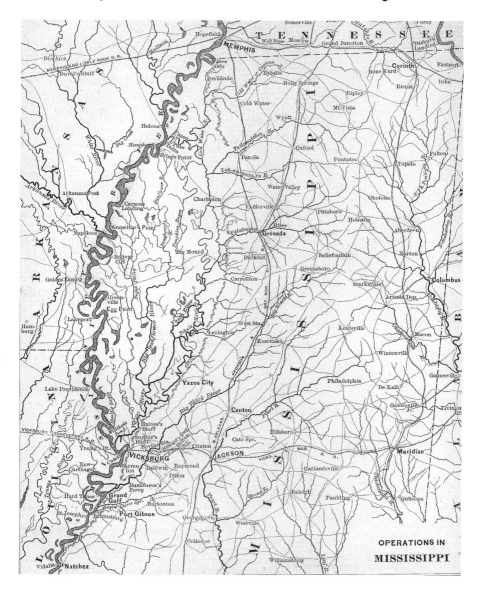

Civil War Map of the Mississippi River from Memphis to Natchez 1863

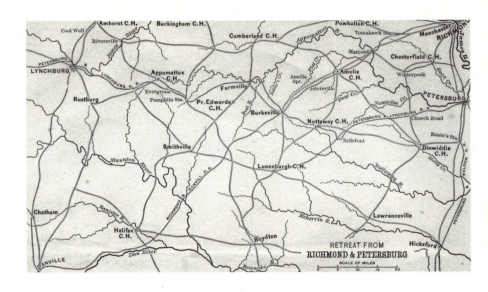

Civil War Map of General Lee's Retreat from Petersburg to Appomattox 1865

Chapter 1

Reporting for Duty

"O be swift, my soul, to answer Him…"
—Julia Ward Howe

Volunteering to serve in the army as a chaplain was a courageous decision for ministers, priests, and rabbis, young or old. The churches had little or no guidance for them; the army had no training program to help them prepare. There was no list of equipment they would need, no authorized assistants to help them, and no sure way to get the ecclesiastical supplies they might want for their soldiers. Most reported without a horse to carry them or a tent to shelter them. Yet, when the Union had a need for regimental and hospital chaplains during the war, more than 2,300 clergy volunteered from a dozen different denominations.

Some came impelled by motives of patriotism and adventure. The war "was a big thing" one soldier said in Virginia, and most young men, including the clergy, did not want to miss the opportunity to be participants and witnesses in the great event. The Union was under attack; all men, brave and true, would stand to the colors.

Others came for the cause of freedom, even in the early stages of the war. The Reverend James B. Rogers, a Baptist chaplain in the 14th Wisconsin Volunteer Infantry, thought that secession and its immediate result, civil war, were acts of treason. After the bloody Battle of Shiloh in 1862, Rogers wrote that slavery was the real cause of the war and "could be prolonged only by dooming to death thousands upon thousands" upon its altar.[1]

As in the case of most armies, it took some time to sort out those volunteers who were qualified, motivated, and physically fit to be chaplains. There were no age or educational qualifications, so regimental commanders were free to conduct elections or simply make recommendations for chaplain appointments based on the needs of the soldiers in their units.[2]

When the officers of the 5th Pennsylvania Cavalry elected Michael Allen, a Hebrew *chaver*[3] from Philadelphia, to be their Jewish chaplain, a visiting YMCA worker complained that Congress had authorized chaplains only from Christian denominations. Allen resigned, but Congress, under President Lincoln's prodding, changed the law. The new act of 17 July 1862 allowed individuals "of some religious denomination" to apply for a commissions as chaplains provided they could present recommendations from an authorized ecclesiastical body or from "not less than five accredited ministers belonging to said religious denomination."[4] Two months after the new law, Rabbi Jacob Frankel of Philadelphia became the first commissioned Jewish chaplain in the army.

Many clergy did not wait for such paperwork because there were more ministers who wanted to serve than there were positions for chaplains. Consequently some 111 ministers of various denominations served as enlisted men in the Union armies before or after being commissioned as chaplains. Another ninety-seven served as commissioned officers at some time during their army service.

Chaplains were mustered with their units; and if the unit was called to duty for three or six months, that became the term of service for chaplains as well. Chaplains could also leave the army by resignation if their health or the

---

[1] John W. Brinsfield, "New Civil War Research: Why Did Chaplains Go to War?" *The Military Chaplain* 76/2 (March–April 2003) 10.

[2] The oldest chaplain who served was John Pierpont of the 22nd Massachusetts Infantry who was seventy-six when he was commissioned in September of 1861. The youngest was George F. Pentecost of the 8th Kentucky Cavalry who was nineteen when he was commissioned in September of 1862.

[3] A *chaver* was an associate rabbi. Michael Meir Allen was certified in the "Orach Haim" code of Jewish law and thereby authorized to conduct synagogue service, but he needed to confer with a rabbi regarding more complicated situations.

[4] Herman A. Norton, *Struggling for Recognition: The United States Army Chaplaincy, 1791–1865* (Washington DC: Office of the Chief of Chaplains, 1977) 89.

health of their family members became a burden for them. It is not surprising that some 123 chaplains served less than three months, 404 for six months or less, and 505 for less than a year. Only 112 Union chaplains served in the army for three years or longer.[5]

Nevertheless, in the first year of the war ministers left their duties to become representatives of the church militant. From Harvard Divinity School to small country churches, Northern clergymen bade farewell to their friends and congregants. Some would return in a few months, some in three years, and some not at all.

[5] One of the relative short-termers was Thomas Quinn of the 1st Rhode Island Light Artillery. Quinn served from 7 November 1861 to 3 January 1862. During those fifty-eight days Quinn had his picture taken twice in a photographer's studio, once as an "assistant chaplain" and once as the chaplain for his artillery regiment.

Memoirs, 1861-1864

The Work of an Army Chaplain

Secretary of War Edwin M. Stanton had no doubt about the proper time and place for chaplains. On 9 April 1862, he issued a congratulatory "order giving thanks for the recent victories and overthrow of traitors" at Pea Ridge, Shiloh, and Island No. 10. The armies were thanked and "a salute of 100 guns from the United States Arsenal at Washington" would be fired in honor of these great victories. At the very head of this order Stanton requested: "That at meridian of the Sunday next, after receipt of this order, at the head of every regiment in the service of the United States, there shall be offered by its chaplain a prayer, giving thanks to the Lord of Hosts for the recent manifestations of His power in the overthrow of rebels and traitors, and invoking the continuance of His aid in relation to this nation by armies of patriot soldiers from the horrors of treason, rebellion, and civil war."[1]

Offering a prayer before his regiment, the chaplain represented Old Testament authority, Christian duty as described by St. Paul, and the expectations of the folks back home regarding each soldier's commitment and actions. The picture was similar to the Whalemen's Chapel where Herman Melville sent Ishmael in Moby Dick. *Galvanized by the sight and sound of Father Mapple preaching from a pulpit built to look like a ship's bow, Ishmael thinks, "What could be more full of meaning? For the world's a ship . . . and the pulpit is its prow." In the army, however, where duty toward regulations was the basis for activity, the preacher and his pulpit received little mention. Aside from describing chaplains' badge of rank as a line officer's uniform of black wool and devoid of brass, the regulations required that they "hold appropriate religious services at the burial of soldiers who may die in the command to which*

---

[1] US War Department, *The War of the Rebellion: A Compilation of the Official Records of the Union and Confederate Armies*, 70 vols. (Washington DC: Government Printing Office, 1880–1901) ser. 1, vol. 10, 22, pt. 1, p. 381.

they are assigned to duty" and "hold public religious services at least once each Sabbath, when practicable."[2]

The story of every army chaplain during the Civil War came down to how he intertwined the conventionalities of everyday life, the church, and the army. Some of the most compelling examples of this appear in a memoir by Charles Alfred Humphreys, a young Unitarian minister who rode off as chaplain of the 2nd Massachusetts Cavalry immediately after he was ordained 14 July 1863 at Harvard's Divinity Hall Chapel.

Humphreys comments that those who attended his ordination expressed their pleasant surprise that it took less than forty-five minutes, but the brief remarks made by two officiants were nonetheless poignant.

The Charge was given by Reverend John Fothergill Waterhouse Ware, whose grandfather was a Boston Congregationalist who had a hand in forming the Unitarian Church. A Unitarian pastor in Boston like his father before him, Ware had been an outspoken antislavery man long before the war.

My Young Friend and Brother,—This occasion is new to our ecclesiastical annals, and there can be no one here who does not feel its peculiar interest and solemnity. The consecration of a young man to the service of God in the Church always impresses; but the service you now choose is not in the Church. What she has to offer of peace, of honor, of struggle, you turn from. It is not the Church that calls you today, but the country; and you stand at the altar, set apart by our prayers, as before by your own, to that service she asks of you. And yet, in serving your country, in taking your part in the lot of the day, are you not serving the Church? God, who has guided your young steps into this way of duty, keep you in it, and bless you!

The work of the army chaplain has never been satisfactorily limited or defined. I suppose that it cannot be. It is for each man to make of it all that he can, and the kind of man he is will determine the chaplain he shall be. Take, therefore, no counsel of those going before you, but go to make your own place, watching for opportunity, and doing your utmost everywhere. At home, where conventions, and customs enclose, a man must yield to them somewhat, if he does not get overlaid by them. Your occasions, your duties, are not, cannot be limited for you. You enter a broad and largely untrodden field. You must make your own work. No man may do more than a chaplain—few have done less than some.

---

[2] Authorized by an Act of Congress on 9 April 1864.

As preacher, your occasions will not be many. In the stir and uncertainty of active campaigning, there is little opportunity, perhaps less inclination, for the stated services of religion.[3] A brief exhortation, with brief prayer, will be all you can ever wisely attempt. Speak earnestly out of your own life to the lives about you. Forget books, and theologies, and all nicety of language—the mere training of schools—and speak straight on, and simply the things which shall lead men out of themselves unto God. Exhort, instruct, rebuke, and have faith that no word uttered can return to you void.

I have heard it said of one of our brethren, "Oh! he was no chaplain at all. He never once said we were sinners." Do not be anxious to call men that word. It does little good. It satisfies the demand of some sects; it has a seeming of piety; but it never helps men to be better. They want broad, wholesome, indisputable truths and principles to stand upon, to build from. Give them these, and your work will be with power and success. Your great work will be in your daily intercourse with officers and men. You are to teach from your life more than from your lips. I say *officers* and men. Do not overlook the former. Many chaplains find their position with the officers exceedingly unpleasant. They are barely endured as an uncomfortable necessity, and they become untrue in this branch of duty for the sake of their peace, and have sometimes terribly lapsed in their dignity and character. The officers are a part of your charge. You are not merely chaplain over the rank and file, but what will try your manhood more, what is of quite equal importance to the service and the country, to the men and the homes, you are chaplain over the officers. Though they may not feel it, or wish to, though you may be tempted to forget it, they are a part of your charge; and it is the emphatic word of one who has, preceded you, that if the officers are not what is right, the chaplain can make them so—while it was the equally emphatic assertion of one high in regimental command to me lately, that where the officers were right, the moral tone of the soldier returning from service would be found to be higher than when he left home. I need not tell you, then, what a duty it is that devolves on you here. If I were you, I would know something about every man in my regiment—not his character only, but his history—what are his home-ties, his previous occupation, and what his future purpose; and then I would keep strictly, not a mere notebook, but a somewhat fuller diary for present reference, and for after use. I would find somehow to get at every man—in some *way* get and keep an influence over him. I think this can

---

[3] In an 1864 diary which is part of his pension file at the National Archives, Chaplain Orton Clark, 83rd Pennsylvania Volunteers, figured he received barely seventeen hours in that entire year to address his regiment.

be done by a constant watchfulness and a little tact. The opportunities are little and many. In camp, in hospital, on the march, on the field, find out some *way* to do something. Great occasions, trying occasions, will *come*. You can *make little ones*—and you know what mighty things little things are. That is the way with men's hearts. Where you can be of any use, do any good, do not hesitate. Let position, and dignity, and convention, and etiquette go. They are small chaff where a soul may be helped. Take your manhood and apply it to their manhood. The soldier is singularly receptive, not of words only, but of influence. A very little thing will give you a warm place in his regard—a great control over him. In earnest himself, he sees clean through a sham; he despises all cant; he does not want to be stooped to; but to any hearty, honest manliness he gives a prompt and hearty return. He is singularly childlike. He will seek you in your tent, and lean on your word as he never would do at home. I have been surprised to find the man, brave, self-reliant on duty, in danger, coming to me as a little child, and as he never would at home; and it is the general testimony that those who have always been a law to themselves—never were led—in the life of the camp, when not in the line and pressure of duty, become singularly dependent; and the man who was at home always cheerful, in service is liable to depressions. His absence from home, the tone of public remark, the fatigue and harassing of the march, the discomfort of bivouac and picket, the tedium of guard duty, the monotony, or scantiness of rations, the thousand annoyances and privations of his condition, tend to depress him. The *morale* of a regiment may depend upon you. You must always be cheerful. Never let them catch you down-hearted or timid. Have a kind, hearty, genial word for all, always. Have you a good, clear, ringing, honest laugh? Use it. It is God's gift to you. It is contagious. It is better than a dram to a fainting spirit. Wherever you are, and whatever the strain of despondency about you, feel that it is your duty to keep a good heart, and you will find yourself the support of many.

My friend and brother! take these imperfect words—not the technical words of a charge, for I feel myself too young yet to assume such a task, especially in this place, where hallowed lips, long dumb, strove to show me the way into my work—as an assurance of the interest with which I shall follow you into a field from whose duties I have myself, it may be unwisely, shrunk.[4] No man I so today envy as the man who goes out to this duty you have chosen. I am sure that you go to it from no impulse, no self-seeking, with no low hopes or

---

[4] Ware was forty-five years old at this time, and he may have refused the offer of a regimental chaplaincy.

aims, but out of a deep conviction, and a feeling, earnest heart. God will lead you, day by day. Day by day, your duties will unfold before you, and fresh opportunities arise. In your quiet, everyday intercourse and life, is to be your success. You will soon be known. Men will talk of you by the campfire, and in the tent. Without looking for any marked, startling results, be sure that your honest labor will not be in vain. It will bless others, and redound in blessing to yourself.[5]

Closing comments came from Edward Henry Hall, who had served as chaplain of the 44th Massachusetts Volunteers, a nine-month regiment, and discharged along with his unit a few weeks earlier. He had already returned to his pastoral post with the Plymouth Unitarian Church. He completed his studies at Harvard Divinity School during 1855 and marked his thirty-second birthday while in the army.

It is my pleasant duty, my brother, to bid you welcome to your new and untried work. I can do it very sincerely. It is a rare initiation into the Christian ministry that lies before you. I congratulate you that your entrance upon your calling falls in times and amid scenes like these; and that you are inclined to push forward at once to the front, where the truth you are to defend is receiving and dealing its heaviest blows.

It is with no common interest that Christianity looks upon this bloody strife. Indeed, she is deeply and mainly responsible for it. It is those stubborn, inexorable truths which she utters; those immutable laws which she proclaims; those seductive ideas at which she hints; justice, freedom, the sanctity of man, which lie at the bottom of the contest, and thrust themselves forward in every new battlefield. These are the mischievous cause of all our woes. But for them, the country might be slumbering still in her selfish materialism, undisturbed by any appeal from outraged justice or offended humanity. Having brought on the struggle, therefore—having rendered it inevitable—Christianity is bound to attend it to its close. Having guarded her sacred principles through all their hidden conflicts, it would be base recreancy to desert them when they enter on an open strife, and the battlefield is shifted to a stage where the world can see it. It is with a purpose, therefore, that Christianity sends her representatives to the

---

[5] Charles A. Humphreys, *Field, Camp, Hospital and Prison in the Civil War, 1863–1865* (Boston: Press of Geo. H. Ellis Co., 1918) 297–301.

front today. Nor can she honorably do otherwise. And happy are they to whom this service is assigned.

You will go, my brother, where the old conflict of ideas has taken on itself a visible and palpable form. While others view it from afar, you will step into its very presence, and see it face to face. While others are speaking vaguely of the high inspirations of the hour, dimly conscious that such there are, you will place yourself in actual contact with them, *feel* their mighty power, and carry off their richest teachings. You will go, too, for a short season—never again perhaps, in this earthly life—where the musings and speculations of our religious faith become vivid and intense realities. For all this I congratulate you, my brother. Have I not a cause?

But I congratulate you as well, that you have chosen to consecrate your calling, at its outset, to the practical wants and living demands of the hour, to show how competent is the faith which you hold to deal with man's daily necessities, to interest itself in his common concerns, to appreciate his human needs, to go hand in hand with him, even into life's struggles and perils, and if suffering comes, to bind up the bleeding wound, and pour in the oil of manly sympathy and tender, loving charity. So religion wins its holiest triumphs.

Shall I not congratulate you, too, Christian minister as you are, that you are to enter on the practice of your faith where it will receive its severest and most pitiless tests? Where none but a masculine, sinewy faith will do? Where religion must strip itself of all its pretences, and abide by its simple realities? Must forget its exclusiveness and lend itself to the largest, most comprehensive charity? Where eyes, quickened to clearest insight, penetrate through every disguise in which mock-piety loves to wrap itself? Where earnest souls sicken at all hypocrisies, yet yield themselves so unresistingly to the power of pure and lofty truth?

And, when all else is said, I congratulate you, as a man and a citizen of this republic, that you are to have a hand in the mighty struggle in which *human freedom*, insulted and imperiled so long, is vindicating its majesty, and crushing its life-long foes to the earth. Great will be your joy, as the years pass by, that you have been an actor in the historic strife; and that you hallowed your calling by connecting it so intimately with the endangered cause of human progress.

Accept, then, my brother, this Hand of Christian Fellowship.[6]

---

[6] Ibid., 301–302.

On 28 April 1864, Chaplain Humphreys wrote to Reverend Hall from a camp in Vienna, Virginia. Able to include it in his 1918 book because it was found among Hall's papers and returned to him, Humphreys called this letter the "fullest expression" of his work as a chaplain. He put down his thoughts having served eight of the nineteen months he would come to serve with the 2nd Massachusetts Cavalry.

You enquire as to my method of labor. I have very little method, but from necessity more than from choice. If there is any single rule that runs through all my work it is this—to be kind to all. If this seems to be a low aim for one who was ordained to speak eternal truths, my only apology is my youth. Exhortation and counsel are more fitted for maturity and age. I think my work will be surer if I do not assume any premature dignity or unwarranted authority, but trust to the pervasive influence of charity and love. I would rather have men say of me: "I wonder what faith he belongs to. It must be pretty near the right one, he is such a nice fellow," than that they should say, "Well, our Chaplain made out a pretty strong case for his belief; you could hardly help believing that what he said was true." I prefer to work by my life than by my speech; I rely more on the little kindnesses, attentions, and words of cheer of every day than on Sunday preaching, or week-day advice and counsel, though I do not neglect the latter, nor consciously undervalue them. The work of some ministers is like the sunlight with healing in its beams and nourishment and strength for every plant and tender herb that comes within the scope of its influences. The work of others is like the burning fiery furnace seven times heated moulding everything to its own will. My aim is to be like the former. The routine of my labor is like this: I hold a service every Sunday morning in a barn floor near by, to which anyone is free to come; there is no compulsion. I do not have a large audience, as I have never made it a special aim to increase it, I am so diffident of any ability in this line, or, I should say, so confident of my inability. I may say this—my services are very interesting to those who have any appreciation of religious duty and any taste for religious services. My aim in preaching is to elevate rather than to convert. I appeal to what is good and true in my auditors. If any are not already turned towards the good and the true, I suppose with them my preaching is vain, and I frankly acknowledge my weakness in this direction. I have the help of a good brass band in the service, and oftentimes the exercises have an unwonted solemnity with that help. I believe music may be made the handmaid of religion. I always speak without notes though never without full preparation, and never more than fifteen minutes. I use J. G. Forman's little hymn and service book for my introductory sentences and my hymns. We sing together one hymn always. The little interruptions (from the basement) of cows mooing, horses neighing, and dogs fighting, do not trouble us much. I have succeeded thus much at least—in making the men feel that there is a deep and solemn reality in religion whether they appreciate what it is or not. After the regimental service I go to the brigade hospital and hold a service in one or another of the wards, and visit all the wards, speaking to every patient. This is all the regular Sabbath work. The remainder of the day is like the rest of the week. The weekdays are spent in visiting the hospital, caring for the mail, and receiving callers, the latter taking up the longest time. I do not make many calls on the men in their quarters; in military life it has too much the appearance of intrusion. The men do not expect it and are seldom prepared for it. But they call freely on me, bringing their complaints, or revealing their experiences, which are often intensely interesting. I have had an ample library all winter, and an unlimited number of games of various kinds. I have kept the men supplied with stamps even when they could not pay for them. I have sent to Washington daily by mail-carriers for little things that the men have wanted. The only general result that I have seen from my labor is that there is a little less open profanity and a great deal less complaining than when I first came. The results in individual cases of course I cannot measure. I do not believe in any adequate gauge of moral influence like that which is flaunted before our eyes by evangelical sectarians in statistics of conversions and degrees of conversion. The results of my work if they could be chronicled would be—a little more kindness of heart in one, a little more elevation of purpose in another; a little more faith here, a little more charity there; here more reverence and there more truth. I trust that some such germs of good will grow and thrive in my daily path.

You ask about my relation to the officers. They are of the pleasantest kind. I have their respect and so far as I know their confidence. I have never asked anything of any of them that they have not readily granted. I am as a brother among them, not assuming any dignity from my profession except when I speak on Sundays. I am too young to rebuke them, too inexperienced to advise them unasked; but when on the Sabbath I speak in the name of my office, in the name of truth and of God, then I can do anything.

I am not much on tract-distributing; how was it with you? I half suspect that this is a failing in me; yet it goes against my feelings unless a very plain way is open for it. I have never held a prayer-meeting, partly because I had no place, partly because I saw little advantage to come of it. Of late I have been trying to serve the Lord on horseback, following the men into the field, lying at night under the tented sky,—which at this season, I assure you, is not so comfortable as canvas,—charging with them into the ranks of the enemy, and sharing all the dangers and exposure of active service. I carry no arms, but try by a cheerful courage to add a little to the effectiveness of those who do. Please let me hear from you.

C. A. Humphreys,
Chap. 2d Mass. Cav.[7]

Other chaplains summed up their feelings and their work in fewer words than Humphreys. Another Unitarian minister in yet another nine-month Bay State regiment, Chaplain John Farwell Moors, 52nd Massachusetts Volunteers, mused about his service in a letter to his wife written 5 April 1863 from Bayou Boeuf, Louisiana. "I begin to be impatient to see the end of all this. I can stand the poor fare, the sleeping on the ground, the hard marches; but the feeling is discouraging that we are doing so little.... Yet I am not homesick nor discouraged. I am bound to stick to it; and I hope, when the time is out, that I shall have satisfied my conscience and the claims of patriotism."[8]

---

[7] Ibid., 15–19. Humphreys died in 1921 at the age of eighty-three.

[8] John F. Moors, *History of the Fifty-Second Regiment Massachusetts Volunteers* (Boston: Press of George H. Ellis, 1893) 104.

"God's Honor—Man's Ultimate Success"

Chaplain Moses Smith,

8th Connecticut Volunteer Infantry

The following sermon was "preached on Sunday, 27 September 1863, by the pastor of the Congregational Church, Plainville, Connecticut, when about to leave his people and enter the army of his country." Ironically, this blaze of belligerence and sanctity came from a man who had been drafted!

Born 16 August 1830 in Hebron, Connecticut, Moses Smith studied at Yale and the Andover Seminary before his 1859 ordination. Conscripted during August 1863, Smith was assigned to the 8th Connecticut Volunteers, a regiment which had been in the field since October 1861, and gone through two Congregationalist ministers as chaplains. Joseph J. Wooley, a pastor of twenty-four from Norwalk, had resigned after barely five months because of his health. It was not because he lacked spirit, because he again served as an army chaplain with the 1st Rhode Island Volunteers during the Spanish-American War! Chaplain John Moses Morris succeeded Wooley. Valedictorian of Yale's Class of 1860, he was commissioned a chaplain immediately upon graduating from the Yale Theology Department in 1862. Wounded in the arm at Antietam and standing with the 8th in the thick of the slaughter at Fredericksburg, Morris badly needed a rest when he resigned after sixteen months. Draftee Reverend Smith was offered a lieutenancy when he reported to the 8th, but he insisted on being mustered on 15 August 1863 as a private soldier. He accepted the unit's chaplaincy when Morris left.

A Sermon: God's Honor Man's Ultimate Success.[1]

---

[1] Rev. Moses Smith, *God's Honor Man's Ultimate Success, A Sermon* (New Haven CT: Thomas J. Stafford, Printer, 1863).

1 Samuel 2:30. "Them that honor me I will honor, and they that despise me shall be lightly esteemed."

"God's Providence," said Napoleon, "favors those that have the heaviest cannon." But Napoleon lived to see that not all cannon are made of brass and steel. God often places heavier ordinance before an army than the science of war ever maneuvered, and woe be to that army, or that general, that assays to meet God's artillery.

There is a vast amount of misconception, and hence of infidelity, concerning God's Providence in this world. Some almost entirely ignore it in their creed, and utterly in their plans and labors; others believe that God takes care of great events, while smaller ones follow in some hap-hazard way. Some believe that God rules by a cold iron law, from which escape is impossible, and to which submission is bare necessity; others, that this world is left for the greater part to its own disposal, God ordaining sunshine and rain, summer and winter, earthquakes and tornadoes, what they term natural events, but men doing the rest, and that bad enough it must be confessed.

Now there is some truth in each of these notions respecting Providence, but very much error in them all. If we could combine the truth that each contains, and add something more from the Bible, we should approximate the whole truth.

First of all then, settle it in your minds that God never acts unreasonably. He may go vastly beyond our powers of understanding why. But He, who has crowned reason king in the rational soul, and made every man, yes, and angel also, to be self-condemned when he fails to obey reason's voice, will not contradict Himself by acting unreasonably.

Secondly, lay aside also that *most unreasonable* idea, that God has created beings, and launched into existence forces that are beyond His control; or, in other words, that God occasionally gets into a difficulty and to rectify His government must either work a miracle, as He sometimes does; or let things go at loose ends, as seems often to be true. God has never created so many things, or so little things, that he cannot and does not personally care for every one and provide that in every possible contingency each shall conduce to the end He originally designed.

And, thirdly, accept this plain truth, that some things may be best in one class of circumstances, that would not be best in another. That, for instance, to a sinful child discipline, chastening might be necessary, might be the dictate of both love and wisdom, when a perfect, holy child would require only development. Hence in this sinful world chastening must be a part of a loving

Father's counsel, and if God is a wise Father, He will ordain and secure so much of sorrow and trial as will conduce to the best good of His creatures.

Establish these three simple truths, neither of which can be denied without making the Ruler of the universe a being to be despised, and you will have what surveyors call a "base line," from which to take bearings and distances in that which is to most persons the mysterious wilderness of God's Providence.

Begin then in thought where God began the work of Providence. If anything exists, He made it to exist. If anything continues to exist, He causes that continuance. Men speak of the powers of nature, but these are the powers of God. Man uses the forces of wind and water; he harnesses the lightning; both mind and matter are his servants; but in all this he is—and I speak with reverence here—he is only letting God work for him.

God loves to work for his creatures. He does, whether they know it or not, whether they wish it or not, and He desires to do a vast deal more for them than they are willing to receive. *He* gives the steam its expansive power, *He* drives the engine of the locomotive or of your manufactory. Strength of material in building or in machinery is but God's constantly exerted power; nay, it is God Himself you are using from the foundation stone to the end of the spindle. If the winds blow sweeping hurricanes, if mighty waves or terrific lightnings are destroying thousands of lives and property, it is but God working—God teaching lessons of reverence, obedience, and love. If He withdraws that power, the calm of Gennesaret follows in a moment. If the engine explodes, if the cylinder breaks, if the ship parts, if life fails, this is only God ceasing to exert His power. Be it, that in those cases men have passed what we call the limit of safety. That limit is one of God's own observing. He could as easily assign and observe another. The laws of nature are but rules of God's working. They are uniform, because God knows the best limit, and the best need not be changed.

But if a good reason for change should arise, how easily it might it be accomplished! God would but withhold some agency, or turn that agency in another direction, and it is done. A miracle is no more wonderful in the power requisite, than is any common event. Nor is there any more difficulty in prayer being answered. All the efficiency of nature for good or evil is God's constantly exerted power, and foreknowing all the requests, and all the necessities of His creatures, He is prepared to answer every petition for the best good of every child. Nor can the agency of wicked men and devils at all interfere with this result. For all the power of moral beings anywhere is each moment committed to them. At whatsoever instant God ceases to give them this power they are silent, they are dead. True, they often use this power committed to them as God does not desire. But the moment they begin to use it in a way that will be productive of only evil, or to accomplish that which God cannot overrule to the accomplishing of more good than by withholding that power, it will be withheld. For even "the wrath of man shall praise Him, and the remainder thereof will He restrain."

There is then no absurdity in saying that heavier guns can be wielded in the prayer meeting, in the widow's closet, than ever thundered on the battlefield; that mightier forces are held by a wrestling Jacob, than were ever marshaled in fleets and armies. There is no impiety in saying that no disaster, murder or war ever occurred; never a woe, or pain, or tear, on earth was experienced, but it was in God's wise plan. It came through the power He allowed to be used, and which he could have withheld; it came because He overrule it for some positive good, even more than would accrued by withholding the power in order to prevent the evil.

The truth lies in a nut shell. God is the grand center of all things, earth and hell not excepted. They that honor Him find all things working together for their good. They that oppose or neglect Him, array against themselves all the resources of Omnipotence; and these include not natural forces merely, but the villainy of men, and the malignity of devils.

Passing events afford a wide scope for the application of the text. We live in a time when history is culminating. Our years are more than antediluvian centuries. No one nation lives alone. The progress of one is a blessing to all. The sin of one is known world wide. If God is honored in one, all lands with heaven rejoice.

But enough for us to apply the text to our own country.

The prominence of America on the scroll of earth's present history renders the influence of our country doubly important. God's Providence in this nation is read in heathen as well as Christian lands. No other country has had such a history as ours. It was planted with the seed corn of God's Church. The choicest blessings of heaven nourished and refreshed it. No land ever enjoyed such material prosperity; no churches such effusions of the Holy Ghost. God set up this people as "an ensign for the nations." Anxious eyes from every land looked to behold the people God delighted to honor. And what did they behold? Look upon a magnificent painting; a single blot mars the whole. The prince of artists may have devoted to that canvas his choicest years. But the folly of an instant is most prominent of all. Recall the lives of such men as David and Peter; one foul misdeed is always first remembered. So of our land. Other nations looked and they cursed God. Slavery was a dark stain upon our national escutcheon, and jealous eyes saw nothing more. It *was* a stupendous wrong. The countless host of blood and treasure expended by both North and South in this mighty war have not equaled it. The debt is, as yet, but partially paid. But far greater than all the bloody, cruel wrong we did to the negro, or have done to ourselves, is the wrong we should have done to the cause of God.

Just when amid the wilds of Persia and on the deserts of Arabia, the proud Mussulman was turning scornfully from such a land, and such a God, his eye caught the flashes from Our battlefields. Call it what *we* will, the nations abroad understand it as the contest of slavery against God. God would vindicate His character. Not for our sakes; we have been a most wicked people. Avarice and corruption, pride and folly, villainy in every form has run rampant in our land. And never more impiously than since this war began. We make no boasts of the piety of the North. I know not but our sins have been as odious before God as those of the South. This government is not to be saved because of its goodness, but for God's own Name's sake. *He* allowed the flood-gates of civil war to be flung open. *He* allowed the wealth and resources of this country to be turned against itself. Nay, He even allowed the avarice of the North to be pitted against the despotism of South, that these vices might *both* be consumed together. My hopes for an early peace are not based upon our large armies, our now somewhat experienced generals, or our apparent victories. *God* holds the reins of these contending forces, and neither will be ultimately successful until from our victorious banners, or our humiliated government, shall go forth the words to every people, "Them that honor me I will honor, and they that despise me shall be lightly esteemed."

To my own mind the prospect is however most cheering. Our defeats upon the battlefields have been great moral victories. Our people have learned that without God they cannot prosper. Our generals have learned that there is "a God of battles," that there is "a Sabbath in war." Our Administration has learned, in the memorable words of distinguished cabinet officer Secretary Chase—and who ever expected to hear such language from a Secretary in Washington?—"One poor man, colored though he be, with God on his side, is stronger, if against us, than the hosts of the rebellion."[2] Nay, more than all this:

---

[2] Salmon Portland Chase (1808–1873) was an Ohio lawyer, senator, and governor. He had been raised by his uncle, Episcopal bishop Philander Chase, and reputedly recited psalms while bathing and dressing. An outspoken antislavery man and one of Abraham Lincoln's rivals for the 1860 Republican presidential nomination, he was appointed secretary of the treasury and was the most radical member of Lincoln's cabinet.

The rebellion itself has repudiated the doctrines of its own vaunted declaration. It called God to witness that its supporters were depending on Him for assistance to perpetuate the enslavement of His children. He was witness. And He has allowed them to repeat the declaration until the world should known it. And now the world beholds that God detests the whole institution; and forces even its boasted champions to begin in good earnest the work of its destruction. That was a day presaging peace to our afflicted land; a day noted in heaven, if not on earth, when the representatives of thirteen Slave States, in Congress assembled, declared that five hundred thousand slaves should be armed as men and allowed to fight for their independence.[3]

I love to hope for peace. I pray for peace. But my Bible tells me, "there is no peace to the wicked." Wicked nations, like wicked men, are never at peace. We as a nation have never been at peace. The fires of opposing elements have been constantly burning from the day our fathers allowed the demon of Slavery a place in a nation of free men. We have sought to conceal or smother those fires, but it has been in vain. They have been burning hotter and hotter until the irrepressible conflict has astonished the world. But God answers prayer. "By terrible things in righteousness," is He answering now. North and South, Americans and Europeans, all conspire in the petition that peace may come to our land. It is coming, bless the Lord. Peace that shall honor God and instruct the world.

Another application of the text is found in the present condition of the church. You may apply it to this individual church, or the churches of Christ in our land. If *this* church, now to be for a season without a Pastor, will honor God, if it will be faithful and active in sustaining the prayer meeting and Sabbath School, if it will endeavor to make good in personal labors the Pastor's absence, God will honor it. The dews and the showers of divine grace will descend upon it, and its numbers and its graces will increase. But if member stands coldly aloof from member, if the venomous tongue of slander lives in the church, if some show that they have cared more for the Pastor than they have for Christ, and now wander off like unstable souls, as they will show themselves to be—*will* any treat *me* so unkindly as to sneak away when my back is turned?—if dying sinners, at home or abroad, be neglected, then will God for His own Name's sake abandon this church. He will not allow Himself to be dishonored

---

[3] Reference to numbers initially proposed for black troops. Nearly 200,000 were ultimately enlisted.

by blessing such a people, but will show by your leanness that He has departed from you.

So in our land. The church has a harvest field broader, and resources vaster, than were ever conceived of before. Two years ago, the Home Missionary could not cross Mason and Dixon.[4] God has allowed bayonets and cannon to destroy that barrier. Catholic and Infidel have fought side by side with the Christian to prepare the way for the complete evangelization of this nation. The "highway" is almost completed, and the chariot of salvation must speed its course. The whole South must be supplied with the Bible—the *unmutilated* Bible. The Colporteur must hasten with his treasures of life.[5] The Preacher must gather the scattered sheep, and Churches and Sabbath Schools must bless all that land of darkness. Nor is that all. Africa is there by her representatives, and not merely are those sable ones to be evangelized and saved, but a nation is to be born; a nation whose glorious destiny is to evangelize their native continent, and it may be to bear the standard of civilization and Christianity to a loftier eminence than Anglo-Saxon has ever attained. Nor is this work in the distant future. God is now honored in the track of our armies. Never was so much prayer for an army as for ours. Never, notwithstanding all the vile ungodliness of our camps, was so much prayer in an army as in ours. Never an army with so many Bibles and Christian books. Even the rebel army has received thousands of Bibles by grant from our Bible Society, and the religious reading of our own soldiers have reached multitudes beyond our lines. Never were so many Christian letters written; and does anyone who loves a husband, a brother, or son, that is on the field of strife probably never to return, does anyone ever write a letter and not baptize it with tears and follow it with prayer? And do you wonder that conversions are multiplied? God seems to have taken from our communities a multitude whom no Christian effort ever reached, and placed them where every word from home is a treasure, in order that the arrows of Christian truth, winged by words of affection, might pierce and save their souls. Hence so often when we have wept, angels have rejoiced and God has been glorified. We all feared, we could but expect, judging from the past, that when

---

[4] Decades before hostilities of the Civil War, there had been formal divisions within the Presbyterian, Baptist, and Methodist denominations.

[5] Religious publishing houses had been active since the turn of the century in distributing reading matter to all parts of the nation, not only through their churches but through a system of door-to-door selling known as colportage. Colporteurs, who would also preach or lead prayers at the drop of a hat, not only brought tracts and books to hospitals but followed armies into the field.

this war should cease, men would come home bold blasphemers, to spread drunkenness and vice in every community.

But God is showing the church that so far from this being necessarily so, if we will honor Him, He will honor us by sending very many of them home to heaven, as we trust He has some of those we mourn as soldiers dead, or making them, as we believe others are, Christian soldiers, to come home renewed men, and serve with us in the ranks of the great Captain, Christ Jesus.

If you will but use the means God has placed in your power, your homes need not be darkened and your hearts saddened by the return of demoralized men. If they do not come home *better* men, then be assured you have not honored God. You have despised Him and shall reap the fruit of your own doings.

Time forbids that I should speak of the blessed revivals in our regiments on the field, as well as in our hospitals, and in the camps of the freed men. But I hasten to make a personal application of the text.

I desire to offer a brief statement of some of the reasons why I am about to leave this people. The relation between a Pastor and his flock I have ever regarded as a sacred one. None but the great Shepherd can give the minister his commission or assign him his field, and no other authority can annul that commission or rightfully change the field.

God sent me to this people. He sent me to feed this flock of Christ. I have ever felt that no other than God might lawfully call me away. I consulted not my ease, my reputation, or my wealth in coming here. I was willing to be "a living sacrifice." I not even conferred with my dearest earthly friends. I carried it all to my Savior. I was satisfied of His will and my service was yours. I desired to honor God. I can truly say, in that thing *I honored God*, and He has honored me in this work. How long I was to remain I knew not, I cared not. I only asked that, when the Master would have me leave, He would make the path clear, and I would be ready to go. He has answered my request. He has made it just as clear that it is my duty to leave this Pastorate, temporarily, perhaps permanently, as He did before to enter it, and I follow that Divine guidance just as readily now; as then.

If you ask me for the reasons why I feel so well satisfied in regard to the path of duty, I can give them only in part, and *perhaps* they will not seem valid to you. But I can say as before, I have not consulted ease, or reputation, or wealth, or even friends very much. No one has ever given me one inducement, though many have dissuaded. I have earnestly and repeatedly laid it before God. I am ready to have it come before Him in the final judgment.

What is to be the result of this step, I know not. Where I am to labor, I know not. How long I may labor, or how soon fail, I know not. I may say, I choose not. Enough for me, God leads and the result is His. If I honor Him, He will honor me. But there are several particulars in each of which I have desired to honor God.

First, in reference to the draft itself. I believe, without hesitation or limitation, that unless there is willful, designed iniquity, "the whole disposal thereof is of the Lord." I believe that God designed to have my name on that list. When the apostles "prayed and gave forth their lots," they had no doubt respecting the meaning of the result. God was to answer prayer, and the case was decided. Just so I—I speak for another—*we* laid this whole matter before God and asked Him who knew all things to determine whether He desired me. And when I was to appear before the examining Surgeon, again we prayed that He who "holds the hearts of all men in His hands" would direct that man. If the decision had been the reverse, would you not have felt that God had determined? And has He any the less now? I think not. I cannot answer for others; far be it from me to condemn others; but for my part I could not answer the question, which will be put to every drafted man at the final day, "why did you not respond when God called?" Whatever it may have been in the case of others, in my case it was like Gideon's twice tested fleece, each time repeating the word "Go." "And what was I that I could withstand God?" Are we not always safe in the path of duty? Nay, are we ever safe out of that path? If there be anyone here whose trembling soul has falsely evaded, or meanly shrunk from the path God has opened for him, let not such a one vainly dream of security at home. The avenger is already on his track. He may die here sooner than he would have done in the army. He surely will be a hundred fold more miserable than all the privations of camp life or horrors of the battle field could have made him. When God called Abraham he *obeyed*, though "he went out not knowing whither he went." Whatsoever others may do, by the grace of God I will do likewise.

In responding to this call I also desired to honor God, by depriving wicked men of one opportunity to reproach the Gospel of Christ. I have ever preached, "according to the wisdom given unto me," a Gospel which I believed, and which I never feared to test. Now it does not follow, because I admire the self-sacrifice of the missionary, or because I urge young men of my flock to become missionaries, that I ought to become a missionary in actual fact; nor, because I have urged the claims of our country, and lauded the patriotic devotion of our noble brothers in the field, that I ought to be a soldier. But there are men, and women too, just ignorant enough, just wicked enough, to fling the vile aspersion on Christ, that His ministers will preach patriotism and incite others to the contest, but not a soul of them would ever himself venture on the battle field. This remark is at once a slander to the ministry and to Him who bids them their preaching. In itself it should never turn a Christian man one iota in his path of duty. But it is a pleasure to find the path of duty sometimes so opening, that false imputations can be repelled. I therefore rejoice in being allowed to testify to this people, that I have preached no more than I have stood ready to practice. "For the kingdom of God is not in word but in power." A power sufficient for every emergency, and victorious for every trusting heart.

It was furthermore that I might honor God, that I was not willing to allow my friends to commute for me.[6] I appreciate the kindness of those individuals who have willingly offered to relieve me. I thank them for their generous proposals, and, had I consulted personal ease or pleasure, I should have gratefully accepted the favor. But Christ put himself on a level with the lowliest of His people—"He was tempted in all points like as they are"—and as a minister of Christ I desire to follow Him. I would not avail myself of my profession or my position to escape any trial which the poorest member of my church could not escape. If my people had paid the three hundred dollars for me, and some poor brother, unable to meet this liability, had been forced to go and then had fallen on the field of deadly strife, with what words could I have given comfort to his widow's aching heart? By the grace of God I can do it now, and no man shall deprive me of this vantage ground. Whatsoever place the Lord opens to me I will endeavor to fill it. No position can be more lowly, more laborious, or more painful, than that in which Jesus was found. None can be where God cannot be honored, and where He cannot honor me.

With a like regard to God's cause, have I been unwilling to send a substitute such as those are who have usually been secured. To say nothing of the utter waste of money, and hazard to our country by sending such creatures in

---

[6] The whole idea of conscription was to offer a distasteful "hard way" of entering the service that would make voluntary enlistment seem more palatable by comparison. It would compel men to volunteer sooner rather than later. The Enrollment Act of 1863 offered no religious or occupational exemptions. An unwilling draftee could turn to the "substitute clause" of the Enrollment Act. Under it, a conscript could pay a substitute to take his place or simply pay a commutation fee of $300. Although the practice of substitution was as old as the Revolutionary War, commutation was a new wrinkle invented by Lincoln's administration. Presumably the $300 commutation money went into the local community's treasury and was paid out eventually as bounty to a volunteer.

the place of true men; creatures who will, if they can, at any moment desert their ranks and betray your sons and brothers to a merciless foe; it is to those older soldiers who have endured so much in our behalf, the unkindest, wickedest act, we could commit. I stay at home and pray for the good morals of the army? Pray for the conversion of our young men in camp? And at the same time send in my place, to tent with those boys, to mess with them, to drill with them, to be their constant associates, a being whose very presence I loathe, whose lips are vile with pollution, and whose hands are stained with blood? It would be open mockery and insult to God.

Has it come to this, that those who could scarcely be tolerated in our village are eagerly sent to be the constant companions of my Christian brethren, of your husbands and sons? Nay, that the very charter of our national and Christian privileges is to be committed to them? Then it is time that I should go, and many more beside me. Had noble men responded in person to this draft, such men as the country needs—shame on the niggard spirit that counts the vilest good enough for our army—such men as in this time of her peril she had reason to expect, and a few of whom she has received, then might I have remained to serve my country at this post. But when I saw what wretched creatures were to fill the ranks where *men* had fallen, when I saw so many around me dastardly preferring to hazard their country and endanger souls, rather than endure a little self-denial, and, if need be, die a noble death, how could I longer remain? The blood of heroes slain, the periled souls of heroes living and the graves of sainted sires, would cry out against it. The very fact, that some of you have refused your sons, your brothers, and your husbands, impels your Pastor by a stronger necessity to labor and to suffer for that army that will save or ruin our land: and not affect our land merely, but bless or curse mankind.

And this leads me to another consideration, in which the honor and the cause of God are manifestly concerned: and with this in view, notwithstanding all the sadness, the hardship, or the pain I may endure—and you may be assured that this has not been overlooked—I have even *desired* to go. From the outset I have regarded this War as fraught with glorious results. We are fighting not for an Administration—*little* souls talk of parties, or presidents, or administrations now; not for the negro, though his emancipation is the Godlike work of making four millions of men; not for the restoration of our whole government, though that will make all the tyrants of Europe tremble; but for *the world*. This contest is not between the North and the South merely, it is between freedom and despotism, between Satan and God.

It is the same struggle in which bled and died the noble sons and nobler daughters of '76. It is the same cause for which holy martyrs in all ages have given their lives; for which apostles suffered, and Jesus Christ was crucified.

I am ready to enter an army in such a service, and, if need be, to die there. Say not my life is too valuable or ten thousand like it. The result, if attained, will far more than compensate all the cost. Every great advance of virtue and religion in this world's history has been an onset against Sin and Satan, and has been secured at the expense of earth's noblest lives. It is a doctrine of Satan, that life is too valuable ever to be surrendered. The doctrine of Christ is, "I count not my life dear unto me." And with reason; for in this way, under God's rule, the great war of earth hastens to its consummation. In that war I enlisted fifteen years ago, and entering the army of the United States is the farthest from being mustered out of that service. It is out being transferred to another post. I expect to honor God there as truly and, I trust, more extendedly than I have done in this Pastorate. I am to enter the ranks; yet do not expect that my principal work will be done in bearing the musket,—although that I will endeavor to do faithfully. Christianity does not teach men to be unfaithful. He is not obeying Christ who engages to fight for his country, and then faithlessly shirks in the hour of danger or falsely aims above his country's foe. If it is my duty to enter the army, then it is my duty to serve, to the best of the ability God has given me, in the position assigned. Do not think that I shall fear to take the deadly aim against those who, it may be ignorantly and thus even conscientiously, are seeking to strike down our God-given government. I am in duty bound to do it. I shall *endeavor* to do it. And you must not call me a murderer either. I owe no enmity against any man. I feel no spirit of revenge even against the arch-traitors of our land. "Vengeance is *mine, I* will repay, saith the Lord." I pray for them all. I will pray for the man I may meet on the battlefield. I do not wish to injure a hair of his head. But if he will attack, or is forced to attack, these institutions, this government ordained of God, he must be repelled; repelled, if need be, with mortal shot. If, defending my country, I must strike him down, it is as I would do to the villain that should be murderously assaulting my family. I would pray for his forgiveness, but defend my country; offer the prayer and send the bullet. Then, should I fall myself on the same field, I would hope to meet even my foes before a common pardoning God.

But I feel that the physical labor is not the main work for me to accomplish. I have been ordained to preach the Gospel, and to that my life is committed. The place where, is for God to assign. If it is necessary that I serve "in rank and file" to find my hearers, then in the ranks let me be. If it is necessary for me with failing health to fall into the hospital to find my congregation, then "the will of the Lord be done." If He has any other position for me, it will be made known. But wherever I am, my great work must be by lip and life to preach Christ. I enter the army to honor God, and living or dying I shall be honored of Him. My hearers, have you all as good a prospect?

One word more and my preaching in this pulpit is, for the present, perhaps forever, ended. Is there one here today, who is not a sincere disciple of Christ? Let my last word be to him. Fellow Immortal, I shall meet you at the judgment. I shall be summoned to witness against you, if you are not prepared to meet God. I have told you, some of you often, of a Gospel able to save you; of a God ready and longing to honor you with a crown of glory, if you will but honor Him. But if you reject Him, He will cast you off forever. Seek Him then, I beseech of you; seek Him with all your heart; seek Him *now*.

Chaplain Smith's sermon is all the more compelling when his record with his regiment is considered. With the 8th Connecticut Infantry when it was part of General Ben Butler's XVIII Corps, he came through the trials of the Bermuda Hundred. When his regiment returned to the IX Corps under General Burnside, Chaplain Smith withstood the desperate fighting which marked Cold Harbor and the siege of Petersburg.

Discharged with the regiment on 12 December 1865, Smith returned to his Plainville flock and remained there until 1869. A church in Chicago came next, but it was destroyed in the Great Fire of 1873. A decade in Michigan followed, with more congregations in Illinois. Smith was a trustee of Olivet College, Chicago Seminary, and Mount Holyoke College. He died in Chicago on 30 November 1904 and rests in Rosehill Cemetery.[7]

---

[7] *Obituary Record of Graduates of Yale University* (n.p., n.d.) 430.

Chaplain George Hughes Hepworth,

47th Massachusetts Volunteers

George Hepworth was destined by his gifts for soaring flights of intellect. His French mother had wished for a son who could preach, so he was a Harvard Doctor of Divinity by the age of twenty-two in 1855, ready to fight the good fight for the Unitarian Church. A pastor in Nantucket from 1855 to 1857, and then in his native Boston for another twelve, he not only saw the Civil War as an apocalyptic showdown between good and evil, but as a historic, God-driven break between two ages. Mustered 7 November 1862 as chaplain of the 47th Massachusetts, a nine-month regiment, he reported for duty in a blue military uniform complete with sword and sash. The following brief but compelling statement reveals what motivated George Hepworth to become a regimental chaplain.

"Good-by For A Year"[1]

From the very first, I desired to go to the war. I felt that no man has any right to look about him for an excuse to stay at home. If blessed with good health, his first duty is to his country; for, without his country's benignant laws and institutions, he is worth just nothing.

When I looked upon those who had put on the harness, I wanted nothing so much as to go with them; and, when I looked about me on those who remained at home, my desire to go grew apace.

I had often reveled in the rich scenes of the last century, when a lifetime seemed so much; when one generation held in its hands the fate of many ages; and when manly men were building the future, as we build a temple. Those were glorious days, and days in which it was a sublime privilege to live. The rusty sword of the humblest farmer was as much needed as the bright Damascus blade of the leader. Every strong-limbed man and every tender-hearted woman contributed to that aggregate force which founded a new empire. "Will those days ever come again?" I asked myself each time I laid the record on its shelf.

Then came through our New-England homes the invigorating reverberations from Sumter. The trumpet-tongued cannon seemed to thunder forth the prophecy of a new life. The church-bells joined in the chorus; and

---

[1] George H. Hepworth, *The Whip, Hoe, and Sword; or, The Gulf Department in '63* (Boston: Walker, Wise, and Company, 1864) 9–11.

pulpit and rostrum sent out their cry, "To arms for Freedom!" and told us that the days of chivalry were at hand, and that every willing knight was needed for the contest. It mattered not that I was the humblest disciple of one who came to still the troubled waters, and to bring peace upon earth. The day had not yet come when it would be quite safe to give up the sword for a pruning-hook: on the contrary, our chief duty seemed to be to change all pruning-hooks into swords.

So I said to my people, "I can stay no longer;" and they kindly answered, "Go, and God speed you!"

On the Sabbath morning when I reached the top of the hill that overlooked our camp, the bells began to ring, summoning the villagers to the house of God. It seemed to me that they had a voice, which said,—

"Chaplain, the work before you is hard, but grand. A thousand mothers, wives, and daughters have given those they dearly love for their country. A thousand homes will support your arms, while a thousand altar-fires will burn low for nine long months; and many, alas! will never be kindled into their wonted brilliancy, because there is war, bloody war, in the land. Look to your duty. Pray for the boy, who, until now, has never known temptation; warn the husband and the father who is walking, as fast as he can, in the road that leads to moral death, and who will bring back to his family, at the end of his term of service, a poisoned mind and heart; and when the dark day lowers, and the air is thick with battle-smoke, speak, with the Master's authority, the 'Peace, be still!' to those who have fallen; and open, with the hand of friendship and of prayer, the door of heaven, that they may enter to receive their reward."

All this the many-toned village church-bells rang out; and I trembled as I remembered that all I could offer to my country were willing hands and a willing heart.

Regimental chaplaincy proved a disappointment to Hepworth, and he resigned after barely three months to become a first lieutenant in the 76th Regiment of US Colored Troops. Reverend Edward W. Clark, a Presbyterian minister of more years, stepped in as the 47th Massachusetts's chaplain.[2]

General Nathaniel P. Banks, a wily New England politician, tried to harness the precocious Hepworth by detailing him to investigate the matter of compensated labor performed by blacks in Louisiana. The young minister

---

[2] Service File of George H. Hepworth, RG 94, Records of the Veterans Administration, National Archives, Washington DC.

produced a report within weeks, but it was an indictment that moralized and pointed fingers, which was not much to the politician's liking. Resigning his commission in the USCT 17 July 1863, Reverend Hepworth published his critical views of the war and the military titled, The Whip, Hoe, and Sword *during 1864. He then embarked upon a successful lecture tour.*

Pastor of New York's fashionable and influential Church of the Messiah from 1870 through 1872, the intense Unitarian announced he had become Trinitarian. Installed as a Congregational minister by none other than Henry Ward Beecher, Hepworth led New York City's Church of the Disciples for six years before taking a year to tour Europe.

Increasingly interested and involved in journalism, George Hepworth left the pulpit during 1885 to become an editorialist and reporter for the New York Herald. *He died 7 June 1902, a respected writer. His grave is in Forest Hills Cemetery, Jamaica Plain, Massachusetts.*[3]

---

[3] Susan Hayes Ward, *George H. Hepworth: Preacher, Journalist, Friend of the People* (New York: E. P. Dutton and Company, 1903) 231–44, 270.

"Religious Army Chaplains"

Chaplain John E. Robie,

21st New York Volunteers

John Robie was a Methodist minister who published religious newspapers. His readers were his congregation. Before his arrival in Buffalo during 1850, he had lived in Auburn and established the Northern Christian Advocate. *He then put out the* Genesee Evangelist *for several years in Rochester. He ended a successful ten-year run of* The Christian Advocate *when he sold it upon being commissioned chaplain of the 21st New York Volunteers in 1861. Even in the field with his regiment, Robie kept up a steady stream of reports to the hometown newspapers back in Buffalo.*[1]

Born 19 June 1811 in Hanover, New Hampshire, Chaplain Robie was in his fiftieth year when he left his wife and two children for the war. Before that, he had served as chaplain in the 74th Regiment of New York State Militia, a unit based in Buffalo. Since the 21st served a two-year term of service, the chaplain saw his share of action with the regiment at Second Bull Run, South Mountain, Antietam, and Fredericksburg. Nicknamed "Deacon John" by his soldiers, he made a few trips back to Buffalo, delivering soldiers' pay to their families, and saw to his sick and dead without losing his wit. "I am appointed postmaster of the regiment," he announced in a letter, "so you see honors increase." He was detailed to act as "post chaplain" at Aquia Creek, Virginia, through March and April 1863. This was a substantial camp on the Potomac with a number of hospitals.[2]

The following letter by Robie is a chaplain's ground-level view of the army. Far from an exciting lithograph of a courageous cleric amid pounding hooves, the flash of gunpowder, and clash of sabers, it depicts an existence marked by day after humdrum day of uncomfortable outdoor life so uneventful that the sound of the chaplain's breathing was always loud in his ears. Beginning with a sarcastic treatment of army red-tape, Robie's account goes on to a careful review of personal gear. Painful trial and error "in the field" spurred the admonition to load saddles with adequate food, wool blankets, and water-proof ground cloth because regimental

---

[1] Johnny Oldboy, "Father and Son, John E. Robie," *Times* (Buffalo NY), 12 June 1927, B3.

[2] J. Harrison Mills, *Chronicles of the Twenty-First Regiment New York State Volunteers* (Buffalo: Gies & Co., Printers and Bookmakers, 1887).

wagons never kept up with marching troops. Likewise his reminder to fill and refill canteens as often as the opportunity arose.

In addition to Robie's suggestion that prayers and sermons be brief, there is significance in obtaining his colonel's approval to read a prayer as part of the daily dress parade. Robie realized that he would reach more of his men if liturgy was part of the regiment's official daily routines. Religion had to be part of their orders or soldiers would ignore it as irrelevant to their new home-away-from-home. Most army chaplains did not want their regiments ordered to attend religious observances, because congregations voluntarily filled their churches back home. Those townspeople, however, were not the teenagers who made up 40 to 60 percent of a typical infantry regiment. With the folks back home far away, a transplanted juvenile desperately wanted to be assimilated into his new world so he could find some friendly guides and protectors. This need could only be answered fully by the close interpersonal ties afforded by his company and regiment. This was army regimentation of the Civil War. Though not as intense as indoctrination of today, it was more than enough to sweep away emotional baggage of childhood and imbue a teenager in uniform with standards by which his combat unit judged the behavior of its members. The chaplain was left out of this. Some of them, expecting the army to be somewhat similar to their experiences back home, interpreted small turnouts for weekly worship as signs of their failure to reach their men, and promptly resigned their commissions.

Religious Army Chaplains[3]

In order to become a chaplain it is necessary (1) to get a certificate of not less than five ministers of one's own denomination that one is a regularly-ordained clergyman with their recommendation of him as a suitable person to fill the office and (2) to get a certified statement of the vote of the staff officers and commandants of companies electing him to that office in a particular regiment.[4]

---

[3] John E. Robie, "Religious Army Chaplains," *Christian Advocate* (Buffalo NY), 2 June 1864, 2.

[4] War Department General Order No. 15 dated 5 May 1861 required that a chaplain be appointed by the regimental commander on the vote of field officers and company commanders on duty at the time the appointment was to be made. Outside of stating that this chaplain must be a regularly ordained minister of some Christian denomination, nothing more was said about qualifications until Acts of Congress on 17 July 1862 amended those of 22 July 1861. Although they made room for non-Christian chaplains, the new guidelines made no stipulations about education or age.

With these two papers, he can obtain (3) a commission from the governor of the state.

He will then join his regiment and, with these three papers, will apply to the mustering officer of the division or corps to which the regiment belongs. This officer will muster him into the service of the U. S. and give him (4) a certificate of muster, the officer retaining papers (1) and (2).[5]

The chaplain will then show (4) to the adjutant of his regiment, who will enter his name on the roll of the Field & Staff with the date of muster.

The monthly pay of a chaplain, which begins with the day of his muster, is $100 plus $18 rations plus forage for one horse.[6]

In active service, his baggage must be comprised in one valise, or carpet-bag, and one roll of blankets—say three or four woolen blankets and one india rubber blanket, bound together by a shawl strap with handle. These will be carried in the staff wagon. Besides these, he may carry whatever he chooses on his horse or on his person.

When lying for any length of time in one camp or at a station, or in winter quarters, he may have a trunk and a camp bedstead, which must be stored with the post quartermaster or expressed home when the regiment takes the field.

When on the march and at all times during an active campaign, he will do well to carry on his horse one woolen and one gum blanket, lest at night the wagons should fail to reach the troops. He should carry a haversack. Not one of the showy and expensive things which officers often buy, but the

---

Stating that "No person shall be appointed a chaplain in the US Army who is not a regularly ordained minister of some religious denomination, and who does not present testimonials of his good standing as such minister with recommendation for his appointment as an army Chaplain from some authorized ecclesiastical body, or not less than five accredited ministers belong to said denomination."

[5] There was so much misunderstanding—not to mention outright chicanery—regarding the status of chaplains as officers that an Act of Congress on 9 April 1864 had to pointedly recognize the "rank of chaplain without command" in the regular army and volunteers. This Act specifically placed chaplains on same footing as other commissioned officers.

[6] In May 1861, the War Department set pay at $145.50 per month, plus three daily rations and forage for one horse. Around the same time, the Confederate Congress set a chaplain's pay at fifty dollars per month. During July 1862, the US Congress cut chaplains' pay to $100 per month, two daily rations, and forage for a horse. A hospital chaplain's monthly pay was also $100, but he received twenty-five dollars more for renting quarters in place of rations and forage.

simplest kind of gum or oil cloth to contain his most-necessary toilet articles and sufficient food if he should fail to get regular meals during the day. The regular provisions and cooking utensils and table furniture of his mess will be carried in the wagons. His canteen should be filled at every good stream or spring on the road. The cheap government canteen is better than the expensive and ornamental ones. The shoulder strap of both haversack and canteen should be as broad as possible, so as not to cut the shoulder. A small tin cup may be attached to either canteen or haversack. A bottle of Essence of Jamaica Ginger should always be at hand.[7]

The chaplain's dress is a plain black frock coat with standing collar such as are commonly worn by Episcopalian ministers, except that the ordinary clerical coat has seven buttons and the military coat has nine. A black felt hat is most convenient. The chaplain is not, however, obliged to wear any peculiar or uniform dress. Some chaplains wear a blue sash at parades and reviews, and many wear black velvet buttons.[8]

As the commanding officer will permit, the chaplain should have prayer daily at dress parade, which occurs just before sunset. The best time for the prayer is when the officers have marched to the center and have faced the colonel, and before they march forward to salute him. The prayer should not be more than three minutes long. A form of prayer will ensure the requisite brevity and be in keeping with the formalities of the parade.

While in camp, the chaplain should visit the regimental hospital daily and spend ten minutes—no more—in scripture-reading and prayer. The best time is in the morning, after the surgeon's visit and before the patients fall asleep again. At the close of this short service, he may distribute tracts and papers. Judicious letters from the chaplain to friends of the sick and deceased will be very highly appreciated.

---

[7] The aromatic distillation of Jamaica ginger was the soldier's stand-by for protection against a host of ills, especially effective in warming the stomach and dispelling chills.

[8] War Department General Order No. 102 dated 25 November 1861 specified that the uniform for chaplains of the army would be a plain black frock coat, with standing collar and one row of nine black buttons; plain black pantaloons; black felt hat or army forage cap, without ornament. This was the uniform worn by captains and lieutenants but done in black and without brass. War Department General Order No. 247, issued too late in the war for much impact, required a chaplain's uniform to include black braid around buttonholes and an embroidered gold wreath on the hat or cap.

On Sunday, but one service can be held, and that not always. The service, including scripture reading, singing, sermon or address, and prayers should occupy 20 or 25 minutes—never over thirty. The ordinary time for the Sunday service in the army is ten or eleven o'clock—the period most free from interruptions. The adjutant will have the church call sounded on drum or bugle at the request of the chaplain, but the best of all church calls is the singing of a hymn by the chaplain in a good strong voice. The ability to sing independently is a prime qualification for the chaplaincy. One who can sing can call a congregation together on a hundred occasions where one who cannot sing must forgo the pleasure of preaching At the close of the Sunday service, tracts and religious papers should be thoroughly distributed. The Christian Commission will furnish them.

On the battlefield, the chaplain should not needlessly expose himself to danger to show his bravery. Least of all, should he undertake to act the soldier, since he is regarded as a non-combatant. Let him assist the wounded and the surgeons who will be, where it is possible and as much as possible, shielded from the enemy's fire.

Possibly these suggestions, of a nearly two years' experience in the army, may be of use to some who propose entering the service.

Mustered out with his regiment on 18 May 1863, Robie returned to Buffalo and bought back his newspaper. He became presiding elder of the Methodist-Episcopal Church's Buffalo District upon his return from the army and served through 1867. He also bought a summer home in nearby Cowlesville, where he died of apoplexy 26 May 1872.[9]

---

[9] Obituary, *Buffalo* (NY) *Commercial Advertiser*, 27 May 1872, 4.

Chaplain Gamaliel Collins, 72nd Pennsylvania Volunteers

The following letter, its author identified by only the initials "G C," is included in Mary A. Livermore's My Story of the War.[1] *Of two army chaplains with corresponding initials who were in the field during November 1861, as well as the vicinity of Conrad's Ferry on the Potomac River, Livermore's correspondent was likely to have been Chaplain Gamaliel Collins of the 72nd Pennsylvania Volunteer Infantry.*

Born 7 October 1816 in Massachusetts, Collins was preaching in Philadelphia when he joined the 72nd during August 1861. Discharged when his term of service expired on 24 August 1864, he then served as a post chaplain in the US Army from 1867 to 1879. He died 24 April 1891 and was buried in City Cemetery, Hudson, New York.[2]

The letter is unique for its suggestions on how a clergyman back home could approximate the experience of being a chaplain without coming to the front.

Hardships of a Chaplain's Life
Alexandria, Va, Nov 30, 1861
You seem to think that a chaplain's life must be an easy one. I grant you it may be if a chaplain shirks his duty. But if he is ready to share the perils of the soldier, a chaplain will find his life full of hardships and exposure. I acknowledge my letters are "light and trifling," as you characterize them; but have you not heard of the boy who whistled to keep up his courage? Let me give you a few facts concerning my life.

I have slept in the open air, with scarcely any covering, so chilled in the morning as to rise with great difficulty. I have slept in a government wagon, with hungry mules foraging around, and snatching the hay which formed my bed. I have slept with crickets, bugs, spiders, centipedes, and snakes crawling about my couch as thick as princes in Germany. For one week I had no food but salt pork, which I detest, and bread which water could not soften. Since I have been in camp, I have not been comfortable the whole of one night, because of cold. I have no abiding-place, nor has the rest of the army. I must

---

[1] Mary Ashton Livermore, *My Story of the War: A Woman's Narrative of Four Years' Personal Experience* (Hartford: A.D.Worthington, 1888) 231.

[2] Service and Pension Case Files of Gamaliel Collins, RGs 94 and 15, Records of the Veterans Administration, National Archives, Washington DC.

be ready to march, rain or shine. Very different this from my life at Hudson, N. Y., where I had my books, my study, and home.

Tell H—[a country clergyman] that he need not come here to see if he likes it, for he can make a few experiments at home. Let him sleep on the floor of the attic a few nights without a pillow or comforter, or in the garden, wrapped in a pair of horse blankets. Let him get a pound or two of the rustiest pork he can buy and some mouldy crackers, and feed on them for a week. Or let him treat himself to a couple of salt herrings, and drink his black coffee without milk or sugar. These will be good preparatory steps before his enlistment. After he has enlisted, tell him he must make up his mind to be a man among men, cheerful, brave, blameless. He must point out the road, and must also lead the way. Like Cromwell, he must trust in God, and keep his powder dry.

Nov. [30]—We have just had a battle, that took place at Conrad's Ferry, which resulted disastrously to our troops.[3] A narrow river separated my men, with myself, from the battlefield; and, as we had no means of crossing the deep, swift stream, we could render our companions no assistance. I remained with my comrades during the night, assisting the wounded, and rendering all possible aid to the fugitives. At the conclusion of the fight, our brave fellows were ordered to save themselves as they best could. Many plunged into the water, and swam to an island in the river, and were afterwards conveyed to the Maryland shore. Many of them were nearly naked. All were cold and shivering. I assisted them to the extent of my ability; and not only encouraged the men, but literally drove them to walk to camp without delay. I feared otherwise they would freeze to death.

About midnight the fugitives ceased to arrive, and I sought for rest in a shock of corn beyond the canal. I had scarcely fallen asleep when I was aroused by heaving [sic] firing of musketry on the Virginia side of the river. I hastened to the shore, and learned that about four hundred of our soldiers had hidden themselves in the early part of the evening, and had just been discovered. They were slaughtered like sheep. Those that could swim, rushed to the river. Many were drowned. The remainder were butchered on the spot, or made prisoners.

I shall never forget what I saw and heard that night on the banks of the Potomac. It was one of the most dreadful nights of my life. I have passed

---

[3] The Battle of Ball's Bluff or Conrad's Ferry on the Potomac River near Leesburg VA was fought on 21 October 1861.

many that were sorrowful. I have watched and waited calmly for death amid the chilling blasts of the North and the fearful tornadoes of the torrid zone. I have kept vigil by the bedside of those dear to me as drops of my heart's blood, and have felt that the light had gone out of my life, when the sunrise saw me sitting by my dead. But I have never endured so much of agony and of horror as during that night, when I saw men butchered by the hundreds in cold blood, simply because they wore a different uniform from their murderers.

Yours truly, G C

Chapter 2

Ministry in the Camps

"I have seen Him in the watch fires of a hundred circling camps…"
—Julia Ward Howe

Life in Civil War camps was organized according to army regulations but controlled by the commanding officer through subordinates, including the provost marshal, the inspector general, and individual regimental commanders. There were also various types of camps depending on the purpose and duration of the encampment. For example, at the beginning of the war governors of states through their adjutant generals set up camps of instruction, and later conscript camps, where soldiers could be equipped and trained. There were also hospital and convalescent camps for the wounded and those recovering from their injuries. There were temporary camps when the army was on the march, and winter camps when the weather and seasons changed.[1]

US Army regulations specified in 1861 that a camp for one regiment of infantry, approximately one thousand soldiers divided into ten companies, would be in the shape of a rectangle 400 paces wide and 481 paces long. Everything in the camp was laid off in paces: space between tents two paces; space between the kitchen and the company tents twenty paces; the advanced guard two hundred paces in front of the color line where the regimental and national colors were posted and arms were stacked; and officers' sinks or latrines one hundred paces in the rear of the regimental train, "concealed by bushes."[2]

---

[1] William S. Smedlund, *Campfires of Georgia's Troops, 1861–1865* (Lithonia GA: Kennesaw Mountain Press, 1994) preface.

[2] War Department, *Revised United States Army Regulations of 1861* (Washington DC: Government Printing Office, 1863) 76.

The chaplain's tent, if he had one, was usually near the surgeon's tent on the right side of the rectangular camp. The commanding officer's tent was in the center of the regimental camp with staff officers' tents lined up on either side. In a cavalry camp the horses were placed in single file, fastened to picket stakes planted in the ground from three to six paces from the tents of the troops.

The daily routine was established by posted orders from the commander. At Camp Massillon, Ohio, the routine for the week of 29 August 1862 specified morning activities beginning with "Reveille" at 5:30, Roll Call at 5:45, and policing or cleaning up the camp until breakfast at 7:00. Then there was drill, guard mounting, officers school, dinner at noon, more drill and inspections, and a dress parade at 5:50 P.M. Supper was at 6:00, more drill for thirty minutes, and then two hours of free time until Tattoo at 9:00 and "Taps" at 9:30.[3]

On Sundays at Camp Massillon, religious services were observed on the ground, conducted by the chaplain "or others requested" from 2:00 to 3:30 in the afternoon. On that day the Articles of War were "distinctly read to each company" so that soldiers were reminded weekly of the laws of war. The gospel and the law went hand-in-hand in the army.[4]

There were, of course, standards of conduct for soldiers. The changing of the guard was to be done in silence or with as little noise as possible. "No talking, whistling, singing, or laughter" by a sentinel was allowed. Likewise there could be no yelling or disorder in the camp, and no firearms discharged within or near the camp except by authority of the commandant of the post. All soldiers found in town without a ticket of permit were arrested, and no intoxicating liquor was allowed in the camp at any time.[5]

When the army went on the march, many of these regulations went into abeyance. Army camps might stretch for six miles along a river or stream so that men and horses could get to fresh water. Other camps for large units might be as long as fourteen miles along a road, as was the case in Georgia in 1864. Moreover, armies tended to march before dawn and skip

---

[3] Each segment of a soldier's day was initiated by a "camp call" done by drum, bugle or vocal announcement. "Tattoo" called companies to assemble for reports and the day's final roll call. "General Order, No. 3. Headquarters. Camp Massillon [Ohio], August 29th 1862." Copy of orders in the Norton Papers, US Army Chaplain Corps Archives, US Army Chaplain School, Ft. Jackson SC.

[4] Ibid.

[5] Ibid.

dinner if necessary. Unit cohesion was critically important for communication and supplies, but distances between units frequently made this difficult.

Chaplains tended to be very busy or, occasionally, bored. The only duties they had, besides the expected worship services and hospital visitation, were to report "to the colonel commanding the regiment to which he is attached, at the end of each quarter, the moral and religious condition of the regiment, and such suggestions as may conduce to the social happiness and moral improvement of the troops."[6]

Worship services and prayer meetings in the field went on all week, typically after supper and before "Taps." During the day, if there was no fighting, the chaplains might visit with other officers, meet with local inhabitants, distribute mail, write letters for soldiers, or jot down some thoughts for a sermon when paper was available. Sometimes, as in the case of Chaplain Horace James of the 25th Massachusetts Infantry, they would offer an oration to remind the soldiers why they were serving in the army.

Nevertheless, once the army moved to the field, camps could be dangerous places. Chaplain John Crabbs of the 67th Ohio Volunteer Infantry counted fifteen men from his regiment who died of disease from 9 February to 15 March 1862. Of these fifteen soldiers, twelve were under the age of twenty-six. Other chaplains wrote of accidents, and at least one possible murder when a soldier was killed by "a falling musket" while asleep in his tent.[7]

Although there were not as many revivals recorded among the Union soldiers as among their Confederate counterparts, there were significant religious meetings in the army. Chaplain Milton L. Haney of the 55th Illinois, Chaplain Alonzo Quint of the 2nd Massachusetts, and Chaplain Amos Billingsley of the 101st Pennsylvania Infantry regiments all led or participated in evangelical services with revival hymns, testimonies, and preaching. At times, even on campaign, the camp became a church.

---

[6] War Department, *Revised United States Army Regulations of 1861*, 507.

[7] See the diary of Chaplain Lyman Ames, 29th Ohio Volunteer Infantry, Military History Institute, Carlisle PA.

Memoirs, 1862-1864

How a Camp is Arranged

Letter from Reverend Henry Rinker, 11th New Jersey Volunteer Infantry

Henry Rinker did serve as a chaplain; but in March 1865, when he wrote this letter to his daughter, he was still a private in the 11th New Jersey Infantry. Rinker was born in Southampton County, Pennsylvania, on 5 April 1825. He entered Princeton as a sophomore and graduated with first honors in the class of 1847. He taught school at Mount Holly, New Jersey, and then spent two years at Princeton Theological Seminary.

Ordained as an evangelist, he spent a year, from 1856 to 1857, in Wisconsin doing missionary work and helping administer Carroll College in Waukesha. He returned to the East in 1857 to become pastor of the Presbyterian Church in Wyoming, Pennsylvania. In 1861 he became head of the Newton Collegiate Institute in New Jersey where he remained for four years. In the spring 1865, he enlisted, at age forty, as a private in the 11th New Jersey Volunteers.

The following letter to his daughter, written in March 1865, contains a description of his camp so she could picture where he lived.

Dear Nanny,

The men have their tents usually some distance from the Regimental officers. Their tents are arranged according to the companies. All those in the same company being arranged in the same line. Then the tents of the different companies are in parallel lines with a wide space for a street between the lines. Often the men take great pains to have everything neat and pretty about these tents and streets. Everything like filth and rubbish must be removed. Men are appointed whose special duty it is to see to this. If you were to visit an encampment of soldiers you would think it was a town built in a funny kind of way.—Thursday morning.

I deferred writing the remainder of my letter till the morning and I am not perfectly certain that I shall have it ready for todays [sic] mail, as I am liable to interruption by other writing. However you must be patient if you do not get the letter quite as soon. The tents that are now put up are mostly what are called summer tents. They are the same as winter tents with this exception—that instead of being spread over little huts or houses built of logs[,] the tents we made to [sic] rise directly from the ground passing over a ridge pole in them idle which pole rests upon two forked sticks one at each end of the pole. The edges of the tents are fastened down with ropes or cords attached to wooden pins or plugs driven into the ground. In the summer tents one end is left entirely open, and in some cases through want of material or for other reasons both ends. The officers generally have a little more stylish tent. That is a kind of house is made of canvas about four feet high—answering the purpose of the log hut in the winter tents of the men—and then instead of a single canvas roof, there is a double canvas roof. The upper roof is six to ten inches above the under. This upper is called a fly. This of course makes a very dry and comfortable tent. One of our clerks sleeps in the office tent which is pretty large & moderately good. The other three—myself one of them—have a separate tent for sleeping. It is not a walled tent, nor has it a fly; but it is quite good and answers the purpose very well. I do not sleep on the ground now when we are in camp. Dr. Welling, our surgeon in chief, who is a good friend of mine, secured me a stretcher which makes a very good bed.[1] You do not know what a stretcher is so I will tell you. It is something on which they carry the dead and wounded men from the battle field. There are two stout poles or bars connected with strong canvas forming a couch or bed. The ends of these poles project from the canvas some distance for the carriers to take hold of. Under the poles are supports about 14 inches long attached by hinges so that they can be set straight or let down. The poles are kept apart by a sort of jointed bar of iron. This is a stretcher. And such is my present bedstead. At night I spread down my rubber blanket over the stretcher—then my overcoat. My pillow is made of my extra underclothing & a camp pillow belonging to Dr. Welling. Then I cover up with two good warm hospital blankets. As a rule I have not taken off my clothing, as the nights are generally quite cold. But when it gets much warmer I shall undress more. The other two clerks in my tent still sleep on the ground just as we do on the march—although an order has been

---

[1] Dr. Edward L. Welling, surgeon for the 11th New Jersey Infantry.

given that all the men in the Brigade must make for themselves bunks. Dear Nanny next time I will tell you more. Excuse me now. Love & kisses from Papa to all.

    Your Papa

"Our First Camp"

Chaplain Levi Warren Norton, 72nd New York Volunteers

An Episcopal cleric who spent most of his life in western New York, Levi Norton was born in Attica, and married a lady from Lowville. He completed his studies at Union College in 1843 and graduated in 1846 from the New York General Theological Seminary. Ordained in 1847 at twenty-eight, Reverend Norton spent a few years in Watertown before settling in Jamestown. In that city, he built St. Luke's Church around 1854 and, from 1857, served as chaplain of the 68th Regiment of New York State Militia. Mustered 24 July 1861 as chaplain of the 72nd New York Volunteers—a regiment in General Dan Sickles' Excelsior Brigade—Chaplain Norton went to Maryland with his unit.

The following letter is one of the very few sent home by Chaplain Norton during his brief time in the army.

Vicinity of Budds Ferry, [Maryland] Oct 22, 61

My Dear Frank,
I have been thinking of writing to you for some days but as you have learned from your Mother's letters we were on the march and little leisure consequently remains at such a time. We started on Friday last about 2 o'clock and marched 10 miles down the Potomac. We made camp before dark and then came a busy time. The first thing is to fix the place for the Col.'s tent and then everything is governed by that. We always encamp in the same order as when we are at home at Camp Caldwell. We have a large body of Cavalry say 200 or 300 mounted men. They are encamped on our right and left. Half goes before us on the march and half in the rear and they go out on the different roads to scout, to see if any troops are near us. There are four or five ambulances to carry the sick, some drawn by one horse some by four horses. Then there are about thirty large four horse wagons covered with heavy canvass which contain the baggage of the staff and companies and the Quartermaster stores and the ammunition. This makes up a train of over a mile in length. It is a busy time when we enter and when we break up camp. All the companies are busy either setting up or striking tents and all the teamsters are at work at their horses and wagons and men are packing or

unpacking and all the sounds you ever heard you hear save those of HOME SWEET HOME.

Our first camp was by the side of a large brook called Broad Creek. Saturday morning after breakfast early all was in motion and soon we were off again. We very soon passed an old church, Broad Creek Church, Rev. Mr. Martin's built nigh two hundred years ago. The bricks were probably brought from England. It is a long low church and surrounded by aged trees and old tombstones grown smooth and weeds adding a melancholy look to the whole affair. I would like to have read the inscriptions but could not stop. About noon we halted for luncheon, and then passed on passing another church built in 1740. Rev. Mr. Chipchase, Rector. I called and he took me into the church. It is not as large as our own an open roof tho and built of North Carolina pine which is very handsome wood resembling chestnut. Mr. C. looked a little scarey at me and perhaps thought I was on the wrong side tho he did not say so. We reached our second camp about 5 o'clock on the plantation of a Mr. Wilmer, where we stayed over Saturday night leaving early Sunday morning. I was sorry we could not stop at Mr. Chipchase's lower church for service or somewhere for one of our own, but there was no rest for the weary. We halted on the grounds of a Mr. Marburry about noon and got dinner and about 3 o'clock the Col. decided to remain near there so we marched to the place and encamped. We had a dress parade about 5 o'clock after which I accepted an invitation to tea and stay all night at Mr. Marburry's. He is a large farmer and has some 15 or 20 slaves, who came into prayers in the evening. They seemed well fed and happy. The night passed away quickly in a feather bed. After breakfast we went to camp & were soon off. A march of eight miles brought us to our present camp before noon. We were now all safe on good ground though it proved bad for rain, being very muddy. As soon as the camp was getting into shape the Q.M. [quartermaster] & I rode to a hill top in sight and from thence we saw the secession batteries. One large one with five openings & guns, another with 3 guns. There is also another in the woods which is not very visible but shoots terribly they say. I could see men over there & it was a goodly sight to look on the rascals for we have never seen them before even afar off. They fired at a schooner in the afternoon several shots, but did not hit it. She got by safely. One of their shells fell on this side & was brought in by some of our men 14 inches long & 2 1/2 inches in diameter. It was a curiosity to see these evidences of rebel batteries close by us & yet I do not suppose they could throw their shells to us. Today has been a raining day. It is now about 3 P.M. & the men are busy enough cutting wood & getting ready for the night. Our Engineer Capt. is out at his special work & we are here to help him if he needs help in his work. I cannot speak for that work here for it would not be proper. Billy brought me on his back all the way here about 40 miles & behaved beautifully.[1] My place is in the rear of the column & just before the rear guard. The Surgeon & myself ride there side by side & the Quartermaster when he is not looking after his baggage train. We take our cooks & provisions with us on such trips & with what we can pick up are very comfortable. We buy chickens & mutton & eggs & butter. We eat in a tent as at our own camp. I hope you are getting on nicely & that we shall soon have the pleasure of seeing some of that cake Mother sent me. You have been very good to put up with that leech and I shall not forget it of you. One of these days I will try & reward you for it. It is a great pleasure to me to know how you have done so well. I hope you will continue to be as faithful—8 o'clock P.M. My Dear Boy as I had finished the last sentence about 4 o'clock a heavy report was heard by us all in camp & I looked up and saw pieces flying by the tents. I heard also a horrible scream from several men & men were running towards the spot. It seems that some of the Dunkirk boys though they would see what was in the shell I told you about & got out about 3 pints of powder & supposing that all was out they wet it & then one of them very foolishly put a coal of fire in the opening & crowded it down with his foot. Off went the power & away went the shell in pieces tearing its way in every direction. Three men were terribly injured, Daly Rouse & Donahue,[2] all Dunkirk boys while others some 8 or 9 were more or less injured. Daly lost his left leg, Rouse his right one & Donahue has a terrible cut in the left side under his arm. A man has just come & said Rouse is dead. I saw the two legs amputated & other horrible wounds dressed for they were badly cut to pieces. It was a sad sight to see strong men prostrated by such a fearful accident. Very likely they may all die, but I hope not. My first impression was that the rebels had found out where our camp was & sent a shell over to us & were doing us up in that way. It has been a terrible rainy day & we hardly have felt like looking out of doors. I hope by tomorrow the sun may shine again & dry off the camp. I must now close & get ready for bed. My dear boy I pray a Kind Heavenly Father may watch over you & all the dear ones at home. Kiss your dear Mother for me

---

[1] His horse.
[2] Michael Daly, Co. E, 72nd New York; John Rouse, Co. E, 72nd New York; James Donahue, Co. E, 71st New York.

& be a good boy. Give my love to all the family. Kiss the dear brothers & sister & remember my thoughts turn to you all no matter where I am or what is going on.
 Goodbye dear Frank
 I am your affectionate Father,
 Levi W. Norton

In December, 1861, Chaplain Norton was stricken with typhoid fever. Hospitalized in Washington, DC, and unable to be with his ten-year-old daughter when she died, he remained there after his 15 April 1862 resignation because he was too weak to travel. When he returned to Jamestown, New York, during May, he may still have been contagious because seven-year-old Levi Junior died on 10 August 1862. That same year, St. Luke's was destroyed in a fire. Reverend Norton rebuilt the church and spent a number of years as a pastor in New Jersey at Metuchen and Rahway. He retired in Jamestown during 1892 and suffered a stroke three years later. He died 23 August 1900 on a trip to Bemus Point with his son and daughter.[3] His remains rest in Lakeview Cemetery, Jamestown.

---

[3] Service and Pension Case Files of Levi W. Norton, RGs 94 and 15, Records of the Veterans Administration, National Archives, Washington DC.

Pocket Diary

Chaplain John Crabbs, 67th Ohio Volunteer Infantry

On 25 November 1861, John Crabbs was mustered as a private in Company I of the 67th at Seneca, Michigan. He gave his occupation as "clerk," but he was a clergyman who had designs on the regiment's chaplaincy. "My occupation has been, and is, twofold," he wrote in a pension application during 1886, "that of a local clergyman with occasional work on the Sabbath, and that of a merchant tailor during the secular days of the week."[1] Before enlisting, he had obtained endorsements from community leaders who sat on the Military Committees of Fulton and Lucas Counties recommending his appointment as chaplain of the 67th Ohio. He apparently did duty as a private soldier until, as he notes in his diary, he was appointed regimental chaplain on 15 January 1862.[2]

Born 22 October 1823 in Jefferson, Ohio, the chaplain was nearly twenty years older than most of his regiment, though this was not an uncommon circumstance for chaplains. Because of his age, however, Crabbs soon fell prey to illness which would mark his army career and cause his resignation.

> *In the Shenandoah Valley campaign against Stonewall Jackson under General Shields, I took severe colds in several instances, and at Harrison's Landing under General McClellan, I went down with dysentery and typhoid fever. When the army evacuated that point, I was placed upon a hospital boat and transferred to the General Hospital at Point Lookout, Maryland. After several weeks, I ventured to rejoin my regiment but was still weak and afflicted with a severe cough which terminated in bronchitis, which compelled me to abandon the service at Bermuda Hundred.[3]*

---

[1] Pension Case File of John Crabbs, Record Group 13, Records of the Veterans Administration, National Archives, Washington DC.

[2] In January 1862, Rev. Smith Curtiss of Toledo, who had been an applicant for the same job, alleged that Crabbs had bribed Col. Otto Burstenbinder, the regimental commander, to secure the chaplain's position. Burstenbinder was eventually fired, but Crabbs remained in place as chaplain.

[3] Pension Case File of John Crabbs, Record Group 13, Records of the Veterans Administration, National Archives, Washington DC.

Pocket Diary 1862

Rev. John Crabbs, Chaplain 67th Regiment, O.V., USA, Morenci, Michigan.[4] If I should fall by disease or in battle, send this book to my wife in Morenci, Michigan—her name is Susan Crabbs.[5] Bishop E. S. Jones, N. Y., Soldiers Hymns. C. L. Pascal, Philadelphia, Manufacturer of Army hats for Chaplains.[6] Number of J. Crabbs revolver 3747. Captain John G. Klink, Pittsburg Landing, Tennessee, Sherman's Division. Married at Suffolk, Va., Nov. 21, 1862.[7] D. Appleton & Co., N. Y., Military writing course.

Sunday, Jan 5, 1862—Morenci, Michigan. Held an hour's discussion with D. Morning on the question of an infinite mind as ruling and regulating the affairs of the Universe.

Monday, Jan 6, 1862—Engaged in the recruiting service of the US Army, received several applications.[8]

Tuesday, Jan 7, 1862—Continued in the recruiting service.

Wednesday, Jan 8, 1862—Enlisted and had sworn into the service Mr. J. M. Rothruck a man who will make a good soldier.[9] Having received intelligence that my services are desired at Camp Chase, I started immediately to take the cars at Adrian, Michigan.[10] Started from Adrian at 3:00 A.M.

Thursday, Jan 9, 1862—Reached Camp Chase at 2:00 P.M. today, found the men mostly well. Entered the ranks for afternoon drill. The

---

[4] "O. V." is an abbreviation for 67th Ohio Volunteers. Morenci MI is west of Toledo OH, on the Michigan-Ohio state line.

[5] Rev. Crabbs married Susan Ilger on 25 September 1845 at Ashland OH.

[6] Chaplain Crabbs evidently made notes as reminders about Bishop Jones's "vest pocket size" hymnals and Appleton Publishing's self-instruction booklet for regimental clerks, as well as the Pascal Company as a source for regulation head gear.

[7] Capt. John G. Klinck was commissioned 3 August 1861 in the US Army as an assistant quartermaster of Volunteers and mustered out 28 July 1865. Chaplain Crabbs may have officiated at a wedding relevant to Klinck, since the 67th was at Suffolk on the given date.

[8] John Crabbs enlisted in the 67th Ohio Volunteers on 25 November 1861 and was detailed as a recruiter in his hometown.

[9] John M. Rothrock, Co. I, 67th Ohio Volunteers, promoted to sergeant on 11 January 1865 and honorably discharged on 1 September 1865.

[10] Named after former governors, Camps Chase and Dennison were the largest military camps in Ohio. Camp Chase was west of Columbus. Adrian MI is about twenty miles northeast of Morenci.

ground muddy and disagreeable. The men are all anxious to receive marching orders to the enemy's country. Drilled the greater part of the day, the ground having frozen the last night so as to make marching comparatively pleasant.

Saturday, Jan 11, 1862—Rain today making our drill unpleasant. The 29th Ohio volunteers now in camp here received marching orders for Eastern Virginia at about 9:00 A.M. They prepared to march, but before they had marched 2 miles they received a countermanding order and with their baggage they returned to camp and are yet here. This is a fine Regiment, well prepared for the field.

Sunday, Jan 12, 1862—Order was issued for Church parade this morning at 9 o'clock but owing to the extreme inclemency of the weather the order was countermanded.

Monday, Jan 13, 1862—Today all the Regiments in Camp Chase had a grand review at Columbus, Ohio, on the occasion of the inauguration of Governor Tod. The 67th received from the Adjutant General and the Governor the praise of being the best Regiment on the ground of its age.[11] The 67th performed a march of about 12 miles during the day.

Tuesday, Jan 14, 1862—Had company drill in the forenoon today and dress parade in the afternoon. The boys somewhat wearied over the march and review of yesterday.

Wednesday, Jan 15, 1862—Had the usual drill and parade today. Received the appointment of Chaplain in the 67th Regiment of Ohio Volunteers with the rank of Captain of Cavalry.[12] Received the congratulations of the officers in view of my promotion.

Thursday, Jan 16, 1862—Entered upon the discharge of the duties of my new office by the distribution of Bibles and Testaments to officers and

---

[11] David Tod (1805–1868) succeeded William Dennison as governor of Ohio on 13 January 1862 at the State House in Columbus. The adjutant general at the time was C. P. Buckingham. The 67th Ohio Volunteers numbered 1,030 when they were mustered at Camp Chase. Eventually a total of 2,393 soldiers served in the regiment from October 1861 to December 1865. Of that total number, 1,410 were between the ages of fourteen and twenty-five.

[12] A chaplain's pay was equivalent to that received by a captain of cavalry: $100 per month. Some Union Army chaplains took this comparison beyond its intent, however, and wore the shoulder straps of a captain as if they were company commanders. A regimental chaplain was not in his unit's chain of command.

men. Commenced boarding today with the officers mess at the headquarters of the 67th Regiment O. V. M., USA.[13]

Friday, Jan 17, 1862—Continued the distribution of Bibles and Testaments to the officers and men in the 67th. Made a visit to the Ohio State House and attended the session of the Ohio Legislature.

Saturday, Jan 18, 1862—Received today my commission as Chaplain of the 67th Regiment O. V. M. USA. Prepared for marching to Romney, VA.[14] Contracted today my chaplain equipment at Columbus, Ohio from Quartermaster:

1 Sword	$18.00
1 Chaplain's coat	23.00
1 Chaplain's pants	10.00
1 Chaplain's vest	5.00
1 Chaplain's cap	4.50
TOTAL	$60.50
Express Charge	.75

Sunday, Jan 19, 1862—Commenced the march today from Camp Chase to Romney, Va. by the Central Ohio RR to Bellair on the Ohio River thence by the Baltimore & Ohio RR to New Creek 28 miles from Romney.[15] Four companies paid off at the State House in Columbus, Ohio, during our march through that city.

Monday, Jan 20, 1862—Detained today at Benwood on the Ohio River, in consequence of high water and break in the railroad. Nothing of note today but the monotony of lying still in camp.

Tuesday, Jan 21, 1862—Detained further today at Benwood for the same reason assigned on yesterday.

Wednesday, Jan 22, 1862—Prepared today to continue our march from the Ohio River to the vicinity of Romney. Great dissatisfaction manifested on the part of the six companies which were not paid off.

---

[13] Abbreviation for the Ohio Volunteer Militia, US Army.
[14] Romney WV.
[15] Bellaire OH is across the river and five miles south of Wheeling WV. New Creek is west of Romney.

Thursday, Jan 23, 1862—Reached New Creek Station at 1 o'clock this morning. Remained quartered in the cars until daylight, when we pitched our tents on the Virginia bank of the Potomac awaiting further orders.[16]

Friday, Jan 24, 1862—The Regiment today ordered to prepare three days' rations so as to be ready for emergencies.[17]

Saturday, Jan 25, 1862—The 67th today called out for drill in light and heavy skirmishing. Reconnoitering parties today near Romney, find no appearance of the enemy.

Sunday, Jan 26, 1862—The day opens with stormy and rough cold weather in consequence of which church services in camp were suspended. Commenced boarding today noon with Mr. Long's family—a very fine family.

Monday, Jan 27, 1862—Nothing new today. The Regiment continues its squad and skirmishing drill preparatory to immediate action as a contact with the enemy is anticipated daily.

Tuesday, Jan 28, 1862—Our pickets today had a contact with the enemies [sic] pickets and took several prisoners. Several batteries of artillery passed us today for Paterson's Creek.[18] In the hospital today with the sick.

Wednesday, Jan 29, 1862—The weather mild today. Men at work building a bridge across the Potomac for the transportation of troops and military stores. The enemy's signal rockets observed last night in the direction of Sheats Mills. Scouts sent out today in the directions of Romney.

Thursday, Jan 30, 1862—Some of our pickets were driven in last night by a body of the enemies cavalry. Three of the enemies scouts captured. A detachment of about 100 of our cavalry sent out this morning in the direction of Romney and met a superior force of the enemy, dispersed them and rescued a union man whom they had taken prisoner by the name of Daniel Waterman.[19] Our cavalry also burned a large mill property known as Sheats Mills. Visited Provost Marshall Playford.[20]

---

[16] On the West Virginia side. West Virginia was not yet recognized as a separate state in 1862. The 67th Ohio was to guard the Baltimore and Ohio Railroad, a vital rail link across western Maryland.

[17] Preparing three days' rations involved cooking salt beef or pork and filling haversacks for the march.

[18] East of New Creek Station on the Baltimore and Ohio Railroad.

[19] From Co. B, 77th Ohio Infantry.

[20] Capt. George H. Playford.

Friday, Jan 31, 1862—Nothing of importance today. The weather cold and disagreeable. The Potomac and its tributaries still swollen which retards the march of troops. Several men of the 67th O. V. sent to General Hospital at Cumberland with mostly measles.[21]

Saturday, Feb 1, 1862—The weather yet cold and disagreeable. Many of the men in camp coming down with the measles. Regiments here ordered all to prepare three days' rations and hold themselves in readiness for marching.

Sunday, Feb 2, 1862—The day opened stormy. Went to the Headquarters and succeeded in getting an order for working on bridge suspended until Monday which intelligence was received with great joy by the soldiers of the 67th. Spent the day in visiting the tents and the sick in the hospital. I was detailed to take the sick to Cumberland tomorrow.

Monday, Feb 3, 1862—Errands: Hospital visited today with 17 men in General Hospital. For the Colonel of the 67th O. V.—1 watch hand, piece of chain, large crystal.[22] For Mr. Sibley at Revere House—C. K. W. Sibley inquire for letters. For Captain Ford, Co B, inquire about Ira Johnson, Marshall Huett, Peter Miller and Elbert Porter.[23] For Lieutenant Carlton— see Bill and money.[24] For Stebing—letters.[25] For M. Roth—postage and envelopes.[26] For Captain Bensey—Lieutenant Miller is he in care of the surgeon? 2 pounds of tobacco.[27]

Tuesday, Feb 4, 1862—Hospital: R. Davidson—better, Peter Miller— better, John Sutton—better.[28] Revisited this morning the 11 sick brought down last night by the train, found them doing as well as possible but not so

---

[21] General Hospital at Cumberland MD.

[22] Col. Otto Burstenbinder, age thirty-two, dishonorably dismissed on 29 July 1862 for maladministration of the regiment.

[23] Capt. Hyatt G. Ford, age twenty-seven, commanding Co. B, who was killed at Kernstown VA on 23 March 1862. The enlisted men were Pvt. Ira Johnson, age eighteen, Co. B, who died of disease in the General Hospital in Cumberland; Pvt. George Hewett, Co. F; Pvt. Peter Miller, Co. B, wagoneer; and Pvt. Albert Porter of Co. B.

[24] 1st Lt. Sheldon Colton, Co. K, discharged for disability on 9 October 1862.

[25] Pvt. William Stebbins, Co. K.

[26] Pvt. Jacob Roath, Co. G.

[27] Capt. Charles A. Rowley, Co. D; 2nd Lt. Louis Miller, Co. D.

[28] 1st Lt. Robert Davison, Co. F; Pvt. Peter Miller, Co. B; Pvt. John Sutton, Co. F.

comfortably situated as deserved. Visited the following who had been brought last week and found them all doing well: Ira Johnson, Mr. Keewit, Peter Miller, A. Porter, James Baxter, J. Wikly, Co B; F. Young, Co I; S. D. Moon, Co G; J. D. Robinson, Co I; Mr. D. Blain, J. Sutton and J. Celey [sic].[29] Captain Mason sent Caley [sic] a heavy blanket.[30]

Wednesday, Feb 5, 1862—Returned from Cumberland after having visited the sick of the 67th. Upon returning to New Creek found that our Regiment was ordered to move to Patterson's Creek. The 55th O. V., 73d O. V., USA came to New Creek yesterday also one battery artillery. Marched from New Creek today and reached French Town 40 miles east on Balt & Ohio at ten P.M.[31] Four regiments ordered tonight for some unknown destination.

Thursday, Feb 6, 1862—For Captain Platt—brandy to the amount of $2.50.[32] Get watch hand, deliver letters and get mail for 67th O. V., USA, bills for Lieutenant Dewey[33] and one whetstone. Prisoner brought in today as a spy. Captain Ford out with a skirmishing party. Rev. Mr. Keith tracts for Army, informant—Rev. Andrew J. Lane.[34]

Friday, Feb 7, 1862—Visited today the deserted country of four large farms belonging to Simeon Dudley.[35] Nine slaves consisting of boys, girls, men, women and children. Their master has been in the South Army since May last. Butter for hospital to the amount of $1.00, tea for the hospital—$1.00. Troops marching 13 & 14 Indiana today.[36]

---

[29] Pvt. Ira Johnson, Co. B; Captain Dewitt Dewey, Co. F; Pvt. Peter Miller, Co. B; Pvt. Albert Porter, Co. B; 2nd Lt. James Baxter, Co. A; Pvt. Joseph Wiley, Co. D, who died at Petersburg on 2 September 1864; Cpl. Friend Young, Co. F, who died of disease at Alexandria VA on 3 August 1862; Pvt. S. Dallas Moon, Co. G, age eighteen, who died of disease in the Cumberland Hospital, 15 February 1862; Pvt. James D. Robinson, Co. I, age twenty-one; Pvt. Myron D. Blain, Co. F; Pvt. John Sutton, Co. F; and Pvt. John Kaley, Co. F.

[30] Capt. E. D. Mason, Co. F.

[31] Baltimore and Ohio Railroad.

[32] Capt. Thomas J. Platt, age twenty-two, promoted to major and assigned to the regimental headquarters in 1865.

[33] Capt. Dewitt Dewey, Co. F.

[34] Chaplain Andrew J. Lane, 62nd Ohio Volunteers, a member of the Pittsburgh M-E Conference, informed Crabbs that Chaplain William K. Keith, 7th Maryland, had a supply of tracts.

[35] Pvt. S. J. Dudley served in the 36th Virginia Infantry.

[36] The 13th and 14th Indiana Infantry Regiments.

Saturday, Feb 8, 1862—Troops marching: 7th Virginia today, 62d Ohio, Col Pond; 5th Ohio and 84th Pennsylvania all to Pawpaw Tunnel camp near Beaches Store.[37] Our present positions: 58 miles from Harper's Ferry; 50 miles from Winchester; 13 miles from Blues Gap; 19 miles from Romney; 100 miles from Manassas; 17 miles east of Cumberland[.]

Monday, Feb 10, 1862—Cumberland, sick relief association. Large attendance of ladies, surgeons, and chaplains. Object to relieve the sick and provide delicacies for the convalescent. Ladies called upon to volunteer in the good work and to signify their willingness by arising whereupon most present arose. The proceeds to be placed in care of the principal surgeon. James Baxter, descriptive list of certificate of enlistment; J. D. Robinson, descriptive list; George Stebbins, discharge. Write for Marvin C. Shaw to Esther Shaw in Chesterfield. For Freman Buckley to Channey Buckley.[38] Look for express for 67th. Find the date of deaths in hospital.[39] Detailed today to go to Cumberland and visit hospital, stay till ordered to regiment.

Friday, Feb 14, 1862—General Lander captured 17 officers and 43 privates at the Bloomers 16 miles from Pawpaw Tunnel towards Winchester.[40] Battle this morning. The enemy attacked by the Ringgold Cavalry and the First Virginia Cavalry.[41] Our infantry did not keep up with the cavalry but was close when the attack was made. Our captured was 2, the enemy 30. We took as prisoners 17 officers including a colonel, a major and 43 privates. Bloomers 16 miles in the rear of Winchester.[42] This all new ground.

Saturday, Feb 15, 1862—Cumberland—Prisoners captured yesterday brought into Cumberland today, their appearance [rest of sentence illegible]

Sunday, Feb 16, 1862—Cumberland—Sick today

---

[37] The camp was at Paw Paw WV, seventeen miles southeast of Cumberland MD. The 7th (West) Virginia Infantry was the unit first referenced. Col. Francis B. Pond commanded the 62nd Ohio Infantry.

[38] Chaplain Crabbs wrote letters for some soldiers including John Buckley and Marvin C. Shaw of Co. A.

[39] More reminders written to himself.

[40] Brig. Gen. Frederick W. Lander died on 2 March 1862 at the Paw Paw camp.

[41] The Ringgold Cavalry Battalion eventually was consolidated with the 22nd Pennsylvania Cavalry Regiment; the 1st (West) Virginia Cavalry of Lander's Division was commanded by Col. Henry Anisansel.

[42] Bloomery Gap WV.

Wednesday, Feb 19, 1862—Sick today
Thursday, Feb 20, 1862—Sick today
Friday, Feb 21, 1862—Not so well today.
Saturday, Feb 22, 1862—Today a beautiful flag costing $80.00 was presented to the 67th O. V., USA by Gen. Lander from the ladies of Toledo, Ohio.
Sunday, Feb 23, 1862—Attended a funeral today of a soldier. Rest and meditated on the scriptures. Attended Church in the evening.[43]
Saturday, Mar 22, 1862—Near Winchester, Virginia. Skirmish with Ashby's Cavalry supported by artillery.[44] General Shields wounded by the bursting of a shell, the left arm being fractured above the elbow, the wound was dressed by Dr. McAbee.[45] This menace of the enemy made it evident that war's work was before us. And our troops were on the lookout. A part of our forces moved forward and occupied the ground where the skirmish occurred until morning.
Sunday, Mar 23, 1862—Kernstown Heights, heavy battle on our side.[46] One brigade about 5000, General Kimball's Brigade 4th, 8th, 67th Ohio, 14th Indiana, 84th Pennsylvania, 3d Brigade, General Tyler a part of the 3d Brigade.[47] On the enemy's side Jackson's Stonewall Brigade, Turney's Brigade, Shetz Cavalry, Ashby's Cavalry, in all 6000.[48] Colonel Down's

---

[43] Regimental records indicate Chaplain Crabbs was absent on leave during portions of February and
March 1862.

[44] Col. Turner Ashby (1828–1862) was Stonewall Jackson's cavalry commander. He was promoted to brigadier general on 23 May but was killed in action on 6 June 1862.

[45] Brig. Gen. James Shields (1810–1879) was wounded and resigned 28 March 1862. Dr. H. M. McAbee was the regimental surgeon of the 4th Ohio Infantry.

[46] The Battle of Kernstown VA on 23 March 1862 was a victory for the Union and one of Stonewall Jackson's rare defeats. Jackson attacked a Union force that proved to be twice as large as he anticipated. When the Confederate brigades were almost out of ammunition, the Union reserve counterattacked and drove Jackson's men from the field in disorder.

[47] Col. Nathan Kimball, promoted to brigadier general on 16 April 1862, was commanding Shield's Division in the absence of Gen. Shields, who was wounded the day before. Col. Erastus B. Tyler was the brigade commander. After the victory at Kernstown, Tyler was promoted to brigadier general on 14 May.

[48] In Jackson's order of battle, Brig. Gen. Richard Garnett commanded the Stonewall Brigade, Col. Peter Turney commanded the 1st Tennessee Regiment, and

Battery, Clark's Battery, Battery L of the 4th Ohio. Conduct of the 67th noble of officers on the occasion. Companies A and I in the skirmish killed and wounded. The 67th occupied the advanced position in the morning.

Monday, Mar 24, 1862—This morning pursued the enemy to Strasburgh fighting almost every mile. Reinforced by Banks.[49] Camped during the night near Middletown, 5 miles from Strasburgh. We found Jackson's dead and wounded. Wounded were scattered all along the road from that battle ground to Strasburgh. Our surgeons stopping at several places to dress the wounds of the Rebels.

Tuesday, Mar 25, 1862—Crossed Cedar Creek by a ford, the bridge being burned, and pursued Jackson two miles beyond Strasburg. Returned to Strasburgh. Dr. J. Westfall, our assistant surgeon, amputated a wounded Rebel's arm, his name was Pat Sullivan.[50] He had a wife and five children in Richmond. I called at the house several days after and found that Pat was dead.

Wednesday, Mar 26, 1862—This morning the cook of Co C was found dead in his quarters. He died of apoplexy. I attended his funeral. He was buried on an elevated spot near our camp. I performed the burial service over his remains and the usual volleys were fired over the grave.

Friday, April 4, 1862—Visited today the cemeteries of Winchester. Observed the burial of several soldiers—how it was done. Visited the grave of General Morgan of Revolutionary fame.[51] Inscribed on his marble slab: "Major General Daniel Morgan, departed this life on July, the 6th, 1802, in the 67th years of his age. Patriotism and valor were the prominent features of his character. And the honorable services he rendered to his Country

---

Col. Turner Ashby Jackson's cavalry. The other reference is probably to Brig. Gen. George H. Steuart's cavalry on loan from Ewell's Division. Jackson's forces numbered 4,200 and suffered 700 casualties. The Union forces numbered 9,000 and sustained 590 casualties.

[49] Strasburg VA. Maj. Gen. Nathaniel P. Banks (1816–1894) had the misfortune to be defeated repeatedly by Stonewall Jackson. It is estimated that Banks lost 30 percent of his soldiers during the Valley Campaign of 1862.

[50] Dr. James Westfall of the 67th Ohio Infantry. Patrick Sullivan was in the Stonewall Brigade at the Battle of Kernstown.

[51] Daniel Morgan was a hero of the battles of Saratoga (1777) and Cowpens (1781) and was awarded a gold medal by Congress for his valor. His home was in Winchester after the Revolutionary War.

during the Revolutionary War, crowned him with glory and will remain in the hearts of his countrymen a perpetual monument to his memory."

Saturday, April 5, 1862—Distribution of prayer books by our Episcopal Chaplains. A soldier asks what he shall do in the night with his prayers if he has no candle?

Friday, Sept 5, 1862—Philena Heald, Box 455, Wilmington, Delaware. Many times will memory recall the hours spent at Ft. Lookout. Kindly thou shalt be remembered my friend, may God bless you and keep you, truly your friend, Philie.[52]

Deaths in the 67th Regiment O. V., USA[53]
Feb 19, 1862 Wm McKess Company B
Feb 9, 1862 W. Freman Company G
Feb 28, 1862 James Burk Company G
Feb 9, 1862 Silas Wels Company E
Feb 24, 1862 Martin Mikel Company H
Mar 12, 1862 Ira Johnson Company B
Mar 4, 1862 Mr. Fuller Company G
Mar 1, 1862 Levi C. Lyon Company G
Mar 4, 1862 Joe Ballard Company F
Mar 4, 1862 M. Fowler Company G
Mar 6, 1862 F. W. Stuart Company K
Mar 15, 1862 S. Birch Company G
Mar 14, 1862 Charles Hancock Company G
Mar 9, 1862 A. Michler Company G
Mar 9, 1862 R. Adamson Company I

---

[52] Evidently a letter of appreciation. Fort Lookout was a name applied to part of Point Lookout MD, a notorious Confederate prison camp.

[53] Chaplain Crabbs listed fifteen men from the 67th Ohio who died in the Cumberland General Hospital of disease between 9 February and 15 March 1862. Many of the names are misspelled even though the dates and company designations are correct. The surnames should be: McKay, Freeman, Joseph Burk, Wells, Wikle, Johnson, Fowler, Louis Lyon, Franklin Ballard, Mead Fowler (second listing), F. M. Stewart, Samuel Burd, Charles Hancock, Alex Muchler, Robert Adamson, and (unlisted) George Winfield, Co. G. Of these fifteen men, eight were eighteen to nineteen years old, and four others were between twenty-one and twenty-five years old. The other three were in their forties.

The pocket-sized diary of Chaplain Crabbs falls silent at the time when his ailments began to hamper his activities. His military service and pension files at the National Archives outline the rest of his time in the army, but afford none of the details which might be found in a diary. Crabbs left Hammond General Hospital at Point Lookout and returned to duty 8 September 1862. He rejoined the 67th at Suffolk, Virginia, where that little hamlet was transformed into a fortified camp from which the Union would strike at the Confederate food supply that came out of eastern North Carolina. Before Longstreet's siege of Suffolk, however, Crabbs and the 67th Ohio were moved to South Carolina and the operations around Charleston Harbor. Able to go home for fifteen days during Christmas, 1862, Chaplain Crabbs was present for duty through 1863. He received a thirty-day furlough on 23 February 1864 after the regiment re-enlisted.

When the 67th Ohio Veteran Volunteers returned to duty, they became part of the struggle for Richmond and Petersburg in the 10th Corps under General Ben Butler. It was during that hot, dusty summer and the vicious fighting in the Bermuda Hundred that Chaplain Crabbs decided to resign. He was granted a disability discharge effective 7 July 1864 due to chronic bronchitis. He returned to Morenci and lived there until his death 15 June 1888.

Chaplain Crabbs's diary is on permanent loan to the US Army Chaplain School at Fort Jackson, South Carolina.

"Two Great Wars of America"

Chaplain Horace James,

25th Massachusetts Volunteers

In the following address, Horace James lives up to his reputation as a "pulpit orator," just as his own life answered his question as to whether the Civil War would produce any "giants among men." Born 6 May 1818 in Medford, Massachusetts, James became a Presbyterian minister by way of Yale, New Haven Seminary, and Andover Theological Seminary, completing studies at the latter during 1843. He immediately took up the role of pastor in sleepy Wrentham, twenty miles southwest of Boston, and remained there until assuming the pulpit of Worcester's Old South Society in 1853. He became a leader of Worcester's Temperance League. Taking a year off during 1858, he toured Europe.

The 25th Massachusetts was raised entirely within Worcester County during September 1861. Reverend James assisted with recruiting by speaking at war meetings, and he himself joined on 21 October 1861 as regimental chaplain. As part of the Burnside expedition to North Carolina, the regiment played a prominent part in the battle of Roanoke Island, where Chaplain James took over for a fallen member of a cannon crew. Soldiers said he was "true as steel." The 25th remained in North Carolina for almost two years and participated in fighting at Trenton, Plymouth, Tarboro, Kinston, and Goldsboro until ordered to Newport News, Virginia, during December 1863. While there, half the regiment re-enlisted and the veteran volunteers went home on furlough. When the command was reunited in late March 1864, it was with a new chaplain—Stephen G. Dodd—because Reverend James had accepted promotion to staff officer as a captain and assistant quartermaster of US Volunteers. While his Worcester boys went on to fight in Virginia at Cold Harbor and Petersburg, Captain James served to honorable discharge on 8 January 1866.

Despite his changed military rank, Horace James continued work he had taken on in 1862 when named Superintendent of Negro Affairs in the District of North Carolina. He established settlements for freed slaves on Roanoke Island and across the Neuse River from New Bern. James City, which grew up on the site of the colony he founded on the banks of the Neuse, was named in his memory.

Chaplain James delivered the following address to his regiment at New Bern, North Carolina, on 4 July 1862. Before the sun went down, he received a request, signed by every commissioned officer in the 25th Massachusetts: "We are induced by *a desire to refer again to the principles therein taught—to its elevated tone and pure patriotism...in behalf of ourselves and friends, to request a copy of the Address for publication."* That same year, 200 31-page booklets titled The Two Great Wars of America, an Oration Delivered in New Bern, North Carolina, before the Twenty-Fifth Regiment Massachusetts Volunteers, July 4, 1862 *were published by W. F. Brown & Co. of Boston.* Today, one copy is in the library of Cleveland's Western Reserve Historical Society, and another in the public library of Worcester, Massachusetts, where James had been a well-known and respected pastor.

The Two Great Wars of America

Friends, fellow-citizens, and soldiers of the Army of the United States: I bid you welcome to the festivities of this hour. With emotions of profound gratitude to God, the Author of liberty and Arbiter of destiny, we celebrate another birthday of the GREAT AMERICAN REPUBLIC.

Looking reverently and affectionately upon her face, yet fair and fresh in national youth, we seem to hear her exclaim in the words of one of her gifted sons, "I still live!" aye, though rent with faction, burdened with debt, involved in war, her plains whitened with military encampments, her very soil furrowed with shot and dank with human gore, while treason is still unsubdued and defiant over a portion of her domain; she doth lift up her voice with strength, and summon her children, in prouder, clearer tones than ever, to assemble together and kneel with patriotic devotion around her altar.

From our hearts we obey; for we love our country, and because of that love for her we are here. We are the constituted guardians of her honor. We bear with us the assurance of her integrity, and are appointed to see that she receives no detriment. We recognize no South, no North, no West, no East, as a separate interest. We know nothing but our Country, however bounded, by whomsoever governed; our Country one and inseparable; our Country guided by the great principles of liberty and law, which were inwrought by skillful hands into her admirable constitution, which have shaped her institutions, inspired her struggles, and are to be still more grandly illustrated in her future history.

We meet to-day upon soil reclaimed to the Union by our victorious arms in a city where one year ago there was no public recognition of our nation's independence, where no peal of bells or salvo of cannon ushered in the festal morning; but a wretched cluster of waning meteors and three dismal bars disgraced the heavens, and a misguided people and an army in open rebellion against the government, contemptuously derided the dignity and sovereignty of the United States.[1]

Thank God! The Old Flag flutters again in the breeze along these shores and waters. In every one of the thirty-four States the "star spangled banner" floats proudly to day. The work of recovery goes bravely on. A series of brilliant successes by land and water is just about to culminate in a battle before the rebel capitol, which will decide the fate of the southern "Confederacy," and virtually end this wicked war.

So we hope. Meanwhile, summoned at such a time as this to the consideration of our country's interests and dangers, may we not appropriately review the great Rebellion and War now upon our hands and compare it with the former or revolutionary struggle of 1776, in respect to its ORIGIN, CHARACTERISTICS, AND PROBABLE RESULTS? My plan of thought, on the present occasion, will lead in this direction.

The wars of 1776 and 1861 are entitled to be called the *two great Wars of America*. In respect to the magnitude of the interests involved, the numerical strength of the forces engaged, and their absorbing power over the public mind and heart, no other struggles that have occurred in this hemisphere are equal to them. One of them is finished, and has passed into history. The other is incomplete as yet. It has, however, sufficiently revealed its character to convince all reflecting men that its influence will continue long after its scenes have transpired, and be an important element in the solution of great social questions, affecting the interests of mankind.

In these two struggles the belligerents have belonged to *the same race*—Anglo-Saxons, fought against Anglo-Saxons in the last century, and the same is true now. We are said to be engaged in *"a civil war,"* and in a very senseless manner some have rung the changes upon the barbarity and wickedness of such a war. So was the war of '76 a civil war. It was one of brother against brother, and sire against son. The British realm and its trans-Atlantic colonies were but one household. Yet Englishmen were not

---

[1] Maj. Gen. Ambrose E. Burnside won a reputation for independent command with his successful expedition against military objectives on the North Carolina coast. He entered Pamlico Sound with ten thousand troops and nearly 100 sailing vessels, steam transports, propeller gunboats, and floating batteries. One newspaper termed it "a large city afloat." Roanoke Island was taken on 8 February 1862, New Bern 14 March, and Beaufort 26 April. Expeditions were then launched from New Bern against Washington, Plymouth, and Edenton NC.

then affected with holy horror in view of its being a fratricidal strife. The truth is that "a civil war" may be as justifiable and as necessary as a foreign war. The moral quality of such a strife cannot be decided by questions or race and descent.

Both these wars *commenced in rebellion*. The patriot of the revolution was no less a "rebel" than the secessionist of the present day. Those who for any reason throw off the obligations of allegiance to the supreme power, are "rebels" in the eye of the law. Whether they shall *continue* to be branded with this epithet depends partly upon the justice of their cause, but more upon their *success*. Rebellion in its early stages is treason; after its firm establishment in power it is patriotism and glory. The rebellion of '76 passed on triumphantly to the latter stage. That of '61 seems unlikely to do so. Unsupported by the recognition of a single member of the family of nations, and giving but doubtful evidence of ability to maintain itself anywhere, it leads as yet the life of a vagabond, its Ishmaelitish hand against every man and every man's hand against it. Whether it shall enjoy any honorable history, or stand upon the record as anything more than a monstrous political apostasy of immense pretensions, but of proven impotence, remains to be seen, and will be speedily determined. It must work out its own salvation, and make its anniversary a nation's gala day, as the first great rebellion has done, or else sink, an execrated thing, beneath the world's notice and contempt. There is no intermediate state for it between a political heaven or hell.

A resemblance between these two wars is perceivable in the *variety of individual opinion* which prevails respecting them. In the era of 1776, there were conservative and radical men, extremists on both sides of the agitating questions of that day, as we see it to be now. This must continue to be the case so long as men are born with varying temperaments, and educated to varying tastes. That the community should be divided into upholders of the American Union and seceders from it, is perhaps no more strange than that there should have been "whigs" and "tories" in the revolutionary war. In every State there are secret sympathizers with the enemy. We may expect that Union principles will spring up in the steps of our victorious armies. They will not declare themselves to any extent except under the gleam of our bayonets and the protection of our flag. Upon their spontaneous utterance we cannot depend. As little can we depend upon the patriotism of a small party in the loyal States, the moment that any reverse is experienced by the national arms. There is even a little clique in the Congress at

Washington, contemptible indeed in numbers but unscrupulous, artful, practiced in debate and in legislative strategy, represented by an Ohio member of ineffable name, who show clearly enough by all their votes and speeches that they would establish the Southern Confederacy if they had the power to do it with impunity.[2] They are traitors to the Constitution and as worthy of political punishment as the tories of the old revolution.

Selfishness, alas! In the forms of personal ambition and the cursed greed of gain, are found hanging like vampyres upon the throat of the best enterprises, sucking the life-blood of the nation, and outraging the moral sentiment of mankind. Patrick Henry gave such men the benefit of his keen satire in the old war. Washington felt indignant at their baseness; but the degenerate race survives.[3] Wolves in sheep's clothing, wretches who can pierce their country to the heart under the guise of friendship, who can assume the livery of the court of heaven to serve the devil in, base enough to make merchandise of a distressed and perplexed nation, to grow rich upon contracts that have defrauded a too-confiding government, and imperiled her most important military movements. The curse of heaven rest upon their ill-gotten stores! [T]he profits of their shoddy cloth and their rotten meat! May their riches become corrupted, their garments be moth-eaten, and the hard earning of the common soldier which they have taken away by fraud, cry out against them before offended heaven.

In refreshing contrast with the acts of mercenary contractors and jobbers who have been developed in such large numbers during this contest, is the *self-denying spirit*, and *cheerful endurance of suffering* which have to such an extent characterized this war. It falls not behind the old revolutionary struggle in respect to these high qualities. On both sides men with families have left their happy peaceful homes, at short notice, uttered a hurried farewell as they kissed away the falling tears, and departed to the seat of war, not knowing, not once thinking, whether they should ever return. Exile has been cheerfully borne, the privations of the camp, the dangers of the field, the discomforts of the hospital. On both sides these have been endured, in many cases by those who suffered deservedly, but with a heroism worthy of a

---

[2] Reference to Clement L. Vallandigham (1820–1871), an Ohio Democrat who sat in the state legislature and Congress before running for governor in 1863. Arrested for sedition 6 May 1863 in a rash move by Gen. Burnside and exiled by order of President Lincoln, he walked into Confederate lines 25 May.

[3] Patrick Henry (1736-1799), colonial patriot, orator, Governor of Virginia; George Washington (1732-1799), first President of the United States.

better cause; all tending to show that the self-sacrificing spirit of the revolutionary heroes is still extant in their descendants. The race of patriots is not extinct. By tens and hundreds of thousands they may be enumerated among the officers and enlisted volunteers of the Union army; and in large numbers, I doubt not, among the rank and file of the Confederate forces. We will not claim that all the personal virtue, as well as the justice of the war, is on our side. Among those arrayed against us, and against their country, are many doubtless, who with mistaken zeal think themselves doing God service. Their treason is the result of a defective education, of degrading social institutions, and a blind confidence in *leaders* who are basely and with lying lips misleading them to their ruin. It is one of the wicked things of this war that so many men with honest intentions are fighting under a misapprehension of the facts; fighting bravely, but with a lie in their right hands. A terrible responsibility rests upon the souls of those few men who have plunged them into this strife, and by pertinacious and unblushing mendacity are still nurturing within them a hostile spirit. Let but a few hundreds of ambitious demagogues at the South be slain or hanged, let that oligarchy of non-producing aristocrats that have taught the South to hate the North, that have made labor despicable, and viewed our mechanism as an ignominy and a degradation; let these few rich slaveholders, in short, who have shrewdly managed to usurp and wield the power of these States, and of the General Government as well;—let but these uneasy plotters of sedition be somehow disposed of, and their influence neutralized, and the masses of the people North and South, East and West, would rush into each other's arms, would flow together like water; and when they had done so, the very floods would clap their hands!

There are several points of *striking unlikeness* between the rebellion of 1776, which resulted in the American Union, and the rebellion of 1861, whose precise destiny has not yet been reached. It may better illustrate the spirit of each of them to present these points briefly in vivid contrast.

They were greatly dissimilar in respect to their *statement of justifying causes*. No political document that was ever penned has echoed around the world more sublimely than the Declaration of American Independence. Its very words are hallowed and classic to the lover of political liberty, as they fall so clearly, so convincingly upon the ear. The cause must needs prevail that was thus supported by facts, by arguments, by appeals to the common sense and sound judgment of mankind. That Declaration alone was worth to the patriot cause an army of one hundred thousand men. The people that could so express their grievances and their rights as they stood at the world's judgment bar, were and of right ought to be, a free and independent people. The government that had so abused them had forfeited all claim to exercise authority over them.

Examine now the annals of the seceded States and of the so-called Confederate Government, and what is their statement of justifying causes for the steps they have taken? I admit the abstract right of revolution. But the reasons must be good and sufficient, and the statement of them must be clear and distinct. For any such statement in justification of the present rebellion we look in vain. The real reasons which prompted it are artfully concealed, and those openly rendered are indefinite and unworthy. We find in them no lack of appeals to heaven to witness their sincerity, such as a devout Arab might make who intended to commit robbery the next hour; but we fail to find in them any appeal which is adapted to convince the sound judgment of mankind. They have jumbled together a verbose and specious justification of their course, in which imagination is largely drawn upon to supply the lack of facts, and upon such a flimsy platform they have concluded to go before the world. Their declaration has convinced no one, for it declared nothing, and done them no good, for it had no force. Bearing a faint resemblance in form to the famous document of Thomas Jefferson, it is so devoid of any spirit kindred to it, as to attract no observation from any quarter.

Totally unlike, also, have been these two movements in their *pervading principle and spirit*. Our fathers strove for simple liberty. Resistance to oppression, not fancied, but real and persistent, was the one impulse that animated them. They had no wish, at first, for separation from the mother country, and no lofty aspirations for power. Had their just demands been acceded to, the American Revolution might have been postponed until now, and the British throne be still the center of our allegiance. But taxes without representation, the Boston Port Bill, the Stamp Act, and other outrageous feats of legislation, together with the intolerable insolence of royal governors from Hutchinson of Massachusetts, to Tryon of North Carolina, were more than they could bear.[4] And when their cup of oppression was full, they thrust it indignantly from them and dashed it to the ground.

---

[4] Thomas Hutchinson (1711–1780), colonial governor of Massachusetts; William Tryon (1729–1788), colonial governor of North Carolina.

What is the animating principle of the present rebellion? I hesitate not to pronounce it the *lust of dominion*. The Southern States were willing to remain connected with the Union so long as they could rule it. By their superior political tactics, and by taking advantage of divided and nearly balanced parties at the North, they have had control of the General Government through most of its administrations, having placed either Southern men, or Northern men with Southern principles, in the executive chair. Thus have the few contrived to outwit the many, and an oligarchy has long governed the country through the forms of republicanism. It was not until this scepter was seen to be departing, in the election of a Northern President, uncommitted to the support of their peculiar institutions, that a remedy for this loss of power was discovered in *secession*. If they could no longer rule, they determined to ruin the government of their fathers, and set up another which should be wholly their own. So long had they been "masters of the situation," that they could brook no change, even though it came in a regular way, and gave the Northern States no particle of power or influence that was not rightly theirs by the Constitution. That instrument had been kept by them inviolate. Contrary to their own moral convictions, the Northern people had held to the original bond, and even permitted a Southern interpretation of that instrument to prevail, merely for the sake of peace. But the Southern oligarchy, accustomed to rule, had pressed their demands so boldly and so far that the North could endure it no longer. So they elected for once a President of the majority, and said to the minority, "It is now your duty to yield." This is the head and front of their offending. Yet for this cause they have passed the ordinance of secession. For this cause they have inaugurated a new revolution. For this cause they fired upon Fort Sumter; for this cause they have already shed the blood of thirty thousand freemen.

And in this respect, in the two contests, the facts appear to be reversed. The weaker party are now the oppressors, and lofty pretenders to power and place. Eight millions are attempting to lord it over twenty millions. The Secessionists of the present day, are the British of the past, and hence their English proclivities are easy to be accounted for. The North is now where the struggling colonies were in the olden time, doing battle for liberty against oppression, for democracy against aristocracy, for *right* against organized, pampered, overbearing, irascible *wrong*. As the foreign foe in those days looked with contempt upon the raw, undisciplined troops of the colonists, and insultingly dared them to mortal combat, so have the haughty

Southrons looked upon the people of the commercial North, and deemed them, with all their wealth and resources, only the mud-sills of society, an inferior people, a cowardly horde, who would be scattered like chaff whenever they should draw their puissant swords. Not the least resemblance can we discover, in spirit or principle, between our revolutionary fathers and the revolutionists of this day. Even if the latter should be successful as the former were, they would establish that tyranny which the others attempted to destroy, and destroy forever that noble fabric of freedom which the others erected with consummate wisdom, and cemented with their blood.

Not more unlike have been these two rebellions in the spirit that animated them, than *in the previous preparation that was made* for them. Our early patriots were found totally destitute of the materials for carrying on a great war. A conflict at arms had not entered into their calculations, and a state of actual hostility found them but poorly provided with all the needful munitions and stores. They rushed into the earlier engagements with their rusty fowling-pieces and their home-made powder horns. In the battle of Bunker Hill, in which the enemy confessed a loss of one thousand fifty-four men out of two thousand engaged, the scanty allowance of each of our soldiers was only a gill of powder, two flints, and fifteen balls not made into cartridges. The patriot army was fed, armed, and paid only by the superhuman exertions of Washington and his associates, in the face of overwhelming difficulties, with neither means nor credit at command, and with absolutely nothing previously provided.

Not so the rebellion of 1861. This jumped into being fat and flourishing from the hoarded savings of I know not how many years. Its leading spirits, fed at the public tables, transacting the public treasury, had been carefully laying for a long time the train that was to be exploded at a fitting moment, and do the works of a generation in an hour. While the country, busy and confiding, pursued its career of prosperity, never dreaming of danger, *Toucey* was sending the ships of the navy on useless expeditions to the ends of the earth, *Floyd* was stealing guns from all the Northern arsenals, and amassing them at various points in the South, *Cobb* was tampering with the credit of the United States, and bringing its fiscal affairs into a state of utter confusion.[5] Parties in the interest of the divisive

---

[5] Three members of President James Buchanan's cabinet: Isaac Toucey (1796–1869), secretary of the Navy, from Connecticut; John B. Floyd (1806–1863), secretary of war, from Virginia; Howell Cobb (1815–1868), secretary of the treasury, from Georgia.

movement, and acting under secret instructions, were moving in all directions with intense activity, doing everything possible to bind the hands and weaken the power of the General Government, and to make everything ready so that their warlike confederacy might leap into being, Minerva-like and fully armed, from the head of the old Republic, and deal at her birth, a death-blow to her sire. Thus have the rebels of the seceded States been plotting, preparing, amassing, and dividing the spoils, robbing, plundering, and stealing, through the connivance or sympathy of their Northern abettors, until it came near to proving the utter destruction of the American State. One cannot contemplate this particular chapter of our nation's history without an involuntary shudder. We were on the brink of ruin. Our capitol was almost in the hands of an armed enemy; and for a few weeks the great republic, paralyzed and powerless, had only a name to live! It becomes us to acknowledge, at this happy hour, with profound gratitude to God, the special providential care which guided us through that dark period, and delivered the nation from those perjured and malignant men. Nothing but their execution upon the gallows will ever atone for their crimes. May the memory of them perish from the earth!

As the two contests I have named differed so essentially in respect to previous preparation, it was to be expected that they would differ also in *fortune of the field*. And so indeed it occurred. The earlier experiences of the revolutionary patriots were defeats. As the war progressed, and the resources of the colonial army were increased, victory began to perch upon their standards. But the confederate cause, of late afflicted with defeat upon defeat, in one long and almost unbroken series, commenced with successes. The army of tyranny in each case advanced strong and defiant in the beginning. But they did their best in the first impulsive onset. The forces of freedom were amassed more slowly, but when once trained in the field, and arrayed for the strike, their cool, determined progress swept all before them. A causeless rebellion, though prospered at the start, must expire in disgrace. But the forces that contend for liberty and law, though worsted it may be, in the first assault, will return with increased strength and confidence to the fight, until they proudly survey the field as conquerors.

The two great struggles which we are attempting to compare, have had but little resemblance to one another in *the number of troops engaged* in them. Then our whole population was three millions, now it may be thirty-three millions. Then we might have had an army of fifty thousand; now it exceeds five hundred thousand. The decisive actions of Saratoga and Yorktown in the American revolution, look puny beside the battles of Manassas, Shiloh, Fair Oaks, and Richmond.

The *expenses incurred* furnish another item of striking comparison. Six years of warfare with Great Britain did not equal, I think, the expenses of a single year of war for the Union. But then we had no navy, no river or harbor defences, no iron-clads nor Monitors. Our fathers crept timidly along according to the then prevalent modes of warfare, and were as ignorant of a rifled cannon, or a balloon reconnaissance, and indeed of a telegraphic message, a steam transport, a railroad supply train, a rubber blanket, a percussion cap, or a Mini ball, as were the old Romans of gunpowder and daily papers. The difference of the two eras, in celerity of movements and brilliancy of exploits, by reason of the great inventions and improvements of modern science, is immense, and to us scarcely conceivable. True indeed, river piles, chevaux de frise, torpedoes, and infernal machines, do not always stop the progress of invading fleets and armies, as our own experience testifies; but the appliances of science and skill, when rightly and promptly employed, offer an immense advantage in the prosecution of war, not less indeed than in the pursuits of peace.[6]

What will be the effect of this conflict in developing *character*, and raising up *great men*, remains to be proved. After the former struggle had ceased, we were enabled to gaze reverentially upon a band of heroes, such as the world had never seen. "There were giants in those days." George Washington, John Adams, Patrick Henry, Roger Sherman, John Hancock, Benjamin Franklin, Alexander Hamilton[7]—what names are these, and such as these! Their pure patriotism, their exalted wisdom, their guiding counsels shaped events for ages. To no set of men since the apostles of Jesus, has so much been committed; of none can it be said that they so faithfully restored their trust. When one looks upon those departed heroes, and is affected with feelings but little short of adoration towards them, he is inclined to ask the question: Will this great national crisis call forth another generation of like minded patriots? When deliverance has come to our whole land, and she

---

[6] Chevaux de fries was a type of defensive palisade used as an obstruction to attackers. Using a log as a shaft, pointed sticks were driven through the log to form an "x" with sharp ends facing the enemy.

[7] President George Washington; President John Adams; Governor Patrick Henry; Judge Roger Sherman; John Hancock, president of the Second Continental Congress; Benjamin Franklin, Minister to France; Alexander Hamilton, secretary of the treasury - all patriots of the American Revolution.

shall again enjoy peace with righteousness, shall we be able to encircle with unfading rays the names of our deliverers, and enshrine them with our revolutionary sires, in the national Pantheon? I would fain hope so. This rebellion will furnish its name of infamy to complete the trio of treason and perfidy, so that *Judas and Arnold* and *Floyd*, may forever sink to their own places in company. Will it not also add the names of *Ellsworth*, and *Greble*, and *Winthrop*, and *Lyon*, and *Lander*, and *Ellett*,[8] and many others yet living, to the roll of patriots whom the nation will delight to honor! It is, my fellow citizens, a privilege to live in such a day as this, for it brings immortality within the grasp of every man.

I hasten to inquire, *what are to be the results of this rebellion* and war of 1861 and 1862[?]. I do not claim to be a prophet, with power to foretell events that are as yet concealed among the mysteries of Providence; but will speak of results as in my own view they ought to take place, provided this wretched insurrection shall be everywhere effectually checked and suppressed. And among them will be, first and foremost, a UNION RESTORED, ESTABLISHED, AND PURIFIED. I say restored. No soldier in the army, or in the navy of the United States, and no loyal citizen at home, is willing to accept anything short of a union perfectly restored. Not one square foot of its territory can be given up, even if it were upon the plains of Deseret, or among the dreary sands of Hatteras. The principles of dismemberment cannot be allowed for a moment. The great rivers and mountain chains of North America, with their system of valleys and streams, are adapted to one and only one people. Secession is a violation of the physical laws impressed upon the face of this continent, as well as the fundamental laws of the republic. As a doctrine, it must perish in infancy, and sleep in the grave never to rise again. All the territory now under insurrectionary rule must be restored, till there is seen but one national flag, one capitol, one currency, one congress, and one executive, and all the machinery of the confederate government, with its executive officers and their unfinished projects are swept into oblivion. As sure as there is a sun in the heavens, our conquering armies will not furl their banners nor sheathe

---

[8] Col. Elmer E. Ellsworth, first Union officer killed in the Civil War; Lt. Col. John Trout Greble, killed in battle, Big Bethel VA, 26 May 1861; Pvt. Theodore Winthrop, author, killed in battle, Great Bethel VA, 10 June 1861; Brig. Gen. Nathaniel Lyon, first Union general killed in the Civil War; Brig. Gen. Frederick W. Lander, died of wounds at Paw Paw WV, 1862; and Col. Charles Ellet, died at Memphis TN in 1862.

their swords, until the union of North American States is perfectly restored from the gulf to the lakes, and from sea to sea.

And when restored it must be *established*. Not set up like Dagon to fall upon its face again, but plated so deeply that no tempest of passion can prostrate it, no lightnings rive its root, no floods undermine its deep foundations. This must be the last experiment of the kind. Secession is too expensive a luxury to enjoy a second time. When our government has reasserted and established its sway over the whole land, it must stand strong as the pillars of Hercules, no element of weakness being left in it, no plague spot upon its fair exterior to spread around its foul contagion.

Aye, we aim at a union *purified*. It does not wholly satisfy us that its integrity is to be maintained; we long to see it improved and strengthened in every element that enters into material greatness. Why should our dear republic be exempted from the great law of growth? If it be not altogether perfect yet, in God's name let it go onward to perfection. Why fetter it in its uprising? Why stint and limit an organization so superior; so freighted with sublime possibilities, so well fitted, as experience shows, to shed a blessed light upon the nations that sit in darkness, and be an element of hope to the world?

There are those who exclaim "give us the *'union as it was'*." It was indeed a glorious union *before*, but we want it grander, purer, stronger, every way. After passing through such a baptism of suffering and blood, should it not become possessed of a higher sanctity? God forbid that our national afflictions should fail to be improved, or be the means of hardening us more and more in national guilt and sin. If they should wean us from our selfishness and absorbing greed of gain, if they should purify our public counsels and our private life, if they should promote the growth of mutual good feeling between man and man, if they should bring judgment to the oppressed, and education and ultimate freedom to the enslaved, and cause all classes to value more highly the blessing of a good, paternal, wise administration of government, then should we have occasion to count it all joy that we had fallen upon these evil times, seeing that they had resulted in a bountiful harvest of blessings to the nation and the world.

Who can be so senseless as to ask for a restoration of "the union *as it was?*" Establish it, indeed with all its previous wealth of beauty and glory, but with as much more as may be possible. Fill it with all the elements of truth and liberty, humanity and benevolence, that can be breathed into it, and this time, if possible, make it immortal.

Nay; I will go farther, and assert that the "union as it was" *is impossible*. A person has had the small pox and has recovered. But his system has undergone a radical change. The marks and scars of the foul contagion are upon him, but his body is no longer susceptible to that loathsome disease. He has not recovered his health "as it was," but is in a sounder condition than before. And when there has been a loathsome eruption upon the body politic, shall the radical evil be left uncured, only *to break out again?* No, no; let us *not* restore "the union as it was," with the same liability to be torn by treason and furrowed with the plowshare of war. Let us now restore to power and activity the same agencies that have proved to injurious heretofore, only to see them produce the same mischievous results again and again. From my heart I pray never to see the union again established *"as it was" just before this rebellion took overt shape,* placed in a condition for another imbecile President to abandon it to its fate; for another perjured Secretary to plunder and rob it, and for another nullifying State to openly insult and contemn its sovereignty. If there be, as we believe there is, one fundamental vice of society in all the rebellious States, which has chiefly tended to nurture this rebellion, and which has continually given it life and excitement, shall we not attempt in some suitable and just manner, to weaken and remove this evil, that it may harm and distract us no longer?

You know to what I refer; and I feel no obligation of delicacy, leading me to refrain from touching briefly upon the domestic slavery of the seceded States in this connection. They cherish it because it supports that aristocratic social system, which they have deliberately chosen, and are confessedly fighting for. We reject and oppose it, because it is subversive of all business prosperity, is a curse to the State which upholds it, an unspeakable injury to the colored people themselves, and a still greater injury to their masters. And although in our military movements, as such, we have nothing to do with this institution, we are in fact procuring and producing its overthrow. We have not *introduced* the Negro into this war. But he is in it, and in every part of it, and can no more be expelled from it than leaven can be removed from the loaf that has begun to ferment. Would that a purified government might escape this annoyance and disturbance in all time to come. Would that one rebellion in the interest of this wretched, wasteful, and worthless system of labor might prove sufficient. Would that all at the South and at the North would examine Negro slavery, not with fanatical zeal, but with calm, considerate attention, and agree together to put an end to it by gradual and compensated emancipation, as a harbinger and hostage of our peace, and a blessed deliverance both to the master and the slave.

When this war shall cease, and a settlement be made of the various matters at issue between the two sections, it will come to pass that a *better understanding will prevail between them than ever before*. The South has greatly misunderstood the North. The few, who, by their social position, give tone to public opinion here, have maliciously belied the North, in order to foster a state of feeling that might lead to a separation. But the intercourse of warfare will do something, and the intercourse of peace yet more, to dispel delusions, to abolish factitious distinctions, and to equalize the social status of the Puritan and the Cavalier. There are those in this army who never will settle again in New England, to reside there permanently, but will enter upon some of these uncultivated tracts of land, do something to develop the neglected resources of this broad section of country, and thus come, with blessings in their hands, to the people of the South. The States now vainly attempting to establish a separate independence, will become truly independent, and truly great, when, giving up their aristocratic notions, they begin to stimulate *free labor*, establish *free schools*, call out the energies of all classes by elevating, rather than depressing them, and *level up* society to a standard of general intelligence and thrift. Herein, and in no other possible course, is to be found their salvation as commonwealths. By this course only can they recover from the terrible prostration resulting from this war. This is the kind of "subjugation" we wish to impose upon them, namely, an exaltation and blessing, a dignity and wealth of civilization, to which they have been heretofore strangers.

I am inclined to take a hopeful view of the future. And in a comparatively short space of time, I seem to see this shameful political apostasy annihilated, and the whole land consenting, either willingly or unwillingly, to one grand central government. Under the new stimulus imparted to all its industries, by the returning demands of peace, I see every wheel, spindle, and pinion again revolving, and the nation, as a nation, learning war no more. With a considerable standing army, yet maintained to promote the common security and confidence, I behold the multitude of our teeming population going forward to possess the land, and covering with beautiful villages and cities the slopes and hillsides and plains of our goodly domain.

By a system of compensated emancipation in part, and in part by the fortunes of war, I hear liberty proclaimed throughout the land unto all the inhabitants thereof. Going forward in the steps of a free and Christian civilization, I see my countrymen attaining to a purer nobler personal life, and thus laying the foundations of national distinction in the beautiful virtues of individual character. I see our government, having survived the shock of war, and having maintained both the form and spirit of a democracy, while other nations in similar circumstances had relapsed into a military despotism, still leading all the governments of Christendom in a grand career of political distinction, still attracting towards herself the admiring gaze of mankind. Having maintained her financial credit in a wonderful manner, in the day of her trial and calamity, and when browbeaten by transatlantic nations, and threatened with an intervention which she neither needed nor desired, I see her unfurling her flag of forty or fifty bright stars, before the eyes of France and England, from the masthead of more vessels than their combined navies and mercantile marine can boast, and disputing with her own mother country the title of "mistress of the seas." And as ages roll on, and her population increases, her debt is extinguished, her wealth accumulates, her cities grow numerous, and her churches, asylums, colleges, and schools may be counted by hundreds of thousands, we shall still behold in her unexampled greatness the influence of her present trials, and new evidence of the exceeding goodness of God unto her. May the brazen throats that today echo her praises, and the star-spangled banners that stream above her soil, be ever the bulwarks of her liberty, the defenses of her manhood, and the dread of tyrants whether at home or abroad.

Peace brought James back to his work as a minister and a whirl of activity. From 1867 through 1870, he was pastor for Lowell's First Congregational Church as well as district secretary for the American Christian Union. Moving to a church in Greenwich, Connecticut, during 1871, he also became editor and part-owner of The Congregationalist. *In 1873, during a tour of the Holy Land, he took sick with what was later diagnosed as consumption. He retired to a hillside cottage in Boylston, just north of Worcester, on the estate of a friend. Horace James died there on 9 June 1875, leaving a wife and child. His grave is located in Wrentham.*

Chaplain Thomas Kinnicut Beecher, 141st New York Volunteer Infantry

"Free of vanity, forthright, with a grim humor and a not too hopeful view of human nature, but stubbornly devoted to helping his fellow man, Thomas Beecher was at once the most unorthodox of the seven sons of Lyman Beecher and perhaps the most truly Christian."[1] *Born 10 February 1824 to the Reverend Lyman Beecher and his second wife, Harriet Porter, in Litchfield, Connecticut, Thomas was the next-to-last child of eleven who survived infancy. A persuasive temperance preacher and founder of the American Bible Society, Lyman held irreverent renown as the "New England Jehovah." Tom grew up among siblings who turned out as extraordinary as the elder Beecher. Catharine and Isabella were lucid, energetic crusaders in behalf of women's rights. Half-sister Harriet wrote* Uncle Tom's Cabin. *Half-brother Henry Ward Beecher went the way of all Beecher males—into the Congregationalist ministry—and became the quintessential orator of 1850s America. A family friend paid tribute to Lyman and his unique brood with the observation that America was then "inhabited by saints, sinners and Beechers."*[2]

With these natural aristocrats of sensibility as models for developing his inherited Beecher gifts, Thomas was destined for the highest achievements, but the Beechers were as troubled as they were compelling. The strength that enabled them to do successful battle against unfathomable causes and unaccountable effects was matched by a mirror-image potential for decline. Lyman experienced lengthy depressive periods which were attributed to "dyspepsia." Most of the Beechers were subject to episodes of "nervous prostration." George Beecher was described as "a cheerful, buoyant man" who was the soul of his congregation, but he stepped outside of his kitchen door with a shotgun one July morning in 1843 and took his own life.[3] *An avid missionary in China before the Civil War, Tom's younger brother James first served as chaplain of the 67th New York Infantry, then as lieutenant-colonel of his brother's regiment, and finally as colonel of the 35th Regiment of US Colored Troops. Discharged with the brevet rank of brigadier-general and married to Connecticut socialite "Frankie" B. Johnson, James endured several re-eclipses of his*

---

[1] Milton Rugoff, *The Beechers: An American Family in the Nineteenth Century* (New York: Harper & Row, 1981) 285.

[2] Ibid., xii.

[3] Milton Rugoff, *The Beechers: An American Family in the Nineteenth Century* (New York: Harper & Row, 1981) 203–204.

sanity until he shot himself while visiting Tom in Elmira.[4] *Thomas K. Beecher had his own share of the family demons but somehow mastered them.*

So much a cynic that family members referred to him as "Thomas the Doubter" and distracted by a mechanical aptitude that ranged from carpentry to making astronomical instruments, Beecher took five years to get through Illinois College at Jacksonville where half-brother Edward was head of the school. He pursued a teacher's career after attending Yale Divinity School, but his faith seemed to crystallize when he encountered Reverend Horace Bushnell in Connecticut while principal of Hartford High School. Three years after his 1851 ordination, Beecher become pastor of the First Congregational Church of Elmira, New York, now called Park Church.[5] *Except for the four months as a Civil War chaplain and a trip to England during 1873, he was minister to that church until his death on 20 March 1900. Near the Park Church on Main Street in Elmira stands a statue of Thomas K. Beecher erected a year after his death. Inside the church, a tribute is engraved upon the altar: "In Memory of Thomas K. Beecher 1824–1900. Workman, citizen, philosopher, minister: nature stamped him by courage, candor, love to be a shepherd of souls."*

Beecher's unique descriptions of his experiences as a regimental chaplain are straight and true. Mustered 12 September 1862 as chaplain of the 141st New York Volunteers, he gave seven reasons for joining.

Of the nine hearty men in Elmira called ministers at least three ought to be doing duty and I am one of those three; there are no enterprises of great importance which I could serve by staying; the 141st Regiment is gathered from companies in which I am known—no other minister could enter the regiment and be recognized so quickly; the determination of the Colonel to have me; I can serve the regiment in various arts and handicrafts; every man in the regiment knows it is no gain—but a great loss—to go with them and this will give me sincerity and authority; it will be easy to see if I succeed and easy to resign if I don't.[6]

---

[4] Compiled Service Record of Chaplin James Beecher. Records of the Record and Pension Office, RGs 94, National Archives, Washington DC.

[5] "Great Man Dead, Rev. T. K. Beecher," *Elmira* (NY) *Daily Advertiser*, 20 March 1900.

[6] *There was a man sent by God. Thomas K. Beecher 1824–1900: Teacher of the Park Church at Elmira, New York 1854–1900* (The Park Church, 1900).

Chaplain Beecher called his prayer meetings "chaplain drills" and held them after the camp call "tattoo" signaled an end to the day's activities and before "Taps" put out all lights.

Chaplain's drill opens with a box-drag by two, of a very greasy box on which hospital pork is cut by day, to a convenient site, whereon the Chaplain stands and swings his lantern. When enough gather around to say 'We,' the Chaplain begins to talk. What he says need not be written, for he has already told all he knows in Elmira. He finds it refreshing to talk to new faces, and get off old things as if they were new. What good times those Methodist preachers have, moving every two years. Next to editing a daily paper, I count preaching three or four new sermons a week to be the most unreasonable tax and draft on human brains. Church-goers! don't find fault with stupid sermons, until you've tried to write one hundred per year for eight years.[7]

When his subject was grave, Beecher could be as compelling as he was humorous.

Another one of our best men—Corporal Fox, Co. H, from Avoca—has fallen asleep, to rest from his labors. I do not use these words as trite euphemisms, but as Christian truths sincerely spoken. I feel as if somehow the dead belong to me. I have no difficulty in remembering their faces and their names. It is not so with survivors. They are busy here and there; I see them by moments at a time, now as guards pleasantly saluting me, now as police tidying our streets, now as fatigue parties shouldering spades, or as home-loving men waiting at my tent door for letters, or as hungry men filing around the kitchen fires plates in hand. Somehow, such meetings do not impress me. They do not strike in and fix themselves. But a man takes sick and at once he seems an acquaintance. He talks to me—tells me his hope and his fear—listens to my instructions and says amen in a whisper to my prayers. He fades day by day, and at last his clean, white sharp-cut face is recognized in the open coffin; they who knew him best are by him—his three officers stand and wait for Chaplain to speak.[8] I cannot explain it—but

---

[7] Thomas K. Beecher, "Letter from Chaplain Beecher," *Elmira Weekly Advertiser and Chemung County Republican* (Elmira NY), 18 October 1862, 1.

[8] Reference to the three officers in every company's chain of command: captain, first lieutenant, second lieutenant.

'tis so—the departed are more mine than the staying—the dead are more to me than the living. If a hundred of these men die, I shall be able to call their roll easily.[9]

Chaplain Tom's most comical moments came in describing his attempts to make a comfortable bed.

Being of an investigating nature, I've been looking experimentally into the subject of beds. Laying aside all traditions and prejudices, I began with first principles and have this night finished my round of experiments. Shall I report?

Our soil here is stiff light yellow clay with a few gravel stones mixed in. There was a grass stubble on its surface. My first experiment was to lay a sheet of rubber down, then a blanket double, then the Chaplain, and over him shawl and blanket. Sleep was good, but crickets peopled the grass and made bad noises and crept with prickly feet up and down one's flesh. Grass not good; clean it out.

Experiment 2d. Drive three stakes in a line, set up a narrow board on edge, throw in straw between the board and tent wall. Rubber sheet, blanket, Chaplain, &c., as before. Result was a pleasant sensation, at first reminding one of beds at home, but by and by the Chaplain feels like meat boiling in too little water: raw and cold above the straw, moist and steaming in the straw. Throw out the straw, clean up the tent.

Exp 3d. Bare, hard dry ground, blankets, chaplain, as in the last experiment. Slept well, except dreams of bridge building and strength of materials. One's body touches at three points—head, thighs, and heels. The trunk represents a fixed arch, the limbs a drawbridge. The strain is too great. The abutments crush and settle. Sleep is good but not much rest.

Exp 4th. Take axe and spade and make up a bed, by artificially molding the ground to the form of the Chaplain. Consider a well-used hog wallow recently deserted, and how nicely it fits and welcomes the occupant's return, and you have the archetype of the Chaplain's fourth bed. Result satisfactory, perfectly so, except that an old campaigner says that the ground is unhealthy.

---

[9] Thomas K. Beecher, "Letter from Chaplain Beecher," *Elmira Weekly Advertiser and Chemung County Republican* (Elmira NY), 21 November 1862, 3.

Exp 5th. A Manilla hammock such as the natives sling up between two trees, and swing in the wind therein, held the Chaplain four nights. Slung between two tent poles, the slack was excessive, and the narrowness oppressive. One seems to shorten at both ends, and to be perpetually "dressing on the center." When first tucked in, the reminding is of a mummy, or a patient in pack at Elmira's water cure. Fault—one cannot turn over, nor get out of bed without help. Send back the hammock to the courteous Colonel.

Exp 6th. A sacking bottom, well stretched. Blankets, Chaplain, &c., as in experiments one, two and three. Result—very cold. Wind sucks under and blows up through. Memo: Plan a good one if one can have five blankets and a shawl. Otherwise very bad in cold weather. Last night, water froze a quarter-inch thick at my tent door.

Exp 7th. The floor, the modeled ground *a la* hog wallow. To this I return from all my experimenting. The ground—the bare ground. Bring me the axe and the spade, let me make my bed. Lie down, Chaplain, make your mark. Friend Bailey, scrape away where he touches, copy the curves—ease off that lump—pick away that stone—there, that fits. The wallow is perfect. In five minutes more, it will hold the Chaplain.[10]

Because most New York regiments were recruited within one or two counties, local newspapers kept readers informed about hometown units by publishing letters from their members. Chaplain Beecher had a hand in raising the 141st New York Volunteers, and his letters spoke to loved ones eager for any news of sons, husbands, and brothers.

Camp Hathaway
Laurel, Md., Oct. 5, 1862
Dear Editor:[11]
Our Sunday is over—the Drum Major has executed what he calls a "'flammer doodle," to call the Companies into line for roll-call. I hear a half-dozen Orderlies calling names, and men answering. This finishes the daily duty. In a little time the lights will be out, and the camp dark, all but the officers' tents.

---

[10] Thomas K. Beecher, "Letter from Chaplain Beecher," *Elmira Weekly Advertiser and Chemung County Republican* (Elmira NY), 1 November 1862, 3.

[11] Thomas K. Beecher, "Letter from Chaplain Beecher," *Elmira Weekly Advertiser and Chemung County Republican* (Elmira NY), 10 October 1862, 3.

Shall I tell you of our Sunday? At first dawn you may easily hear that 'tis Sunday, for the camp is far quieter than usual, even though a soldier's duty does not cease on any day. Indeed, a duty that begins with a solemn enlistment oath, may well be counted a religion, and have its place upon even the Lord's day.

At quarter of ten, our Adjutant forms parade, while the Chaplain fixes a box pulpit out in a neighboring meadow. Then the battalion marches out and forms in front of the Chaplain—close, compact and attentive. A short prayer of invocation—a hymn—a passage or two from the articles of war—a short lesson from Scripture, with very few words of explanation or reminder—a prayer—and the sung doxology, complete a catholic regimental service.

As we close, the village bells tell us of other assemblies, at which many of us attend. At the Episcopal Church my brother and I attended, and for the first time in our lives took the sacrament of our Lord together.—That the liturgy laid hold of our hearts—that the Scripture lessons seemed strangely fresh and instructive—that pensive and devout memories crowded up unspeakable—and that we prayed tear blind, "Thy kingdom come, Thy will be done on earth as it is done in heaven"—need not be told to you. No wonder that soldiers, sailors and all travelers love liturgies. To hear in a strange land the same words one has learned to love at home; to remember the uncounted thousands who are using those same words with us, brings one to a conscious "communion of the saints"—"The holy church throughout all the world doth acknowledge Thee."

This afternoon and evening there have been volunteer and irregular meetings of our men in both camps. Our last was at the lower camp, where Companies B & C are sojourning. By the light of the moon the Chaplain read the hymn, "Rest for the Weary," and by the light of memory, "Shining Shore," verse by verse read and sung with heartiness. As we sang "Shining Shore" I heard an organ and the voices of many people, in a little meeting house, and listening, I couldn't sing any more, but let the song go on to the end. Then came a little talk. I cannot tell you how quiet and truthful we all seemed as we stood under the cedars together, and tried to see and feel and pray for true religion,—the grace and strength of God in the soul. And so Sunday has ended.

Our Colonel had a pet horse—a graceful sorrel—a noble creature—the gift of a personal and patriotic friend. Mounted on this horse, the Colonel visited one by one our railroad pickets yesterday. One or two trains passed close beside them, and no harm was done; but a third, more swift and thundering, with whistle screaming, struck the horse and threw him aside, useless and dying. The Colonel barely escaped—having hastily dismounted. If you have ever seen a fine horse, intelligent and affectionate, lie a dying, and looking up from his deep eyes into his master's face for help, you will know why to this hour the story of the accident moves a noble hearted man to tears.

Yes, we have had our second gun-shot accident. A man of Co. F has shot away the thumb and finger of his right hand. He's a good and brave man, and is doing well.

'Tis past ten. The walls of our tents are black with flies, driven in by the cold. We may have our first frost by morning. We three tent-mates will have to snug up close together and keep warm as little pigs do, for we have no extra blankets.

The whole camp is dark, save the light of the guard's fire. Let me hasten to fold this sheet, put out my candle, shut my eyes and see the procession of my dear friends at home, and pray for them as they pass. God bless and keep you—keep you strong and single minded.

Hastily but truly yours,
Tho's. K. Beecher

The following letter was sparked by comments of Frederick Barritt, a soldier in the 23rd New York Infantry, another regiment raised in Chemung County. After describing how the army celebrated Thanksgiving despite shortages of food and tobacco, Barritt criticized the government's "extravagance and useless expenditures." Taking particular aim at regimental chaplains, he wrote, "These functionaries are generally of a class who command from $400 to $600 a year as working clergymen in country parishes, but here they often become lazy, fault-finding, selfish, and parsimonious, rarely visiting the sick—as distant as possible from death-beds and especially from battlefields—rarely preaching and more rarely asked to preach—sometimes infidels—they are in very moderate esteem as a class, and they ought to be. Public sentiment calls for their abolishment."[12]

Camp 141st N. Y. V., Minor's Hill, Va
December 14th, 1862.

---

[12]Frederick Barritt, Letter to the Editor, *Elmira Weekly Advertiser and Chemung County Republican* (Elmira NY), 13 December 1862, 3.

Dear Editor[13]—The readers of your paper have had rest long enough. It is time that Chaplain's drill should begin again. By the by, speaking of Chaplain, reminds me of Fred Burritt, your correspondent, and his private letter about chaplains. I wish to say amen to the general sentiment, as to the uselessness of chaplains in the military service. Of work properly belonging to a chaplain there is not enough in six regiments to employ one man. I would not work two hours a week if I confined myself to my proper official duties.

One field officer, who is at the same time a soldier and a christian [sic], does more for the religion of a regiment than ten men in sober black, serving as official authority-less chaplains. In any properly ordered regiment, there is a duty for every hour of the day. All the men of the regiment are "under the law"—and if good soldiers they are perfect in that righteousness which is after the law. To be strictly obedient to discipline is a better religious training than most ministers preach or church members practice. Any common young man, bred for the pulpit, will find himself usually below the regimental standard of righteousness. He will find himself the most disobedient man in the regiment. And he will therefore be as far from the men as any officer, while, unlike other officers, he will have no tie of authority.

If then the chaplain be a young man, as they usually are, he will, little by little, come to be merely an idle staff officer, on duty at funerals and on Sunday—at other times free to come and go, much to the envy and disgust of the men and the dissipation of his own principles.

I am not surprised that so many chaplains prove hard drinkers and otherwise disgraced. I do not know of any young man whom I would dare thrust into the chaplain's place, amid its thousand temptations.

The chaplain ought to be, for weight of character, a higher man than the commandant. All other officers have an authority because of their shoulder straps and commission. The chaplain must be as "one having authority" in himself alone. Instead of sending adventurers and sheepless pastors, our churches should yield up their weightiest men, or send for army chaplains none at all.

Further, unless the commanding officer completely respects and trusts the chaplain, far better have no chaplain at all. The head of a regiment is the

---

[13] Thomas K. Beecher, "Letter from Chaplain Beecher," *Elmira Weekly Advertiser and Chemung County Republican* (Elmira NY), 20 December 1862, 3.

Colonel, the heart of it should be the chaplain. From the head comes orders, from the heart exhortations. If a divorce exists then the orders are hard and dry, and the exhortations devoid of influence.

Much more I might add, but I do not purpose an essay upon army religion. I intended at first merely to say that in my judgment the army would gain by dismissing all chaplains, and trusting to the voluntary acts of officers and men. I would this day prefer to have my commission revoked, and my stay with this regiment, and my support, made to depend upon my military parish. Such, I understand to be the practice in the rebel army.[14] If it were also in our own there would be many hundred chaplains flying home, and I doubt not many hundred working with new diligence and success among the men of their regimental congregation.

I write thus freely and decidedly because my position and opportunities have been unusually advantageous as a chaplain. I have nothing to ask for personally or officially from my officers or my men. And yet, even while enjoying the most advantageous social position in my regiment of any chaplain whom I have yet heard of, I am clearly persuaded that, as a chaplain, I am nearly or quite useless. Were it not that there has been a world of other work, I should long since have relieved the regiment of my presence—and the treasury of my support.[15]

And now as to religious reading and other literature furnished by the million pages for distribution, I have a word or two. The paper, pictures, type and plentifulness are beyond praise. But the contents are often times ridiculously unapt and worthless among soldiers.

Society papers, of which I can obtain thousands, are full of items and letters addressed to Christians and churches at home to keep up an interest and promote contributions to the society funds.[16] One half the matter is thus useless in camp. Why the directors and Secretaries do not print two

---

[14] At this time in 1862, Confederate chaplains were paid eighty dollars per month along with a daily ration.

[15] Tom Beecher resigned his commission effective 10 January 1863 because he did not relish his role as a chaplain and because his congregation urged him to return to Elmira.

[16] Reference to the United States Christian Commission, US Sanitary Commission, and other benevolent societies organized for military relief. The heated competition for donations between these philanthropic groups led to publications filled with success stories that did not directly address soldiers. Others offered advice geared for civilians, not soldiers in combat.

papers—one for donors, the other for the reading army—is to me a mystery. The children of this world are wiser in their generation than the children of light. The secular newspapers address the reader. The New York *Ledger* contains no appeals to Mr. Bonner to support it! Nor long columns to prove how interesting it is. It depends for its circulation upon satisfying readers. But our religious prints depend upon satisfying the good men and women who keep the "sanctified press" a running by their contributions. And so editors and compilers make up the matter for the information of the paying patrons, rather than for the benefit of the receiving soldiers.

Besides all this, I desire to testify that no landsman can write for sailors, nor any easy going pen-driver write for soldiers. In camp we deal with things, not with ideas and sentiment. And all stories and exhortations which pass a creditable muster when paraded in a peaceful community, lack pith and point, when read in camp.

Here am I, chaplain in my tent. 'Tis Sunday. God is my witness that I'm in earnest for my men, and their comfort, here, and salvation hereafter. Here I sit, and looking out my tent door (on Sunday) see eighty men on two camp streets, busy running hither and thither, like ants on a hill. They are two companies just in from twenty-four hours of picket. They are hungry—I hear the plates rattle. They will be sleepy in ten minutes more, for they were alert all night. They are cheerful now for their work is over. They must wipe and polish their guns; unsling and unroll and stow their blankets; kindle fires in their tents; look up their scanty property that has laid ownerless for twenty-four hours.

It is Sunday. What have I? What can I get for them to read of any religious profit? There they are—hearty, robust men in the open air, rude, and full of life. Always greeting me with a smile of welcome. Let me see my papers. "Little Emily and Her Cat," and picture. "Salvation by Jesus Alone"—that tells about some noble man somewhere, very rich and very experienced, who declared at last that faith was the only repose. "For Army Circulation," which will tell our men that a chaplain writes "the soldiers crowd around me to get your publications," and add (by editor) we have sent over 000,000,000,000 pages, &c., since the war began, and there is still a demand. Will not our friends redouble, &c., &c.

If I try a pile of tracts I shall fare as badly or worse. The fact is that schoolmasters must edit school books from the school room. Preachers must write their sermons for their own parish, and army literature must be written by men in the camps, and about things which none but a campman will ever think. I wish I had an article or two with such titles as these. "Company Kitchens and Burnt Rice," showing two things. 1st, How to boil rice. 2nd, How little good it does to curse the cook and use nasty words. Another, "Rusty Rifles," which might tell of inside and outside rust, and point a moral, such as our Lord enounced about the whited sepulchres. "Rubber Blankets" would furnish a theme for instruction and a parable. "D-m the Chaplain" would be a rude but a very useful title for a short article. I have heard the phrase but not in our own camp. Yet I doubt not it has been used by some of our own men, when they failed to get excused from Divine Service. "Who Prays In Our Tent?" "Dress Parade and General Judgment." "Shifting Camp and Dying." I'm amazed at the prolific suggestions of camp life toward religious teachings, and disgusted with the sterility of religious literature sent to camp.

Here let me add that 'tis quite certain that anything at all profitable among men in the army must needs be more rugged and *slang-y* (if you please) than would be allowed by the rules of elegant rhetoric. Who would talk to men must use the dialect best understood by the men to whom he speaks. Hence I urge anew, the propriety of our societies publishing two papers—one for the nice tastes and generous purses of wealthy benefactors—the other for the instant and urgent needs of soldiers knocking about in the open air, and eating army rations from tin plates with their fingers.

No, I shan't distribute any more papers to these men, except for familiar economic uses as waste paper.

I am not in the mood to gossip. Nor is this the proper day for writing it. Let me then merely add that our men and our camp are daily improving in military qualities. There are none of us seriously sick, and few that are sick at all. The day is warm and hazy. We sit with open tents and no fires. We are well fed and some of us well worked. And I am happy to add that the reputation of the regiment at Brigade Headquarters improves daily.

I pray God that all of you who read, may so live as to be able to say the same of yourselves, as your daily reports go up to the Headquarters of the universe, where abideth our God and Father. Amen.

CHAPLAIN

Letters of Chaplain Peter Paul Cooney,

35th Indiana Volunteers

Peter Paul Cooney was born during 1822 in County Roscommin, Ireland, and came to America with his parents when he was five. Raised on a farm in Monroe, Michigan, he first studied at Notre Dame, then at St. Charles College in Maryland. Cooney was ordained at age thirty-seven and entered the Order of the Holy Cross.[1]

The rule of life for priests and brothers of Holy Cross required they be "Men with Hope to Bring." Their motto was "The Cross, Our Only Hope." Holy Cross men were expected to preach in rural and foreign missions while also schooling poor and abandoned children in useful occupations as well as in Roman Catholicism. Father Basil Moreau organized the Congregation of Holy Cross in France during 1840, and the following year saw Father Edward Sorin, CSC, leave France for the US with a group of brothers. In America, Sorin's group began a new foundation for their community—the University of Notre Dame at South Bend, Indiana.

It was at South Bend that Chaplain Cooney was mustered on 4 October 1861 into the 35th Indiana Volunteers, nicknamed the "First Indiana Irish Regiment." Forty-three Catholic clerics held commissions as regimental chaplains in the federal volunteer force during the Civil War and twenty-five of them served in predominantly Irish regiments. Nine others were appointed hospital chaplains, along with one more commissioned as a post chaplain.

Cooney served forty-four months with the 35th Indiana. He is cited twice in the Official Records. *After the fighting at Murfreesboro, Colonel Bernard F. Mullen wrote, "To Father Cooney, our chaplain, too much praise cannot be given. Indifferent as to himself, he was deeply solicitous for the temporal comfort and spiritual welfare of us all. On the field he was cool and indifferent to danger, and in the name of the regiment I thank him for his kindness and laborious attention to the dead and dying."*[2] *In his after-action report about a charge on Montgomery's Hill by his division of the 4th Corps at the Battle of Nashville, Brigadier General Nathan Kimball cited "Father Cooney, chaplain of the Thirty-fifth Indiana Infantry, who remained in the front with his regiment,*

---

[1] Thomas T. McAvoy, "Peter Paul Cooney Chaplain of Indiana's Irish Regiment," *The Journal of the American Irish Historical Society* 30 (1931): 97–98.

[2] US War Department, *The War of the Rebellion: A Compilation of the Official Records of the Union and Confederate Armies*, 70 vols. (Washington DC: Government Printing Office, 1880–1901) Vol. 20, part 1, p. 612.

encouraging and cheering the men by his words and acts." "Meek, pious, brave as a lion, he worked with his regiment in the Valley of the Shadow of Death."[3]

Chaplain Cooney experienced some high times in the Army of the Cumberland because of the attention shown him by Major General William S. Rosecrans, a professed Catholic. After the fighting at Murfreesboro, Tennessee, he guessed he must have been the bane of Protestant chaplains: "Every morning before the battle would commence (for there were five days fighting) I would come out before the regiment drawn up in line of battle; and after offering a prayer and making an act of contrition, all repeating with me, I gave absolution to them while kneeling. The General saw us the first morning and he was so edified with our example that he sent an order to the Protestant chaplains to do the same (Poor fellows, what could they do?)."[4]

Cooney's letters home to his brother Owen afford a detailed picture of his regimental activities as a chaplain.

Equipment and Uniform[5]
I brought a fine horse with me, and a brother as my servant from South Bend. The brother is a fine young man who was with me in Chicago and he is now a brother. He begged the superior and myself, on his knees, to let him come with me to take care of my horse and wait on me.[6]

I got the horse rigged in military style a few days ago in Louisville and the whole rigging, saddle, etc., cost me forty dollars. My horse I think is the finest in the regiment, he carries his head so high that the other day when I was riding him he struck me with the back of his head in the nose.

I have not changed the form of my coat etc., but I have to wear ornaments on them which give me quite a military appearance. There are gold chords down the sides of my pants and on my shoulders there are black velvet pieces about four inches long and two inches wide, surrounded with gold lace in the shape C+N. The Cross in the center is embroidered with gold thread. The C N, the first and last letters of the word "chaplain" are embroidered with gold also. The buttons on my coat are bright black gutta percha buttons and around my hat I wear a gold band with gold tassel. The whole makes a very appropriate uniform

---

[3] Ibid., Vol. 45, part 1, p. 183.

[4] Rev. Thomas McElroy, "The War Letters of Father Peter Paul Cooney," *Records of the American Catholic Historical Society of Philadelphia* 44 (1933): 152.

[5] Ibid., 54–55.

[6] Cooney refers to another member of his religious order who is acting as his body servant. Army practices allowed officers to have them.

for a priest. The Bishop of Louisville was very well pleased with it a few days ago when I went to see him.[7] I wear my Roman collar as before. Around my waist I wear a blue silk sash about five inches wide with tassels. The shoulder pieces were embroidered by the sisters.[8] The others wear the same kind of shoulder pieces as the other officers, without the Cross.[9] I added this as becoming a Catholic chaplain.

A captivating glimpse of an Irish regiment and their priest appears in the following letter. During September 1862, the 35th Indiana was attached to the 23rd Independent Brigade, Army of the Ohio, guarding Major General Don Carlos Buell's right flank as he marched from Nashville to Louisville in pursuit of General Braxton Bragg's Army of Tennessee. Instead of locking horns with Buell, who was entrenched at Nashville, the Confederates marched past him, headed for Kentucky. Taken by surprise, Buell sought to make up for lost time by setting a grueling pace. During the third week in September, the opposing armies began to concentrate near Munfordsville, Kentucky. Cooney describes these days.

Louisville, Kentucky[10]
October 2, 1862
My dear Brother:
After a long silence I am happy to have an opportunity to write you a few lines. Since I last wrote my health has never been better. It seems as if my health grows better as my hardships and fatigues increase; for all that I had to undergo since I entered on this new field of duty could not equal what I had to endure last month.

---

[7] Canon law of the Catholic Church obliged military chaplains to receive approval from the bishop in whose jurisdiction they found themselves, otherwise a chaplain's ministering of sacraments would be illicit. This meant Union chaplains had to reach bishops in Southern cities.

[8] Reference to Roman Catholic nuns in the US branch of Sisters of the Holy Cross who established Saint Mary's College, in South Bend IN long before the Civil War.

[9] Cooney saw other chaplains wearing the line officer shoulder straps of captains on their uniforms. He evidently wore the black frock worn by other priests except for the gutta-percha (contemporary name for a hard thermoplastic) buttons and his unique shoulder straps. Neither approach was according to army regulations.

[10] McElroy, "The War Letters of Father Peter Paul Cooney," 67–69.

We started from McMinnville, Tennessee on the last day of August and we have been marching nearly ever since. We arrived here a few days ago, having traveled, without stopping but for the necessary rests, over three hundred miles and, nearly the whole time in a dense cloud of dust, so that we looked like so many millers. There were between sixty and eighty thousand soldiers with us, making a fearful army. When we arrived here Munfordsville, Kentucky, we prepared for a battle, as the Southern troops were nearly as many as we were at this place and they have the benefit of a strong fortification. We stopped a day and a night to prepare for the battle between two large armies. I heard confessions all that night—no sleep. I sat eight hours without getting off my seat. It was a very cool night; for the nights, as a general thing, are colder in the South than in Michigan or Indiana but the days are warmer. About twelve o'clock, my legs were perfectly benumbed, until one of the poor soldiers brought me a blanket to roll around my thighs; for they think more of an inconvenience to me than I do myself. You might hear them whispering to one another words of sympathy for me. They little knew the joy that was in my breast, midst all these trials, when I considered how much God was doing with the hands of his unworthy son.

If you were to see my confessional that night you would laugh. In the evening one of the soldiers came to me and said: "Father, will you be hearing tonight?" "Indeed I will, my dear, with God's help," I answered and I jocosely asked him in presence of the others. "Did you not know I was hearing all day?" "No Father," said he, very innocently and he noticed the joke only when the next commenced to laugh. I find it an advantage sometimes in camp to crack a joke with them; it cheers them up and enlivens the monotony of camp life. "What will you do Father," said one, "for a place to hear confessions in?" (For we were in the open field) "Never mind," I answered, "come this way four or five of you." They came and we made three stacks of guns, four guns in each, in this shape V, and the bayonets were locked into each other. Then we got three blankets, two covering two sides hanging on the bayonets; the other covered the top, leaving the front open. And in this I sat all night. This is a piece of architecture that you will not find in Monroe.[11] Here the poor fellows came, impressed with the idea that perhaps this would be the last confession of their lives. Some of the officers gave me their wills and then went to confession. But it would take volumes to tell all.

---

[11] Cooney had a sort of field confessional put together in keeping with the Catholic practice of individual confession of sins in private. Nothing like this appears in any other Civil War documents.

Here, dear Brother, in such places life is valued as it ought—as worth nothing. That night I baptized a non-commissioned officer who was to that time an Episcopalian.[12] But we came to Munfordsville the next day and the rebels had run away. We caught only the hind ones who could not keep up. All the march we were up at two o'clock in the morning; and generally it was ten or eleven o'clock before we could get to bed, without tents, but the broad canopy of heaven. I alone had a tent along but some nights it would be five miles behind in the wagon train. So you see we have "high living" when you come to add to this, that the men had to march some times eight hours without anything to eat. The whole army started yesterday from here towards Bardstown forty miles from here to meet the enemy. I follow them tomorrow morning. I shall take a trip home to rest about the end of the month. I think the drafting system is given up, so you need not be troubled about it. Pray, pray, dear Brother, for me and for yourselves and heaven shall be our reward.

Your Brother,
P. P. Cooney, Chaplain
35th Reg. Ind. Vol.

The following letter is interesting in its description of the Major General David S. Stanley's conversion. In it, Cooney depicts advantages gained by his convert's clout.

Blue Springs, Tennessee
(Near Cleveland, Tenn.)
April 26, 1864
My dear Brother:
I am very surprised that I did not receive a single word from you since I left home. I have, I think, written you at least three or four letters. I hope that carelessness is the only reason why you did not write; and if you were sick or otherwise unable to write, you should have got some one to write me even a *few lines*. My health is and has been very good, thanks be to God. I have been for the last two months very busy in preparing the men to complete their Easter duty, otherwise I would have written oftener, to you. Our division consists of about twelve thousand men and there are Catholics in every regiment. Protestants attend the sermons by thousands in the open field. I have baptized many of them

---

[12] In the *Records of the American Catholic Historical Society*, this sentence has the following footnote: "Probably a conditional baptism."

and prejudice to the Church is gone almost entirely. A short time ago I baptized and gave his first Communion to the Major General commanding our division. He is now a most fervent Catholic and his example is powerful over the men of his command. I have every assistance from him in anything that I require for discharge of my duties. He is extremely kind to me. After coming here it was very chilly and even cold and I had neither stove nor fireplace to warm my tent nor could I get any; nor brick or stone to build a chimney. During "holy week" we have about *ten inches* of snow on the level.[13] Though it lasted but a few days, it was very damp and chilly.

He was at Mass on Holy Thursday and saw that I had no stove. He went to his headquarters and took a stove from one of his officers and sent it to me. The officer gave it cheerfully, although a protestant, when the General told him that I had to hear confessions and say my office in a cold tent, without fire.[14] I have been very comfortable since, I have a fine tent in which I say Mass every morning. The General is vice-president of a temperance society that I have established in the regiment. We meet the first Sunday of every month. At our last meeting after I had finished my lecture to them on temperance, I invited the General, who is also a member, to say a few words to the members. He cheerfully consented and he made quite a speech on temperance. You may imagine the influence of a Major General in full uniform over the minds of officers and men who were present. The General's name is D. S. Stanley.[15] He was brought up in Ohio and is an officer of the Regular army. I was at his headquarters yesterday evening, and he gave me his photograph which I send you. He wrote his name on it. I would like to have it fixed with one of mine the

---

[13] Holy Week is the final week of Lent, recalling the death and resurrection of Jesus. Palm Sunday is the first day of Holy Week, the Sunday before Easter. Holy Thursday, or Maundy Thursday, recalls Jesus' last meal. Good Friday observes the death of Jesus, and Holy Saturday is a day of vigil.

[14] Catholic priests are expected to read a daily Divine Office from their breviaries.

[15] Maj. Gen. David Sloane Stanley, commanding 1st Division, 4th Army Corps, was born in Cedar Valley OH, 1 June 1828. Graduated from West Point in 1852 and posted to cavalry, he was on the Indian frontier when the war broke out. He eventually led the 4th Corps and was blamed by Gen. Sherman for not annihilating Confederate Gen. Hardee's force at Jonesboro. Wounded at the battle of Franklin, he remained in the army. Governor of the Soldiers' Home in Washington DC after his 1892 retirement, he died there 13 March 1902.

same as that of Major General Rosecrans', as a remembrance of their piety and our companionship in the trials of this war.

Another battle is expected in a short time. The main body of the Rebel army is at Dalton, Georgia, about eighteen miles from this place. I hope God will protect me in the future, as he has in the past. After the coming battle I will go to Indiana with the men's money and from there home for a few days, God being willing. I have the fifty dollar note you gave me dated January 2, 1860 payable in two years. When I go home I shall want this amount and the amount of the other note (100). Make our arrangements accordingly.

I hope you are all well. Practice your religion Dear Brother, attend to your business at home. I was glad to see by the papers that there would be no draft in Michigan. I shall write you soon again. Write soon. My love and blessing to my mother and all.

Your affectionate brother,
P. P. Cooney, Chaplain
35th Reg. Ind. Vol.

Absent over two months in 1864 due to cholera, Cooney was gratified when the men of his regiment petitioned his return. Chaplain Cooney was discharged 6 June 1865 when his term of service expired.[16] *He returned to South Bend and filled a pastor's role there until another obedience took him to Watertown, Wisconsin, followed by an assignment in New Orleans, Louisiana. Briefly elevated to Provincial Superior of CSC, Peter Cooney died 7 May 1905. He was buried at Notre Dame.*[17]

---

[16] Compiled Service Record of Peter Paul Cooney. Records of the Record and Pension Office, RG 94, National Archives, Washington DC.

[17] Thomas T. McAvoy, "Peter Paul Cooney Chaplain of Indiana's Irish Regiment," *The Journal of the American Irish Historical Society* 30 (1931): 102.

"Army Chaplains" by Benjamin F. Taylor

Benjamin Franklin Taylor was not a chaplain. He was born in 1819 in Lowville, New York, where his father was principal of the Black River Academy. He spent some time in Michigan after graduating from Madison University in Hamilton, New York, taking work with the Chicago Daily Journal *in 1845. He was still with that newspaper when the Civil War broke out and he went into the field as a special correspondent. Taylor frequently succeeded in finding what he described as the "little human smile that brightens war's grim visage, like a flash of sunshine on an angry day."[1] Many of his wartime pieces were published in an 1872 collection called* Mission Ridge and Lookout Mountain with Pictures of Life in Camp and Field.

In describing the regimental chaplains in the Army of the Cumberland, Taylor gave a universal description of those men at their best as well as their worst. For its brevity, it is the best picture of the regimental chaplain to have come out of the Civil War. Taylor began with a brief description of how easy it was to lose track of time and completely miss Sunday after Sunday.

Army Chaplains[2]

It would amuse you to see a man, almanac in hand, trying to find out the day of the month but compelled to call for aid at last. That thin day-book of time, if you have ever happened to think of it, presumes on your knowing one of two things, the day of the month or the day of the week. Ignorant of both, the almanac and the Koran are pretty nearly alike—sealed books. There is no place like the army for losing your reckoning. The days flow by in an unbroken stream. A month passes and you fancy it a fortnight, and it is no unusual thing to see a boy going about among his comrades hunting up the day of the week. The Sabbath, that sweetest blossom in the waste of time, is trampled by hurrying feet unnoted. It came and went yesterday and you find it out tomorrow. You are at sea, and though you may never have been a saint, yet when the Sundays keep dropping out of the calendar like withered leaves, it makes you somewhat uncomfortable for a sinner.

"But how about the chaplains?" you ask. I have met three dozen men whose symbol is the cross, and of that number, two should have been in the

---

[1] Benjamin Franklin Taylor, *Mission Ridge and Lookout Mountain with Pictures of Life in Camp and Field* (New York: D. Appleton & Company, 1872) 139.

[2] Ibid., 119–25.

ranks, two in the rear, one keeping the temperance pledge, one obeying the third commandment—to be brief about it, five repenting, and eight getting - common sense. The rest were efficient, faithful men. Not one chaplain in fifty, perhaps, lacks the paving-stones of good intentions, but the complex complaint that carries off the greatest number is ignorance of human nature and want of common sense. Four cardinal questions, I think, will exhaust the qualifications for a chaplaincy: Is he religiously fit? Is he physically fit? Is he acquainted with the animal "man"? Does he possess honest horse-sense? Let me give two or three illustrative pictures from life. Chaplain A. has a puttering demon; he is forever not letting things alone. Passing a group of boys, he hears one oath, stops short in his boots, hurls a commandment at the author, hears another and reproves it, receives a whole volley, and retreats, pained and discomfited. Now, Mr. A. is a good man, anxious to do duty, but that habit of his, that darting about camp like a devil's darning needle with a stereotype reproof in his eye and a pellet of rebuke on the tip of his tongue, bolts every heart against him. Chaplain B. preaches a sermon—regular army fare, too—on Sunday, buttons his coat up snugly under his chin all the other days of the week, draws a thousand dollars, and is content. Chaplain C. never forgets that he is C., "with the rank of Captain." He perfumes himself like a civet cat, never saw the inside of a dog tent, and never quite considered the rank and file as his fellow human beings. Of these three, the boys hate the first, despise the second, and damn the third.

"Demoralize" has become about as common a thing in the army as a bayonet, though the boys do not always get the word right. One of them—"one of 'em" in a couple of senses—was talking of himself one night. "Maybe you wouldn't think it, but I used to be a regular, straight-laced sort of a fellow, but since I joined the army I have got damnably *decomposed!*" Now, a drunken general and a "decomposed" Chaplain are about as useless lumber as can cumber an army.

There is Chaplain D., well equipped with heart but with no head "to speak of," and, with the purest intentions, a perfect provocative to evil. It was next to impossible for a man to put the best side out when he was nearby. Like a curious two-footed diachylon plaster, he drew everybody's infirmities to the surface. I think the regiment grew daily worse and worse. Where ever the Chaplain was, words were sure to be the dirtiest, jokes the coarsest, and deeds the most unseemly. The day before the battle of Chickamauga, the regiment had signed, almost to a man, a paper inviting him to resign. But on the days of the battles, he threw off his coat and carried water to the men all day. In the hottest places there was Chaplain D., water here, water there. In assisting the wounded and aiding the surgeons, the chaplain was a very minister of mercy. That "invitation" lighted the fire under somebody's coffee kettle on Monday night. The Chaplain had struck the right vein at last—the boys had found something to respect and to love in him, and the clergyman's future usefulness was insured. The bond between chaplain and men was sealed on that field with honest blood and will hold good until doomsday.

One noble Illinois chaplain, who died in the harness, used to go out at night, lantern in hand, among the blended heaps of the battlefield, and as he went you could hear his clear, kind voice, "any wounded here?"[3] And so he made the terrible rounds. That man was idolized in life and bewailed in death. Old Jacob Trout, a Chaplain of the Revolution who preached a five-minute sermon before the battle of Brandywine, was the type of the man that soldiers love to honor. His faith was in "the sword of the Lord and of Gideon," but his work was with the musket of Jacob Trout. I do not mean to say that the Chaplain should step out from the little group of non-combatants that belong to a regiment, but I do say that he must establish one point of contact, quicken one throb of kindred feeling between the men and himself, or his vocation is as empty of all blessing and honor as the old wine-flasks of Herculaneum. No man can misunderstand what I have written. The chaplaincy, at best, is an office difficult and thankless. It demands the best men to fill it well and worthily, men whose very presence and bearing put soldiers upon their honor. And it is safe to say that he who is fit to be a chaplain is fit to rule a people. How nobly many of them have labored in the Army of the Cumberland! Ministers of mercy, right-hand men of the surgeons and the Nightingales, bearers of the cup of cold water and the word of good cheer, the strong regiment may be the Colonel's, but the Wounded Brigade is the Chaplain's.

Writing of sermons, did you ever make one in a field preaching at the Front? If not, I must give you a homely little picture I saw yesterday, which by the calendar was Sunday. Blundering past a rusty camp, the tents stained

---

[3] Methodist minister James M. Morrow, 99th Ohio Volunteers, who died 12 January 1864, age forty-five, in Dayton, where he had been taken after a 5 January train wreck. He was on his way back to the front after carrying soldiers' pay from Shell Mound TN back home to their families. He never recovered his senses long enough to acknowledge his wife, Angeline, or sons Charley and Jim.

and rent, I came upon a group of about as many as met of old "in an upper chamber," and not an officer among them, unless it might be a sergeant. They were seated upon logs, and the Chaplain was just leading off in a hymn that floated up and was lost, like a bird in a storm, amid the clash of bands and the rumble of army wagons in the valley below. The Chaplain wore a hat with a feather that he might have been born in, for all I knew, for during the entire services, praise, prayer and. preaching, the voice came out from beneath the hat with a feather in it. Perhaps it would have struck you as irreverent, but it may be that he feared the misfortune of the wolf who talked hoarsely with little Red Riding Hood because he had a cold in his head. At the heels of the Chaplain as he preached, a kettle was bubbling over a fire and a soldier-boy on his knees beside it was apparently worshiping the hardware. But he was no idolater for all that, since a closer look discovered him fishing in it for something with a fork. Around the preacher, but just out of sermon range, boys were smoking, darning, chatting, reading, and having a frolic. The voice of a muleteer came distinctly up from below, as he damned the hearts of his six in hand—for no teamster I ever heard was so wild as to swear at a mule's soul. The passing trains of ammunition crushed the Chaplain's sentences in two, and, now and then, whistled a truant word away with them, but he kept right on, clear, earnest, sensible—no matter for the hat with a feather in it—and I could not help feeling a profound respect for the preacher and the little group around his feet.

To mingle with the men and share in their frolics as well as their sorrows without losing self-respect. To be with them and yet not of them. To get at their hearts without letting them know it. These are indeed tasks most delicate and difficult, requiring tact that a man must be born with, and a good honest sense that can never be derived from Gill's "body of divinity." "How do you like Chaplain S.?" I asked of a group of Illinois boys one day. "We'll *freeze* to him every time," was the characteristic reply, and not unanticipated, for I had seen him dressing a wound, helping out a blundering boy whose fingers were all thumbs with his letter to "the girl he left behind him," playing ball, running a race, as well as heard him making a prayer and preaching a sermon. The surgeon and chaplain are co-workers. I said the former should report to the Women and I half believe that the Chaplain should do likewise.

It would be of great interest to know the identities of Taylor's chaplains, because he clearly knew them or of them from stories told around campfires. Since he was in the Army of the Cumberland from September 1863, through September 1864, he had from 87 to 101 chaplains in the mix, and there were representatives of the famous as well as the notorious. On the "good" side were chaplains like Joseph Conable Thomas, 88th Illinois Volunteers, who pioneered the idea of a portable regimental library and later became the US Christian Commission's general library agent. He allegedly liked three things, in the following order: "His Master whom he serves, the souls of men, and reading matter, the latter chiefly by getting it in the reach of men." Chaplain Peter Paul Cooney was a Catholic priest born in Ireland who served forty-four months with his beloved 35th Indiana Volunteers. Chaplain William H. Black, 23rd Kentucky Infantry, who is named in the Official Records for his work with the wounded at Murfreesboro and during the Chickamauga campaign; he also received silver and gold watches from his regiment in thanks for his services. Chaplain John Poucher, 38th Ohio Volunteers and later 40th Regiment US Colored Troops, "the ranking chaplain of the Army of the Cumberland, entrusted with arranging for burial of the dead from all post hospitals, as well as shipping wounded by boat and rail."[4] Not to mention Thomas Budd Van Horne, 13th Ohio Volunteers, who wrote the *Army of the Cumberland's* history.

On the shabbier side of the ledger was 81st Indiana Regiment's Chaplain Francis A. Hutcherson, who was court-martialed in July 1864, for having watched soldiers pillage houses at Marietta without stopping them—other witnesses said the chaplain was among the pillagers.

---

[4] Pension Case File of John Poucher, Record Group 15, Records of Veteran Administration, National Archives, Washington DC.

Chapter 3

Ministry on Campaigns

"He hath loosed the fateful lightening of His terrible swift sword..."
—Julia Ward Howe

On 1 May 1864 Secretary of War Edwin M. Stanton reported an aggregated total of 970,710 soldiers on the rolls of the Union Army. Of these, 117,000 were in field or general hospitals and another 81,000 were prisoners of war or otherwise absent from duty.[1]

The official commands of the army in 1864 included twenty-one departments or headquarters ranging from the smallest command, the Headquarters of the Military Division of the Mississippi with 476 officers and enlisted men, to the Army of the Potomac with 120,380 officers and men available for duty. Included in these numbers were approximately 600 Union chaplains assigned to regiments and hospitals, about one-fourth of the chaplains who served at sometime during the war.[2]

Because the Union forces were so geographically dispersed, chaplains had very different experiences depending on their location and the operations their units were conducting. For example, the chaplains who served in the Department of the Gulf in the campaign for Vicksburg recorded different events than those who served in the Department of West Virginia or the Department of Washington. For that reason, accounts of ministry while the chaplains were on campaign included several variables

---

[1] Report to the Congress of the United States as cited in J. William Jones, *Southern Historical Society Papers* (Richmond VA: George W. Gary, 1876) 8.

[2] Herman A. Norton, *Struggling for Recognition: The United States Army Chaplaincy, 1791–1865* (Washington DC: Office of the Chief of Chaplains, 1977) 108.

such as their location, available supplies, the weather, the number of soldiers they had in their regiments, the resistance of opposing forces, and the duration of the operations in the field.

In the main, most chaplains tried to meet the religious and morale needs of the soldiers even in dangerous and difficult places.[3] The most dangerous time, of course, was during a battle when many chaplains insisted on joining their soldiers on the front lines. Chaplain Orlando Benton of the 51st New York Infantry was killed at New Bern, North Carolina, while "nobly encouraging the men to do their duty."[4] Chaplain Horatio S. Howell of the 90th Pennsylvania Volunteers was killed on the steps of the Lutheran Church in Gettysburg during the retreat through the town on 1 July 1863. Chaplain Milton L. Haney of the 55th Illinois Infantry received the Medal of Honor for leading a counterattack during the Battle of Atlanta in 1864.

Among the fighting clergy, the Methodists were especially active. The 73rd Illinois Infantry, which saw valiant service at Chickamauga, was known as "the Preacher's Regiment" because there were fourteen ordained Methodist ministers in the ranks including the chaplain. The commander, Colonel James Jaquess, was also a preacher, a member of the Illinois Conference of the Methodist Church and the former president of two Methodist colleges.[5] Chaplain John H. W. Stuckenberg, a Lutheran professor who served with the 145th Pennsylvania Infantry at Gettysburg, wrote that he was literally "surrounded by Methodists."[6]

The majority of chaplains of all denominations, however, were not combatants. Their place of duty was with the soldiers before battle, at the aid station or hospital during battle, and with the casualties after battle. Even in the rear duty was hard, which may help explain why the average tenure for a chaplain was just a bit less than eighteen months.

---

[3] Perhaps one reason the total number of 116 chaplain casualties in the Union armies was one of the highest in the nation's history.

[4] Roy J. Honeywell, *Chaplains of the United States Army* (Washington DC: Office of the Chief of Chaplains, 1958) 123.

[5] Association of Survivors of the 73d Illinois Infantry Volunteers, *A History of the Seventy-Third Regiment of Illinois Infantry Volunteers* (Springfield: Regimental Association, 1890) 535. Copy in the US Army Military History Institute, Carlisle PA.

[6] See David T. Hedrick and Gordon B. Davis, Jr., *I'm Surrounded by Methodists…Diary of John H. W. Stuckenberg, Chaplain of the 145th Pennsylvania Infantry* (Gettysburg PA: Thomas Publications, 1995).

The memoirs of the ten chaplains that follow record their campaign ministries in Maryland, Virginia, Pennsylvania, North Carolina, South Carolina, Georgia, Tennessee, Mississippi, and Alabama from 1861 to 1865. At least two identified themselves as abolitionists before the war; but all were dedicated to the preservation of the Union and taking care of the soldiers who were in their care, no matter how difficult the ordeal.

Memoirs, 1861-1865

Chaplain Frederic Denison

When he joined the 1st Rhode Island Cavalry on 7 November 1861, Frederic Denison was forty-two, married, and pastor of the Central Falls Baptist Church with a home in Pawtucket. Before coming to Central Falls, he had been at a church in Westerly for eight years. He resigned from the cavalry regiment on 19 January 1863 and next day assumed the chaplaincy of the 3rd Rhode Island Heavy Artillery. Home on leave from May through September 1863, he then reported to the portion of his regiment stationed at Fort Pulaski, which guarded the sea approach to Savannah, Georgia.

A Chaplain's Experience in the Union Army

At the outbreak of the Rebellion I was chaplain of the Pawtucket Light Guard, in Pawtucket, R.I., a body of militia organized as a skeleton regiment. When Rhode Island called for troops to take the field for the suppression of the Rebellion, I offered my services to the Second Rhode Island Regiment of Infantry, but found that another chaplain had just been chosen. I was afterwards elected chaplain of the First Rhode Island Cavalry (then First New England Cavalry), and, leaving my pulpit in Central Falls, in the autumn of 1861, entered the field with that command early in 1862, and served with it in Maryland and Virginia till January, 1863, when, on account of illness incurred by exposure, I was transferred to the Department of the South (South Carolina, Georgia, and Florida), where I served with the Third Rhode Island Heavy Artillery till the expiration of that regiment's term of service. But few chaplains, if any, had larger experiences and opportunities for observation. I served under Colonels Lawton, Sayles, Duffié, Metcalf and Brayton, and Generals Abercrombie, Banks, McDowell,

Pope, McClellan, Burnside, Hooker, Hunter, Gillmore, and Foster.[1] I necessarily became acquainted with many chaplains. During the war there were about two thousand volunteer chaplains serving about two million volunteer soldiers.[2] The service they rendered calls for some special mention and special study.

Not only have chaplains usually accompanied regiments to the field in accordance with the provisions of military law, but they have always been much desired by the soldiers. Men do not become irreligious and faithless by joining an army and marching out to mortal fray. Rather, as a rule, and especially among volunteers, their deepest religious convictions are intensified and their manhood is heightened. Being called to stand as a shield for the right and to face death for great principles, they desire the purest, highest, strongest inspirations of religion. They instinctively court the guidance and protection of God. This was specially true in our Union army.

From large observation I can testify that soldiers have a high regard for devoted and faithful chaplains. Gratefully do I record the fact that I received every mark of regard and confidence that a chaplain could desire. I know that soldiers, though often jocose and seemingly blunt in speech, have great tenderness of heart and are open to the highest hopes and aims of our imperishable natures. In general, no class of men exceeds them in the elements of manhood and a recognition of divine relations. This certainly may be said of the great majority of those who volunteered to enter the Union army during the first two years of the war. Men who enlisted for

---

[1] Commanders of units and armies in which Denison served. Col. Robert B. Lawton, Lt. Col. Willard Sayles, and Col. Alfred Nattie Duffie were commanders of the 1st Rhode Island Cavalry. Col. Edwin Metcalf and Col. Charles R. Brayton led the 3rd Rhode Island Heavy Artillery. Brig. Gen. John J. Abercrombie was the first general officer to whom the 1st Rhode Island Cavalry reported. They then served in the Department of the Shenandoah under Maj. Gen. Nathaniel P. Banks, Department of the Rappahannock under Maj. Gen. Irvin McDowell, the Army of Virginia under Maj. Gen. John Pope, and the Army of the Potomac under Maj. Gens. George McClellan, Ambrose E. Burnside, and Joseph Hooker. During 1864, Denison served with the portion of the 3rd Rhode Island Heavy Artillery stationed at Fort Pulaski in the Department of the South. That department's commanders were Maj. Gens. Quincy A. Gillmore and John G. Foster.

[2] Of the 2,399 commissioned chaplains who served in the Civil War, 2,154 were regimental chaplains in the US Army Volunteer Force.

bounties were of a different moral grade. But even these at times desired the services of chaplains. As a general fact, the Union army was pervaded by a deep religious spirit. Officers and men felt, as did the people of the North and West, that it was a duty they owed to God as well as to mankind to uphold our free institutions and defend the republic. There was no fanaticism or rant in the army, but there was a genuine and strong religious faith that prompted to the noblest sacrifices and deeds.

According to the *Army Regulations* chaplains are enrolled as staff officers and hold the rank of captains of cavalry. As to their specific duties the *Regulations* are almost silent, leaving them to be determined by circumstances and the will of commanding officers. In a cantonment or single regular camp, a place is assigned the chaplain as to his tent and his place on parade and in review. He moves regularly with the staff.

To quote the *Regulations*, the chaplain is "appointed by the colonel on the nomination of the company commanders," and "the wishes and wants of the soldiers of the regiment shall be allowed their full and due weight in making the selection." None but regularly ordained ministers of some Christian denomination, however, shall be eligible to appointment." They were duly commissioned by the states from which the regiments came.

It was taken for granted that the chaplain would assist the surgeon and the hospital corps in taking care of the sick and wounded, while his specific duty was to minister in religious concerns, and conduct all services of worship. It was also accepted as a proper matter that he should serve his regiment as postmaster.

Unfortunately the *Regulations* are silent in regard to the chaplain's uniform and equipment.[3] Most of the chaplains in the service wore no arms whatever, and generally they dressed in black suit, cut somewhat after a clerical and somewhat after a military pattern—a cross between the garb of a priest and that of a captain, and without army buttons. In fact they were variously dressed and wore various kinds of hats and caps. I chose a complete captain's uniform with staff shoulder straps of my rank, and wore cap, sash, belt, and sword, the sword being of the rapier pattern. I had also a full patterned captain's overcoat. Why I was thus uniformed and armed will

---

[3] Rev. Denison's twenty-one years in the Connecticut militia made him into a uniform devotee who conveniently overlooked War Department General Order No. 102, issued 25 November 1861. It specified the uniform for chaplains of the army as a "plain black frock coat, with standing collar, and one row of nine black buttons; plain black pantaloons; black felt hat or army forage cap, without ornament."

appear hereafter. Being for the time unmistakably of the church militant I also carried a seven-barreled revolver. The chaplain of Berdan's sharpshooters carried a rifle and was as good a shot as could be found in that famous regiment, and was severely wounded on the front in Virginia while supporting his command.[4]

It was certainly a mistake that the uniform and arms of chaplains were not laid down by military regulations. So far as outward appearance was concerned, it was sometimes difficult to distinguish chaplains from sutlers or civilians. No reason exists why a chaplain in war time should not be distinguishable by his dress like any other officer; nor why he should not be prepared to act upon the defensive. Surgeons, quartermasters, adjutants, and all aids wear arms. Why should not chaplains? If they exhort men to fight, why not fight themselves, if they have a chance? Chance they can have if they keep with their commands. Unhappily in most cases during the war, being unarmed they were not found on the extreme front. Still the actual duties they performed were many and important, though they were not found in line of battle. Usually in times of action they were aiding in furnishing supplies for the front and in caring for the wounded, sick, and dead. Yet always they labored under this serious impediment and discouragement that there was no specific place in line of service assigned them, while all other officers had definite places and duties. But more on this point hereafter.

I come now to the mention of some of my experiences. In giving these, of course I give much that was common to chaplains in general, and so I illustrate the kind of service of which I am treating. My service began early in the autumn of 1861, under Col. G. W. Hallett, in Camp Hallett, in Cranston, R. I., with the First Battalion of the First New England Cavalry (afterwards the First Rhode Island Cavalry). While here, where the troops were being organized and drilled, I conducted regular religious services on Sabbaths, supplied the soldiers with reading matter, acted as postmaster and aided in securing camp comforts. When the three battalions came together at Camp Arnold, near Pawtucket, under Col. Robert B. Lawton, I continued the same kind of service with additional duties in the camp hospital. Here I wrote a series of army hymns which were published by certain benevolent

---

[4] Chaplain Lorenzo D. Barber (1821–1882) was "the fighting Methodist parson" of the 2nd USV Sharpshooters. He was hit in the leg on 30 November 1863 while using a telescopic sight to pick off members of a Confederate battery at Mine Run. Congress nearly denied his benefits because of his combatant status.

citizens of Providence, such as Dea. William J. King, Mr. Amasa Manton, and Mr. Ansel D. Nickerson, of Pawtucket, for the use of our regiment, and other commands that entered the field. These twelve or more hymns were in 16mo form and were pasted into the soldiers' pocket Bibles. Nearly all the men were also supplied with *Cromwell Soldiers' Pocket Bibles*. Here occurred our first death by disease and my first service in an army funeral. It was while serving in Camp Arnold that certain officers of the Pawtucket Light Guard, under the leadership of Gen. Olney Arnold, presented to me by belt, sword, and guantletts.[5]

My open field service began early in 1862, immediately on the arrival of our regiment in Washington, D. C., where I volunteered to accompany Gov. William Sprague and a detachment of sixty men of our command under Capt. J. J. Gould, to push out to the Bull Run battle-field, then seven miles beyond the Federal front, to rescue the bodies of Rhode Island officers who fell on that field in July, 1861. On our way out, by stress of storm, we halted at Centreville, where I gave a short address in an abandoned church, where from the pulpit appropriate passages of Scripture were recited. I recollect repeating the passage, "Thou shalt proclaim liberty throughout all the land to all the inhabitants thereof," which some of the men even then thought to be prophetic, and which proved to be so in respect to Mr. Lincoln's proclamation issued during that year. I assisted in gathering out of the ashes the bones of Maj. Sullivan Ballou, whose body the rebels had exhumed, and beheaded and burned.[6] After this expedition we were immediately called to take the front. We moved out from Washington to Warrenton Junction, where without tents we suffered severely from snow, rain, cold wind, and deep mud. From this exposed and painful bivouac I wrote home to our daily papers to secure donations of socks, comforters, and cavalry mittens. Before leaving Rhode Island I had so described these one-fingered mittens, and the manner of knitting them, that the patriotic women soon sent us a supply. I deemed it a part of my duty to care for the bodily comfort of our men. I remember that my servant, John Harris, made reconnaissances on my horse and fell in with rebel chickens that I sent to our field hospital, where we had many sufferers.

I now became the correspondent of the regiment for our Rhode Island papers; and my letters were entitled "Notes By The Wayside." These letters

---

[5] Maj. Gen. Olney Arnold of Pawtucket RI was aide to Gov. William Sprague and responsible for training the militia.

[6] Maj. Ballou served in the 2nd Rhode Island Infantry Regiment.

brought the regiment into notice and secured many comforts. By means of these and a daily journal that I was careful to write and preserve, the history of the regiment, in no small part, during its first year of service, was afterwards prepared. In fact through all my service I kept a journal which proved to be of large service in writing the histories of the regiments I served, though the thought of such use of my entries did not enter my mind at the time. And it has been a special satisfaction to me since the war that single entries in my journals have been the means of securing pensions to soldiers and their widows—in one case securing the back pay and pension to a widow for more than $700.00. This leads me to remark that every regiment should have its chronicler. And who so well fitted for this task as the chaplain?[7]

As my regiment was put upon the front as van guard, and for reconnaissance, scout, and skirmish duty, and so was frequently divided and constantly occupied, regular Sabbath worship was sometimes precluded, which left me to serve the command in other ways. I always continued with the headquarters. While Colonel Lawton remained with us less care was given to worship than afterwards when Lieutenant-Colonel Willard Sayles came into command. The latter was always careful to make arrangements, when possible, for Sabbath services. As to having religious services in the field, as a general fact much depended upon the disposition and will of the commander.

It was while under Lieutenant-Colonel Sayles that I thoroughly studied what were, and what ought to be, a chaplain's duties and relations to a regiment in war time. There was no appointed or recognized place for him on a march, in a bivouac, or in a line of battle; he was a supernumerary, a kind of fifth wheel to a coach, being in place nowhere and out of place everywhere. Seeing this awkward and uncomfortable position and feeling it keenly, and wishing to have the moral support, in myself and from the regiment, of being on duty somewhere and somehow, I volunteered to serve Lieutenant-Colonel Sayles as an aid-de-camp. He readily accepted me as such, as he appreciated my previous nondescript situation. Thereafter I was at ease. Thus I was by his side when we bivouacked and when we marched over the mountains to contend with "Stonewall" Jackson in the Shenandoah Valley. While on marches I carried orders to different portions of the

---

[7] At least eighty-one Union chaplains wrote unit histories or book-length reminiscences.

command. From Front Royal I was sent, by order of General McDowell, with dispatches to Washington, and from thence by the Secretary of War to Rhode Island to find Governor Sprague.

On the return of the regiment over the mountains we encamped, to refit, near Manassas Junction. Here we always had regular and full religious services. Here, besides perfecting our postal arrangements, I aided in organizing more completely our regimental band of music and acted as treasurer for the regiment in supporting the band. Here I continued to act as an aid and carried reports to General McDowell.

When Col. Alfred N. Duffié came into command of the regiment, being a Frenchman not thoroughly master of the English language, though a good French scholar and master of the cavalry arm of service, he was very glad to accept me as an aid and was anxious to have me always with him. I was also able to assist him in translating his French into idiomatic English, and in grammatically arranging his orders and reports. He employed my services as an aid very freely, and often called my pen into requisition. He was a Catholic, but of very liberal views, caring more for "the substance of doctrine" than for any particular forms and dogmas. He ordered the regiment, as such, to attend divine service every Sabbath when such service was possible, and told me to follow my convictions and methods in conducting the worship. Of course these services were never of a denominational or ecclesiastical character, but simply and clearly Christian. On one occasion a Catholic soldier asked to be excused from service on the alleged ground that he was a Catholic and I was a Protestant. The Colonel replied: "You are a Catholic; very well; I am glad; I am a Catholic; I attend service; I hear the chaplain; he does not hurt me; he will not hurt you; you are not excused; go to your place."

When we again took the front, in July, 1862, and led the left wing of the van in Pope's advance to the Rapidan, I always rode on the Colonel's immediate left, and in bivouac I rested near him. Very frequently I carried reports to McDowell and returned with orders. Here, as all along before, my uniform and arms were appropriate, and at first very many thought me to be a veritable captain. In preaching I always studied to adapt my address to the occasion. On the Sabbath before going into the battle of Cedar Mountain, as we knew that we were about to measure arms with the foe, I preached from the text "Father, save me from this hour; but for this cause came I unto this hour." Comrades often spoke of this discourse as helpful on the eve of that battle. As became the duty of an aid I was on the extreme front by the side of

Colonel Duffié in the Cedar Mountain fight while our regiment held the skirmish line and took the enemy's first fire, and remained thus between the two armies for several hours.

A word may here be said in explanation of the fact that in hours of battle I was with my commander instead of being engaged in looking after the wounded. In our regiment we had a band of musicians who were a permanent detail in all times of action to care for the injured and bear them to the field hospital. Still I sometimes served somewhat in this work, but the Colonel always wished me by his side. In the Cedar Mountain battle I proposed to gallop up on the skirmish line to recover one of our wounded men.[8] The Colonel forbade me on the ground that I would make myself a target for the enemy's bullets. On the morning of that battle, knowing that the struggle was at hand, we being then on the front, the Colonel gave me a written order pencilled on paper resting on my saddle skirt, as to the disposition of his body in case he was killed. He promised to rescue my body in case I should fall. This piece of paper I cherish as it illustrates the relation and feeling existing between my commander and myself.

After we fell back from Cedar Mountain to the Flat Lands near Raccoon Ford,[9] I returned with my servant to the battle-field to see that the dead of our regiment were buried, and did not leave till they were laid in the trench graves with the other loyal dead. The sight of that war-plowed field, a full mile in length and of about the same width, strewn with decaying bodies and the debris of battle will forever be with me. I am the only one of our command who saw the grave of Lieut. J. P. Taylor, and who can now identify the spot.[10] He too had served as an aid in the battle and so sacrificed his life.

To better understand the temper of the old planters of Virginia and to discover the situation of affairs, the Colonel usually took me with him in visiting the plantation mansions, such as Mr. Bowen's near Rappahannock Station, and Mr. Wharton's near Mitchell's Station. Alone I visited the Kelly mansion at Kelly's Ford, and Mr. Vaugh's on the Flat Lands. It required a

---

[8] Gens. Stonewall Jackson and A. P. Hill defeated Maj. Gen. N. P. Banks at Cedar Mountain on 9 August 1862.

[9] In Culpeper County VA.

[10] Lt. James P. Taylor, Co. C, 1st Rhode Island Cavalry, age forty, died from the effects of sunstroke at a house being used as a field hospital early on the morning 10 August 1862. Chaplains were routinely contacted by families seeking to retrieve the remains of loved ones for burial back home.

little tact in cross examination to bring out the "true inwardness" of these old Virginians.

While on the Flat Lands in Culpepper County it fell to my lot to advise and pray with a deserter who had been sentenced to be shot. He had for the sake of bounties enlisted three times and deserted twice. During the night after his sentence, which was to be executed the next day, he was in great distress. I dealt with him plainly and faithfully as in the sight of God and not of men. Before morning I discovered marks of true penitence and evidence of a thorough change of disposition. I interposed for his pardon and secured it. He was ever after true to his pledge of reformation and loyalty to the service, and counted me as his true friend and benefactor.

What is known as Pope's campaign was one of great severity and hardships. We had little rest and scant rations for nearly four weeks, yet I managed to keep with the headquarters, and was by the side of the Colonel when we opened the battles of Groveton and Chantilly.[11] In leaving the battle-field of Groveton in the middle of the night I remained to see that every ambulance was as full as possible of the wounded. Many had to be left at last. On the morning of August 30th, the last day of the second Bull Run battle, while as an aid, accompanied only by my servant, on my way towards Centreville to seek supplies for our starving men, I had the fortune, near Cub Run, to pick up six full armed rebel soldiers of Jackson's corps, and to take them with me into our lines and hand them over to the provost, Capt. William H. Sterling, of the Seventh Ohio Infantry. Then I appreciated and found the full justification of my uniform and sword. The captives took me to be a captain of the line with a squad of cavalry at my heels.[12] But for my special volunteer effort that resulted in securing supplies from Centreville, my regiment would have lacked rations on the last day of the Bull Run fight, when they had already been short of food for two days.

In this trying campaign when regiments were rapidly pushed to different places and points, and often mixed and broken, some chaplains lost their regiments, or were lost from them, and were left to wander alone and bewildered in search for their commands. Some of those whom I met were

---

[11] The battle at Groveton VA occurred on 28 August 1862, Second Bull Run (or Manassas) on 29–30 August, and Chantilly on 1 September.

[12] Of fifteen Union chaplains killed or mortally wounded, at least six were mistaken for combat officers in their captain's uniforms. The most famous of these incidents was the death of Chaplain Horatio Stockton Howell, 90th Pennsylvania, on the first day of Gettysburg.

in real distress and tearfully asked what they could do, as they learned that I always was with my regiment. I urged them to immediately study the duties of aids and volunteer in that office. They were good men, anxious to do their duty and serve the army, but the most of them had no military education at all and knew not how to assume the role I recommended. This was unfortunate for them and for their regiments, for soldiers never need the countenance and help of chaplains more than in days of forced marches and of battles. I am sure that, as a general thing, chaplains performed much important service in helping the wounded and in aiding the surgeons in their ministries to the sick in the hospitals. They were certainly very active and efficient in duty of this kind after the second Bull Run battle, when I remember to have counted about fifty four-horse ambulances in one train moving off the field loaded to their utmost capacity with the wounded that were utterly helpless, while all the injured that could possibly walk were moving in lines by their side. Our regiment acted as rear guard in falling back from that bloody field.

While we were acting as rear-guard to Pope's army between Fairfax Court House and Alexandria I had occasion to appreciate the regard the regiment had for me. In a temporary halt, after the enemy had been checked, when we all were thoroughly exhausted, I swung from my saddle and fell asleep in a cluster of chincopin bushes.[13] As the rebels again pressed upon us the regiment fell back in the darkness and I was left alone and asleep. The Colonel, on missing me, sent back a sergeant to search for me, and I was aroused just in time to escape a trip to Richmond. The exposures of the cavalry in those days were constant and great.

The only instance in which my regiment, as such, worshipped under a roof was in Poolesville, Md., Sept. 28, 1862, when we entered the churches of the town. At all other times we held our services in the open fields or in groves. In the regiment there was always the ability and the heart to maintain sacred song. I think the soldiers always had a true regard for religious worship.

During the march of the Army of the Potomac over the Bull Run mountains, in the autumn of 1862, under General McClellan, and afterwards under General Burnside, on account of rain, snow and fatigue, as we had no tents, many fell on the sick list, and myself among the number. I was therefore sent with a heavy train of such by rail from Warrenton to

---

[13] Chinquapin or dwarf chestnut trees.

Washington. From thence I had a brief furlough to Rhode Island. On my return I brought to the regiment, then encamped near Falmouth, opposite Fredericksburg, various comforts from our home friends, such articles as mittens, comforters, caps, socks, flannels, books and papers.

But the space assigned to this paper will not allow a more extended mention of my large experiences in Virginia. On account of reduced health, not wishing to leave the service till the rebellion was broken, I was transferred to the Department of the South, a milder region, to serve with the Third Rhode Island Heavy Artillery Regiment, in the Tenth Army Corps, then under Gen. David Hunter. I parted reluctantly with the gallant and devoted cavaliers with whom I had shared hard and important service. In fact the cavalry was my favorite arm of the service.

But I was generously and very warmly received by the noble Third Regiment, in February, 1863, at Hilton Head, South Carolina, where several of the twelve companies were holding the entrenchments.

I took with me gifts of friends to the regiment, such as Testaments, books and papers; and also hundreds of copies of Army Hymns that I had written for the command, similar to those I wrote for the cavalry. Among the books were about three hundred copies of the Douay New Testament, obtained by solicitation from a wealthy Roman Catholic gentleman in New York city, for the us of the Catholic members of the regiment. This donation was a happy surprise and won for me at once the regards of the Catholics. Col. Edwin Metcalf, then in command of the regiment, rendered every possible facility for the furtherance of my duties; and all the officers were cordial and earnest in aiding me. Never can any of us forget the pleasant hours of worship, after parades, on the ample ground, within the strong and large entrenchments.

Usually our religious exercises were held in forts and entrenchments, always in the open air of course. Commonly they consisted of Scripture reading, prayer, song and a discourse. The singing was by the regiment. As these services usually followed a parade when we had the advantage of the music of the band and the presence sometimes of the wives of officers, our song was well sustained. I think these were in substance the services generally held by chaplains in all arms of the service. They were the same in Virginia. On board the naval vessels the Episcopal form of worship was commonly employed, but not always.

At different times the battalions and companies of our regiment were separated and sent to different parts of the department extending from

Charleston, S. C., to the southern coast of Florida. I finally received a general pass from the generals commanding the department by which I moved, as duty called, from Morris Island to St. Augustine. The most of the regular services were held in the entrenchments and forts of Hilton Head, at Fort Pulaski, on Tybee Island, and on Morris Island. Occasionally I was present on the gunboats.

When I reached South Carolina President Lincoln's Proclamation of Emancipation had just gone into effect, and thousands of freedmen were found within our army lines. These were to me a great study. Shortly they began to give color to our military affairs. The First South Carolina Regiment of colored troops was being organized and drilled under Col. T. W. Higginson, the first regiment of the kind raised in our country and mustered into the service. I visited this regiment on Port Royal Island. The strong prejudice against this sort of troops that was at first manifested, especially in the regular army, was soon modified by the humorous logic of Colonel Halpine, "Miles O'Reilly," in his popular ballads, and by the good conduct of the troops themselves.[14]

On Hilton Head the negroes were very numerous, and they worshipped within the entrenchments in a rude sort of chapel of their own construction. I sometimes preached for them and assisted them in other ways. Their religious leader was Abraham Murcherson, a man of ability and character, formerly a slave in Savannah, who could read somewhat, having stolen a knowledge of letters while in slavery. He baptized more than a thousand of his people in Port Royal harbor. The camp or village of these freedmen, west of the entrenchments, was named Mitchelville in honor of their friend, Gen. O. M. Mitchel.[15] There was something highly pleasing and exhilarating in their sacred music. As they rose up and swayed to and fro

---

[14] Charles Graham Halpine (1829–1868) was born to a Church of Ireland priest and attended Trinity College in Dublin before coming to the US in 1850. A newspaperman in Boston and New York City, he was briefly a private in the 69th New York State Militia but through influential friends became a staff officer for Gens. Dix and Hunter. His satirical *Adventures of Private Miles O'Reilly* were serialized in the New York Irish-American newspaper. His defense of black soldiers was a cold-blooded joke that everybody (except blacks) appreciated. *Sambo's Right To Be Kilt* persuaded whites to accept black troops without disturbing their prejudice against negroes.

[15] Maj. Gen. Ormsby M. Mitchel assumed command at Hilton Head SC on 15 September 1862.

to keep time, their rich voices, full of tender and strong emotion, made sublime melodies that rose and fell like the rhythm of the sea. Their poetry of their own composition was quaint and rude. Commonly however, they used the hymns of the white people. They were all anxious to learn to read, and I assisted them as far as possible in their endeavors, by books, paper and pencils. In the meantime, both at Hilton Head and Fort Pulaski, I wrote out near forty of their peculiar original songs—rude ballads and refrains, half sacred and half secular; an odd mixture indeed. These, now found in my army journal, in years to come, will be deemed historically valuable as the relics and reminders of a southern slavery.

Gen. Rufus Saxton was appointed military governor of South Carolina and issued orders relative to the legal marriage of freedmen, and also established at Beaufort, Port Royal, a savings bank for such as might have money to be safely kept.[16] I aided General Saxton in carrying out the marriage laws, solemnizing the contracts and giving the parties certificates of their union and keeping the records. Copies of these certificates are now found in my journal. Some of the marriages were amusing. Under the old slave system, as I found, in regard to marriage, the slaves were treated shamefully; it was really a mockery and only brutalizing.

I became well acquainted with two remarkable negroes of large native ability; Robert Smalls, who ran the rebel steamer *Planter* out of Charleston in the night and became captain of the steamer in the Federal service, a well poised, gentlemanly, able, energetic man; and March Haynes, who escaped from Savannah and was employed by General Gillmore in secret service, a pure, shrewd, brave efficient man, who kept us informed of affairs within the enemy's lines. On one of his expeditions Haynes was severely wounded, and I visited him in the hospital. He too learned to read while a slave, acting as a stevedore in Savannah.

While at Hilton Head, the headquarters of the Department of the South, as Chaplain Hudson was sick one Sabbath morning,[17] General Hunter sent for me, with only a half-hour's notice, to preach at the headquarters before him, his staff and other officials. I distinctly recollect that I preached upon the great and universal law of sacrifice from the text,

---

[16] Maj. Gen. Rufus Saxton (1824–1908) had as his main mission to "arm, uniform, equip, and receive into the service of the US" no more than 5,000 "volunteers of African descent."

[17] Chaplain Henry Norman Hudson (1814–1886), Episcopalian, 1st New York Engineers.

"Except a corn of wheat fall into the ground and die it abideth alone; but if it die it bringeth forth much fruit." The general thanked me very heartily for the service.

At different times I officiated at Fort Pulaski; once for a number of weeks in succession when there were about seven hundred soldiers of various regiments in and around the fort drilling and preparing for the front. Here my duties were varied and full of interest. The regular services were held in the fort on the parade. Occasionally meetings were held outside in the hospital and in the quarters occupied by the blacks. Among the troops here were several hundred Catholics. Gen. Gillmore was a Catholic, and encouraged several priests to enter the department. With two of these I could not affiliate on account of their love of drink, and I did not consent to have them officiate where I was post chaplain. When I visited St. Augustine, I learned that the priest who there officiated in the cathedral was a pure, devout, able man. Therefore when he came up the coast I urged him to spend a few days with me at the fort and hold such Catholic services as the men desired and as he thought best, explaining to him that I was a Protestant who both believed and preached the doctrine of perfect religious liberty, and that while I might not join in all his services, he should have time and place, as should the soldiers, by consent of the commandant, Maj. J. E. Bailey, for his desired exercises. He was surprised by my liberality and heartily accepted my invitation, and remained several days till he had met, in a double casemate and in their quarters, all the Catholics of the post. For this course some of the Protestant chaplains in the department were disposed to criticize me, but the Catholics were pleased and benefited.

In the meetings I held among the blacks, often assisted by Surgeon J. W. Grosvenor, I explained portions of Scripture, as but few of them could read.[18] They often desired to hear the story of Daniel in the den of lions, the three worthies in the fiery furnace, and like vivid portions of the Bible. Some of them would exhort and pray with remarkable fervor. Here I learned to estimate the character and worth of March Haynes as he lay wounded.

While at Fort Pulaski a curious fortune befell me on this wise. Capt. J. C. Chaplin, commander of the naval steamship *Dai-Ching*, lying off the mouth of the Savannah, visiting the fort, was introduced to me.[19] His

---

[18] Assistant surgeon Joseph W. Grosvenor, 3rd Rhode Island Heavy Artillery.

[19] The gunboat USS *Dai-Ching* was commanded by Lt.-Commander James Crossan Chaplin in the South Atlantic Blockading Squadron until lost to

curiosity was excited by my name. When his ship lay in the Potomac in 1862, he heard of my luck in bringing in six rebel soldiers. On inquiring of Major Bailey he found I was that chaplain. Immediately he repeated his greetings in complimentary phrase. In a few days I was invited on board his ship with such post officers as I might select, and boats were ordered to convey the party. We had a splendid reception on board the ship. One of the ship's officers, in behalf of the other officers and men, in a very fine, patriotic speech presented to me a beautiful United States flag, made on board, of best bunting, mounted on a staff with halyards and surmounted by a truck and metal star. I had some difficulty in making a proper reply. Then followed various speeches and abundant hospitalities. That flag was ever after used by me to drape the coffins of soldiers at their burial. It was also at times used as a headquarters flag on expeditions up the river and among the islands. On one of these expeditions it received some injury. I now cherish it as a precious memorial of the war.

Our chief places for the burial of our dead soldiers in the Department of the South were outside of the entrenchments, to the south, on Hilton Head, on the north side of the demilune at Fort Pulaski,[20] in the cemetery at Beaufort, and on the south end of Morris Island.

In a portion of my quarters in the gorge wall[21] of Fort Pulaski I fitted up and furnished a very respectable reading-room for war times. Here the soldiers, when not on duty, met, especially in the evenings, for study. Here also they met at times to practice sacred music for our regular worship. With my consent, to whom the matter was referred by the commandant of the fort, the men instituted a series of concerts and a species of theatricals more comic than classical. These were practiced in a room near the magazine, and for a time were very popular as they broke the monotony of garrison life in the evenings. I always regarded an innocent laugh as a kind of tonic for soldiers. Heaven knows we had serious hours enough.

I also served my regiment as assistant allotment commissioner of Rhode Island, for safely sending home, at the expense of the State, moneys of the officers and men; and in this office, that demanded time, labor, and care, I transmitted without the loss of a cent, more than a hundred thousand

---

Confederate gunfire on the Savannah River during January 1865. Chaplin survived the war.

[20] A demilune was a configuration of the fort's works composed of two walls forming a salient angle towards the country.

[21] A gorge wall faces the inside of a fortification.

dollars. On my being called upon to handle bounty certificates, I discovered certain tricks and frauds of certain bounty brokers and swindlers. I refused to be a party to these transactions and exposed the rascalities. This drew down upon me the maledictions and threats of the swindlers, and for my firm conduct I for a time suffered the displeasure of the governor of Rhode Island who had been deceived by the acts of the knaves. The fight was quite sharp. I persisted and saved the State and the soldiers thousands of dollars. The legislature of the State finally supported my proceedings. I regarded it as my duty to defend the soldiers from northern enemies as well as from southern rebels.

One day, as assistant allotment commissioner on Morris Island, I received from officers and men allotted moneys, amounting to over fifteen hundred dollars, and, as we all were constantly under fire, I felt anxious for the security of the money. Not being able to pass to the rear when it came night, I called Maj. George Metcalf and pointing out to him a fine bunch of rice grass said to him that before I laid down I would bury the money on the south side of the grass bunch, and if, during the night, a rebel shot should muster me out I wished him to unearth the funds and send them to Allotment Commissioner Smith, in Rhode Island. But I wore my head till morning and sent the money north.

Perhaps my comrades of the Third Regiment will expect me to mention a matter which they were the first to make public by causing it to be published in *The New South*, a little newspaper printed at Hilton Head. Our commander had wisely prohibited gambling, and kept his eye on every violation of the order. In this order all the officers stood with him. One night, in the entrenchments, as I could not sleep, and was walking the parade[22] at a late hour, I discovered a light in a tent at the extreme of a company street. Supposing some one must be sick to justify a light at that hour, I moved down towards the tent. On approaching it I heard voices that did not indicate distress, and by pausing and listening I learned that the boys were playing cards for something beyond mere amusement. One voice cried out "Who will go it?" "Who will go it?" A not unhappy thought came to me as suited to the occasion. I slipped my hand into my left breast pocket and took out my copy of the New Testament that I usually carried, and throwing back the tent front entered with a smile on my face and perhaps a

---

[22] A parade was a wall, or traverse, erected to protect the flanks of a defensive position.

mischievous look, and laying the Testament on the cards and the money, said cheerfully, "I've got it, boys," and instantly withdrew. In a twinkling the lights were out, and the boys scattered. Naturally they expected I would report the affair to our commander, but I never mentioned the matter to a single soul until the boys themselves gave the story away to the editor of *The New South*, since they said it was too good to keep. My treatment of the case, it was asserted by the boys, effectually killed gambling for the future, and some have told me that since that time they have never been able to even play cards without seeing that New Testament appear on the scene.

There is a way of doing good without giving offence. Once sitting at the mess table by the side of a brave but rough lieutenant, who had an unfortunate habit of making remarks to himself which would be disrespectful if applied to the Supreme Being, as the officer thoughtlessly enjoyed this form of speech, I nudged him lightly and whispered, "Draw it mild, lieutenant." He received the suggestion kindly and thanked me years afterwards, and a little time before his death in Woonsocket, he again mentioned the matter and said that he never afterwards allowed this habit to lead him astray without hearing the suggestion, "Draw it mild."

When a company of exchanged prisoners from the infamous Andersonville prison reached our lines and were landed at Hilton Head I assisted in caring for them. They were in a ragged, emaciated, wretched condition. Among them was Chaplain H. S. White, of the Fifth Rhode Island Regiment, whom I immediately took to my quarters and furnished with clean and civilized raiment and other comforts.[23] The stories of these prisoners, supported by their personal condition, were sufficient to brand the rebels with eternal infamy.

This mention of prisoners reminds me that when I learned that the Confederates had put a large number of captured Federal officers under the fire of our guns in Charleston to save the city, and among them were some officers of the First Rhode Island Cavalry and others that I had known in Virginia, I procured and sent to them boxes of cooking utensils, clothes, and

---

[23] Chaplain Henry Sumner White, 5th Rhode Island Heavy Artillery, (1829–1915) was eulogized as "one of the wheel-horses of Methodism." Captured 5 May 1864 at Croatan Station NC, he was held for only a day at Andersonville, but for longer periods at Macon, Savannah, and Charleston. Exchanged during September 1864, he rejoined his regiment until discharged 22 December 1864. He later detailed his experience in eighteen letters written 1864–1865 to the independent Methodist newspaper *Zion's Herald*.

other comforts. In doing this I had a sharp war of words with the rebel officer of exchange. I gave him to understand that his refusal to receive and deliver the articles would be published to the world as a specimen of Southern chivalry. He wisely yielded. By the way, to meet the barbarity of putting our officers under fire, we prepared a stockade here on Morris Island and put a like number of rebel officers under the fire of the rebel guns. This step ended the barbaric game.[24]

My duties on Morris Island during the bombardment of Fort Sumter and the city of Charleston were numerous and onerous. At times I was the only chaplain on the island, and was therefore called to officiate for different regiments in Sabbath services and the burial of their dead. Here, too, came some duties in the field hospital and some cooperation with the devoted agents of the Sanitary Commission and the Christian Commission, whose ministries to the soldiers on the front in action and to the suffering in the hospitals were of great value. So greatly did we prize the labors of these volunteers and active commissions that our regiment finally put into the treasury of the Sanitary Commission one thousand dollars out of our post fund. Of these beneficent commissions, and the volunteer female nurses in the hospitals who came from the North, some of them from the most favored and affluent families, it would be difficult to speak in too high terms of praise.

I recall our worship one Sabbath when in the midst of my discourse a sixty-four pound shell came over from Fort Moultrie and, plunging into the sand, near the musicians on the right of the line, exploded and gave us a nice shower of sand, but did not interrupt our exercises or mar the thread of my discourse.

I was sometimes sent along the coast on special duties to facilitate postal arrangements. I recollect my running down from Charleston to Hilton Head on a navy dispatch steamer whose captain had a habit of drinking even when he was not thirsty. Anxious to do the polite thing and

---

[24] Six hundred Confederate officers, later popularized as "The Immortal 600," were placed in front of federal gun positions as "human shields" on 22 August 1864. This was retaliation for putting captured federals in a part of Charleston which was under Union artillery fire. On the same day, the Red Cross Conference concluded in Geneva, Switzerland, after producing an international agreement to protect victims of war. The *Geneva Convention for the Amelioration of the Condition of the Wounded and Sick of Armies in the Field* had been signed by sixteen countries, which did not include the US or the Confederacy.

seeing me well uniformed as a staff captain, he invited and urged me to share his inspiriting hospitality, and as well nigh indignant at my refusal, though I courteously explained that I never used that sort of reinforcement. He seemed to think I lacked the qualities of an Officer. I speak of this to indicate some of the temptations that beset army and navy life.

It fell to my fortune once to be put in charge of a squad of rebel prisoners, captured on the Savannah River, to take them to Hilton Head. When the men were delivered to me they said they had given up all their arms, but I had my suspicions, and before I allowed the steamer to leave the wharf I had them examined and found on them several slung-shots and a five barreled revolver. Naturally I chose to confiscate these warlike implements much to the disappointment of the prisoners whom I safely delivered to the provost at Hilton Head.

During the war certain officers of the regular army in Washington, not having too much grace in their hearts, or good purposes in their heads for chaplains, sprung through Congress a law cutting off the pay of chaplains when they were absent from their regiments or posts. On learning of this, and seeing that chaplains who were sick, or wounded, or prisoners, were cut off as to pay, I took counsel with Chaplain H. L. Wayland, from Connecticut,[25] and others, and wrote a letter to Hon. Lafayette S. Foster, of the Senate, who laid my communication before Hon. Henry Wilson, Chairman of the Committee on Military Affairs. When my letter, spreading out the facts of the case, and the conditions of certain wounded and captured chaplains was stated before Congress, the evil legislation was at once repealed and the old law was restored.

From over-work and loss of sleep on the Charleston expedition and in hurrying to the relief of our men who were injured in the destruction of the gunboat *Washington*, I was prostrated by my old army disease and carried to the General Hospital on Hilton Head, and was finally sent North for a few months to recuperate. In returning, on board the large transport *Fulton*, under Captain Fulton, we had a remarkably pleasant Sabbath, when, by request of the captain, I preached on the ship's deck to a congregation of near six hundred soldiers and civilians. My test was, "Without faith it is impossible to please God." The singing of this company on the sea in war

---

[25] Chaplain Heman Lincoln Wayland, 7th Connecticut Infantry (1830–1898), was a Baptist minister who served as a home missionary in Nashville for the two years following his resignation on 1 January 1864. Throughout his life he was a tireless advocate for civil and religious liberty as well as civil service reform.

times was something inspiring. And during the sermon a land bird, that had been driven to sea, lighted on the starboard arm of the main yard and sang like a little seraph, and to which I pointed, thus illustrating the text of faith in God. All hearts felt the lesson.

I might speak in great praise of certain chaplains in the Department of the South, particularly of Rev. H. L. Wayland, of the Seventh Connecticut, and Chaplain H. C. Trumbull, of the Tenth Connecticut.[26] The latter accompanied a night attack on Fort Sumter and was captured.

My experiences in five of the rebel states, and my large acquaintance with the national troops from nearly all the loyal states, enables me to speak correctly, I think, of the disposition and feelings of the opposing armies, a matter about which many have had curious and erroneous opinions. Our soldiers were animated by principles, not passions; by patriotism, not party zeal; by loyalty to the republic, not a theory; by regard for the rights of all and the life of the nation, not revenge or retaliation. The Confederates had less of great principles and more of party spirit and passion; they hated the views of the North and hugged State sovereignty and slavery; while they were brave and zealous they were often, to their prisoners, harsh and cruel; they fought for themselves and not for humanity.

But enough. I have mentioned these facts and incidents to illustrate the nature and kind of services rendered by chaplains, and have indicated the relation of these services to the welfare of the army and the nation. Some chaplains did all they could under the circumstances. All might have done more if the *Army Regulations* had been different—more full and definite as to place and duties.

Chaplain Denison was discharged 5 October 1864 when his term of service expired. He subsequently returned home to serve as president of the Rhode Island Soldiers and Sailors Historical Society. "A Chaplain's Experience In The Union Army" started out as a paper read before the Rhode Island Historical Society. It was later included in a series titled Personal Narratives Of Events In The War Of The Rebellion *of which the Society published 250 copies during 1893. He also contributed articles titled "The Battle of Cedar Mountain, A Personal View" and "The Battle of Groveton." By the time of these pieces, Denison had attained some*

---

[26] Chaplain Henry Clay Trumbull, 10th Connecticut Infantry, (1830–1903) Congregationalist. He did not accompany the 18 July 1864 night attack on Battery Wagner but was captured the next day when he strayed into Confederate territory while helping to bury the dead and remove wounded on Morris Island.

notoriety as having written the histories of his two units: Sabres and Spurs, the First Regiment Rhode Island Cavalry in the Civil War, *published in 1876 and* Shot and Shell, the Third Rhode Island Heavy Artillery Regiment in the Rebellion 1861-1865 *in 1879.*

Denison died 16 August 1901 and was buried at Elm Grove Cemetery, Mystic, Connecticut, in a grave that has since lost its marker.

"A Soldier's Funeral"

Chaplain Alonzo Hall Quint, 2nd Massachusetts Infantry, USA

He was a cerebral man. Born 22 March 1828 in Barnstead, New Hampshire, an only child, Alonzo Quint obtained his undergraduate degree at Dartmouth in 1846 and completed studies at Andover Seminary during 1852. The following year, he became pastor of Mather Congregational Church in Roxbury, Massachusetts. He had a wife and child before the war broke out and sat on the Massachusetts Education Board. From 1859 through 1876 he was owner-editor of the Congregational Quarterly *and was secretary of the Massachusetts Congregational Church Association during those same years and up to 1881. He was also belonged to several historical societies.*[1]

The ranks of the 2nd Regiment of Massachusetts Volunteers held sons from the state's wealthiest and most influential families, and Chaplain Quint knew them all. He maintained a detailed daily journal in the field so he could write two books that the soldiers or their survivors would want as remembrances. The Potomac to the Rapidan *was published in 1864 and* The Record of the Second Massachusetts Infantry *during 1867. Mustered 20 June 1861, Chaplain Quint was with the 2nd at the battles of Winchester, Cedar Mountain, Antietam, Chancellorsville, and Gettysburg. During August, the chaplain took sick and went home, never to return to his regiment. Quint's term of service was allowed to expire, and he was never replaced. The history of the regiment was completed using accounts provided by its members. The 2nd Massachusetts spent some weeks in New York City as part of the force sent in to keep the peace after the Draft Riots. From there, they joined the Army of the Cumberland during the Atlanta campaign and marched through Georgia with the Army of the Tennessee.*

A Soldier's Funeral[2]

The ordinary routine of campaigning of course goes on. We have few hardships; the food is good and abundant now; the climate is delightful; there is little sickness.

---

[1] Appleton's *Cyclopedia of American Biography*, 6 vols. (New York: The Press Association Compilers, Inc., 1915) 5.

[2] Alonzo H. Quint, *The Potomac and the Rapidan* (Boston: Crosby and Nichols, 1864) 21–23.

But this routine is sometimes changed. It was today.[3] In the midst of active drill, the step ceased, the bugles were silent, the ranks took their iron position. It was when the band of another regiment passed by, pouring out their melancholy wailing for the dead. It was a soldier's funeral, and among the thousands in our camps, there was a reverent silence.

My thoughts went back to the first funeral at which I had officiated. It was at Harper's Ferry, while our regiment occupied that post. There had been brought into our hospital a soldier of the Fifteenth Pennsylvania, —then on its way home at the expiration of its three months' service,—whom that regiment left with us one afternoon as they passed through the place. That evening, as I passed at a late hour through the hospital, I noticed this new face, and on inquiry found the facts. He was sick with typhoid fever, very sick. Little more than a boy in years, he was to me, then, nameless, not one of ours, but he was a suffering soldier, and may God bless everyone of such. I did not press him to speak, but he recognized the name of our Saviour, and looked up as if waiting to hear. It was too late to question, too late for human comfort. I dared say little, but I could not but think that some friends, father, mother, perhaps a yet closer one, whom I never saw, and doubtless never shall see, whose very residence I know nothing of, might be glad to know that some of the blessed promises of our Lord were whispered in his ear, and that a few words of prayer asked for the soul of this dying man, whose hand I held, the favor of our Father and our Saviour. That night he died.

He was buried the next evening in the way of soldiers, which, to one unaccustomed to the sight, is deeply interesting. A suitable escort (for a private, eight rank and file, properly commanded) is formed in two ranks opposite to the tent of the deceased, with shouldered arms and bayonets unfixed; on the appearance of the coffin the soldiers present arms. The procession then forms, on each side of the coffin being three bearers, without arms; immediately preceding are the eight soldiers, with arms reversed (the musket under the left arm, barrel downward, and steadied by the right hand behind the back); in front is the music, than whose dirge no sadder sounds ever fell upon my ear, as they proceed to the place of burial. With slow and measured step, and muffled drum, they move. At the grave, the coffin is placed upon one side, the soldiers resting upon their arms, the

---

[3] This entry in Quint's journal was written 21 September 1861 near Darnestown MD.

muzzle upon the foot, the hands clasped upon the butt, and the head bowed upon the hands. The chaplain, who has walked in the rear of the coffin, conducts the burial service; "earth to earth, ashes to ashes, dust to dust." Three volleys are fired over the grave, and the last kindness to the comrade is over. The graveyard left, immediately the band strike up a cheerful air, and take their way back to camp and to living duties.

It was thus we buried the stranger soldier. He had no friend who knew him there. No kindred wept by the side of the grave. His bed was made alone, in a deserted graveyard, on the bold cliff that overlooks the two rivers united in the mighty stream which pours its affluence into the Atlantic. But the soldiers subdued their roughness, and laid him down tenderly. The frequent oath was unheard. The solemn silence was scarcely broken by the low words of command. When the sharp volleys echoed up and down the valleys, the shadows had already fallen on the lordly rivers, the Potomac and Shenandoah, rolling by, far below us; but the gorgeous evening sunlight was richly clothing the dark green forests of both Maryland and Virginia heights, towering over us. His grave was cut in a hard and rocky soil; but out of that soil the evergreen was thriving and the wild flowers perfumed the air. It was on the very day his regiment was mustered out of service, that we buried him; and turning backward to our fragile homes, we found the order already given, "Ready to march;" and soon we struck our tents, and forded the dark and foaming river which separated the rebel from the loyal state. *He had forded a darker and rougher river, which, we hoped as we left him, no longer kept him in a world of sin, and out of the land of perfect peace.*

And so will throngs be buried, in this sad and mournful war. But out of the great clouds of private sorrow will rise the triumph of our country's glory.

Worship In Camp[4]

The Sabbath service is held at half-past four o'clock, P.M. under the lengthening shadows. The drum and fife play "church call;" the companies are formed as for parade. Each marches to the sound of music, to its place, till the regiment forms three sides of a square, leaving, perhaps, fifteen feet each side of the preacher. Just within the square are the field and staff officers, and the band, which plays a voluntary. At a word of command, the

---

[4] Horatio B. Hackett, *Christian Memorials of the War* (Boston: Gould and Lincoln, 1864) 126–28.

singers leave the ranks and stand near the band. In the service, the men stand until the time for sermon, when, at the word, "Rest," all are seated but still in order. The sermon closing, all instantly rise, uncovered, for prayer and benediction. These ended, "Attention! Company A, left face, march!" and, to the music of the band, the men march to their tents. There is no lack of attention, and never a disrespectful look.

Sabbath evening, at half-past seven o'clock, is our prayer meeting, lately established. It is held, now, on an open space, near the tents of our band. Each time, it has been a dark evening. A few candles cast a dim light. The flame of near or distant camp-fires shines fitfully on the browned faces of hardy men, bringing into deeper shadow the somber blue of their uniform. They stand closely—a hundred of them. A familiar revival hymn, perhaps "Behold, behold, the Lamb of God," or "We're going home, to die no more," attracts others, for music is a great charm in camp. A prayer, reading of Scripture, a short address from the chaplain, singing, and then all are invited to speak, or pray, or sing. One comes forward quietly into a little vacant space, and in a low voice testifies to the grace of God. Then another; and one prays, or singing breaks forth; or one, in whose heart the springs have been long choked up, bears witness that the fountain is once more gushing, and mourns over his sins. Here and there are visible tears rolling down some rough cheek; "it seems so like home," or "it makes us feel human," or "it reminds one of a praying father."

The hour passes. Tired? No; though no cushioned seats have rested them,—they have all been standing the whole period. But they have rested on the grace of God; and they look forward with yearning hearts to the Wednesday evening prayer-meeting.

Rev. Quint became pastor of North Congregational Church in New Bedford during July 1864 and remained there until his death 4 November 1896 in West Roxbury. He was elected to the state legislature for a three-year term in 1881 and served as secretary for the National Council of US Congregational Churches from 1871 through 1883. His gravestone in Pine Hill Cemetery, Dover, New Hampshire, is inscribed "Chaplain of 2d M. V. I."[5]

---

[5] Ibid. (Massachusetts Volunteer Infantry)

Chaplain John Chandler Gregg,

127th Pennsylvania Volunteers

A member of the Philadelphia Conference of the Methodist Episcopal church when he was mustered 20 August 1862 as a regimental chaplain, Gregg was thirty-two and had been preaching for five years. Ordained a deacon in 1857, and an elder in 1859, he served as a pastor in Hummelstown and then in Bainbridge, Pennsylvania.[1] He began his account of the Battle of Fredericksburg, Virginia, with prayer meetings for soldiers.

Fredericksburg[2]

On December 10th, 1862, our camp was thrown into a state of unusual excitement, by orders received that we must prepare to move on the 11th. Our prayer and experience meetings on that evening were well attended, and deep seriousness seemed to fall upon the hearts of all. The men knew that they were now near the foe, and that a desperate battle was impending. Thoughts of home, and the many friends they had left behind; thoughts of the future,—the numerous risks of the battle-field, the probability, nay, the almost certainty, of some of the present company falling—all combined to bring a crowd of solemn reflections to every mind. We had a good meeting, and many expressed the hope, through Jesus, if no more permitted on earth to mingle our songs and supplications, that we should have a glorious meeting in the land of everlasting rest.

According to previous notice, the morning of the 11th found us early astir. The roll of drums, and the hurried formation of ranks of armed men, with the evolutions of artillery getting into position, produced a scene of bewildering confusion, while occasionally the startling sound of cannon broke upon the ear, and quickened the blood coursing in our veins. By six o'clock, A.M., the whole army was in motion, and ready for the command "forward," to the field of carnage and blood. It was a thrilling spectacle to see the thousands of officers and men, all obedient to one governing mind, wheel into their positions, and move away from their pleasant quarters, to try once more the issue of battle.

---

[1] John Chandler Gregg, *Life in the Army, in the Departments of Virginia, and the Gulf, Including Observations in New Orleans, with an Account of the Author's Life and Experience in the Ministry* (Philadelphia: Perkinpine & Higgins, 1866) 50–51.

[2] John Chandler Gregg, *Life in the Army*, 76–89.

The Army of the Potomac was at this time in splendid condition, and capable of great achievements for their country and its glorious flag. Mingling with the enthusiasm of the movement, there could be observed a spirit of intense seriousness among the men. Many requested an interest in our prayers, and on every countenance could be plainly read the feelings of the heart, which were to conquer or die.

Our section of the army was halted at the Lacy House, just in front of the city of Fredericksburg.

We found the engineers busily engaged in laying pontoon-bridges across the river. This was a hazardous undertaking, and cost many a noble life. Again and again was the work interrupted by a murderous fire, kept up by rebel sharp-shooters on the other side; but, just as often, our brave fellows dashed on, and at length completed their task about three o'clock in the afternoon.

During this time, besides the sharp firing of musketry which was constantly kept up, about seventy-five of our cannon, which had been ranged on the heights, were belching forth their thunder, and raining desolation on the city, and rebel works around it.

A brave band of men volunteered, and crossed the river in a boat, to silence the rebel sharp-shooters. They were watched by thousands of eager eyes, as, amid the storm of bullets now directed on themselves, they landed and quickly stormed the rifle-pits, with such boldness and determination, that the skulking murderers either ran or surrendered.

One of that number was a private of Company I of our regiment, and few exploits of the war have evinced more true heroism than this expedition.

The bridges being now in order for the passage of troops, while our heavy ordnance was making the ground to tremble beneath our feet, and amid the yelling, cheering, and the wildest excitement, there was a dash made to cross the Rappahannock, and support our brave pioneers who held their ground on the opposite side. We could hear their shouts, and very soon they had reinforcements, which enabled them to advance and take possession of the city.

Quite a large number of our men were killed and wounded while engaged in laying the pontoon bridges, and among the slain of that heroic few who first crossed, was the noble Chaplain Fuller, of Massachusetts, killed, it is said, by a minie bullet, and that fired by a rebel woman.[3]

Our brigade was the first column of troops ordered to the other side, and our regiment was the third in the order of crossing.

The enemy, of course, directed his fire on the bridge while crowded with our troops. Shot and shell came hurtling fast and furious on their devoted heads. Captain Fox, a gentlemanly, intelligent, and Christian soldier of our regiment was mortally wounded, by a fragment of shell, and died in a couple of hours.[4] I performed the melancholy duty of assisting to bury his body the next day, under rebel artillery fire. Our Colonel was a target for the foe, and was fired at, but led the One Hundred and Twenty-seventh bravely on regardless of danger, until he entered the city, about half of which was occupied by our forces that night, and the balance next morning.

December 13th, the battle commenced in earnest, in the rear of the city, and also on our left, where General Franklin, having crossed below, engaged the enemy.[5] Our regiment was ordered into the fight at about one o'clock, P.M., and remained in an exposed situation for several hours. A galling fire of rebel infantry and artillery, from concealed points, swept through their ranks, until they fell back under cover.

During this first day's engagement, Colonel Jennings was severely wounded in two places, but, like a brave man, he refused to leave the head of his regiment. Captains Henderson and Ball, and also Lieutenants Henry and Orth were wounded. Lieutenant Shoemaker was killed.[6] He was a man of intelligence and courage. A number of other officers were injured, and several of our men were killed and wounded. I regret having no correct list

---

[3] Chaplain Arthur Buckminster Fuller, 16th Massachusetts Volunteers, was a thirty-nine-year-old Unitarian minister who completed studies at Harvard Divinity School during 1847. Transcendentalist Margaret Fuller was his sister. He was killed 12 December 1862 after he joined the street-fighting in Fredericksburg.

[4] Capt. William Fox, Co. K, 127th Pennsylvania Volunteers. *History of Pennsylvania Volunteers* by Samuel P. Bates (Harrisburg PA: B Singerly State Printer, 1870)states that Fox was first of the regiment to be hit, killed instantly while crossing the river.

[5] Maj. Gen. William Buel Franklin (1823–1903) led the Left Grand Division at Fredericksburg.

[6] Col. William W. Jennings, Capt. James Henderson, Capt. John J. Ball, 1st Lt. Jerome W. Henry, 1st Lt. John F. Orth, 1st Lt. James S. Shoemaker.

of their names to insert here, as their bravery entitles them to the most honorable record posterity can bestow.

December 15th, our regiment was again under fire, Lieut.-Colonel Alleman commanding. The exposure and carnage was even greater than on the previous day. The Lieutenant-Colonel, Lieutenant Novinger, and several of the men were wounded, and our list of killed was considerable.[7] In the three days' fighting our regiment lost, in killed, wounded, and missing, about one hundred and seventy-five officers and men.

I was near enough at times to the rebel lines during these three terrible days, to hear their unearthly, fiendish yell, such as no other troops or civilized beings ever uttered. It was not a hearty cheer, or hurrah, or roar, but a kind of shriek as dissonant as the "Indian war-whoop," and more terrible.

Major-General Franklin's Division on our left succeeded in capturing seven hundred prisoners, and in driving the rebel forces some distance at one time during the battle.

During the night of the 15th, the whole army retreated back across the river, without gaining any material advantage, and after having lost immense numbers of the bravest and best men in our ranks.

Why were we defeated? In my judgment it was, first, because the rebel army had had every advantage over us. They fought behind stone walls, and had natural entrenchments which made their position a very strong one, while our men were compelled to attack them and fight in an open field.

Secondly. I fear there was a great lack among our general officers of that concert of opinion and action which was necessary to success. *Jealousy and disloyalty* had much to do with the defeat of our noble army before Fredericksburg.

The commanding general, I think, should not be charged with this disaster. Great injustice has been done General Burnside, by placing the entire responsibility on his shoulders.[8] He is a skilful [sic] commander, a brave soldier, and a high-minded Christian gentleman.

The sum total of our losses in the three days' fight, is reported at fifteen thousand men, which estimate includes the killed, wounded, missing, and prisoners, who fell into the hands of the enemy.

---

[7] Lt. Col. H. Clay Alleman, 2nd Lt. Marcus Novinger.

[8] Maj. Gen. Ambrose Everett Burnside (1824–1881) was relieved of Army of the Potomac command after he publicly admitted blame for the failure at Fredericksburg.

It is no wonder that both officers and men of the Army of the Potomac should feel dispirited as they fell back to their old camps again, after such a fearful sacrifice of life and limb. But still there was a determination to "pick flint" and try again. That secesh rag must be humbled to the dust. Those haughty rebels must come to grief. This gigantic rebellion *must* be put down, and the Union must and *shall* be preserved. Such a determination could easily be read in every face.

After General Hooker took command, an order was issued, allowing whisky rations to be distributed to the army. As soon as I became aware of this arrangement, I asked our Colonel if he was going to allow the issuing of whisky rations to the men of his command, remarking at the same time, that he had under his care the sons of many praying fathers and mothers, and that I thought this course would demoralize the men, and awaken in them such an appetite for strong drink as would be highly dangerous, and might lead some of them to ruin. The gallant and noble-minded Colonel informed me in an emphatic manner that there should not be *one drop* of whisky distributed among either officers or men of his regiment. I thanked him, and repaired quickly to my tent, where on my knees I gave glory and praise to God for having such a Colonel, and that he had a proper respect and care for the moral welfare of his command.

He differed very widely from many others of his grade in this particular. What a blessing it would have been if all had been actuated by the same principle.

As the dull, weary days of winter rolled on, the officers and men devised many a scheme of innocent fun and amusement in Camp Alleman. Snow-balling was one of the most popular and exciting pastimes resorted to. Sometimes our regiment and the Sixty-ninth New York, that was encamped very near us, would get up a regular pitched battle, and instead of the "minie," would try to demolish each other with volleys of snow-balls. At times the Sixty-ninth would bring out their time-honored and bullet-riddled battle-flag, and challenge our boys to try and capture it. Again our men would display their colors, and dare the others to come and take it. While the two regiments were engaged one day in a regular "set-to," a secesh citizen was riding past, and received a tremendous whack from a snow-ball which was thrown by one of the little drummer boys. The instant Mr. Secesh was hit, he jumped from his horse and ran towards the boy, as though he intended to knock him down. At that moment two of our men who were watching the movement stepped forward, and informed the

Johnny Reb not to dare to lay the weight of his finger upon that little boy. So the insulted Virginian, concluding that discretion was the better part of valor, remounted his poor old steed, and rode on his way a wiser if not a better man.

While we lay in Camp Alleman, First Lieutenant Wm. R. Orth died. He was an exemplary young man, of amiable character, and was much respected and beloved for his many fine traits. Having lived as a Christian should, he departed with a hope bright and full of a blessed immortality.

Saint Patrick's day was a notable period in the army, especially among the Irish Catholics. The pious of this persuasion had a grand time of religious services in the morning, and this was quickly followed by a general spree. Drunkenness, horse-racing, and fist-fighting became the order—or rather the disorder of the afternoon, and the day closed in a regular "Tipperary" fashion.

I met Major-General Howard on one occasion, under circumstances that I shall never forget.[9] This pure patriot, and brave soldier, is known to be a sincere Christian, and everywhere feels it to be both a privilege and duty to stand up for Jesus. The occasion I refer to was on a certain Sabbath. I was preaching to my men on the subject of the last judgment, and on concluding my sermon, learned that General Howard had been one of my hearers. I at once introduced him to the officers and soldiers who composed my congregation.

The General stepped up and addressed them, saying, "Officers and men of the One Hundred and Twenty-seventh Regiment, Pennsylvania Volunteers, I am glad to see so many of you out to hear preaching this Sabbath morning, and I would to God, that all the men of my command were true followers of Christ Jesus, the Lord. Soldiers, allow me to express, with your Chaplain, the sincere desire of my heart, that we may meet at the right hand of the Great Judge in that day, which he has described to us. Soldiers, may God bless you all."

That short address made a deep and lasting impression on our men, and caused them to think more highly of the General than ever before. He is not only a true friend, but an active and practical helper of the Chaplains, in their sacred calling in the army, and has been known to kneel by the side of the wounded and dying soldier, and tell him of Christ and salvation.

---

[9] Maj. Gen. Oliver Otis Howard (1830–1909).

I was put in possession of the fact one day, that the Brigade Commissary was selling liquor to officers and men, by the canteen full, and determined at once to stop the traffic.

I rode down to General Howard's head-quarters, and made known my case. He promptly issued an order prohibiting it.

A few days afterwards some of the officers of the Brigade, and a certain officer of my own regiment, informed me that General Howard had ordered the Commissary not to sell them any more whisky. They, of course, knew nothing of my connection with his business, and did not dream that I was the cause of stopping their rum, at this particular time. If they but knew how much poisonous strychnine was probably in that stuff, they ought to have regarded any one as a benefactor and philanthropist who put forth exertions to stop the trade, and prevent the evil consequent on using it.

One Sabbath morning there were two Virginia gamblers who came into our camp, and induced some of the men to play cards with them. When Colonel Jennings heard of it, he sent a guard down to the spot where the gamblers had begun operations, and had the two "professionals" marched up in front of his tent. He then gave them a reprimand, and by his suggestion they were both honored with a ride upon a rail. In this he served the scamps exactly right, only, in my judgment, it would have set off the matter a little more effectually to have allowed them, and all their kin, a coat of tar and feathers before mounting them. This would have capped the climax, and made a good Sabbath sermon on the sin of gambling and its consequences.

Our "Christian body" continued to maintain its identity and efficiency. We had preaching every Sabbath when the weather would admit, an experience-meeting every Sabbath night, and prayer-meeting every night of the week in my tent. God honored the means employed, and blessed us with a gracious revival of religion in camp, which lasted several weeks, and resulted in the conversion of a number of souls.

We had many seasons of refreshing from the presence of the Lord, and it is a matter of joy to me that many of our men returned home from the service of their country better than when they enlisted. It is my prayer that they all may be made partakers of saving grace, become valiant soldiers of Jesus, and when discharged on earth, that they may live forever in the kingdom of God.

Discharged 29 May 1863 when the 127th Regiment's term of service was up, Reverend Gregg sought appointment as a hospital chaplain of US Volunteers but was not appointed until 18 March 1864. Initially sent to Saint James Hospital in New Orleans, he worked there from May through October 1864. His next assignment kept him in New Orleans, as well, at the Corps D'Afrique Hospital. Though he labored there through June 1865, he never tired of writing "cordafreak" in place of the correct and proper French. The chaplain did all he could for his African-American patients; his dedication to them stood in odd contrast with his outspoken nativist and anti-Catholic views. Diagnosed with breakbone and malarial fever at the beginning of 1865, he hung on at the hospital into the summer. In need of a cane to walk and his vision blurred, Gregg went home on sick leave 28 June 1865. He resigned his commission at home and never returned to duty. Reverend Gregg ultimately lost sight in his right eye but still managed to write a popular account of the war titled, Life in the Army, in the Departments of Virginia, and the Gulf, Including Observations in New Orleans, with an Account of the Author's Life and Experience in the Ministry, *which was published during 1866. Death came 4 December 1886.*[10]

---

[10] Pension Case File of John Chandler Gregg, RG 15, Records of the Veterans Administration, National Archives, Washington DC.

Gettysburg
A Tribute to Chaplain William Corby
88th New York Infantry, Army of the Potomac

One American in ten was a Roman Catholic during the Civil War.[11] It was a Protestant nation with Methodists making up nearly half the population. On 29 October 1910, the portrait statue of Father William Corby, rendered by Philadelphia sculptor Samuel Aloysius Murray, was unveiled on Hancock Avenue at the Gettysburg National Battlefield. The movement that resulted in the placement of this monument began after the 1888 reunion of veterans at Gettysburg on the battle's twenty-fifth anniversary. Father Corby served as chaplain of the 88th New York Volunteer Infantry from 15 December 1861 to 27 September 1864 with a brief return to the regiment in March 1865. He was in the thick of the fighting at Antietam and at Gettysburg with the Irish Brigade.

In his memoirs, Father Corby said his chaplaincy was "much like getting married…we made the engagement for better, for worse; for richer, for poorer, till death do us part."[12] He felt these relationships were made possible among Catholics by their belief in the sacramental power to bring consolation "when all earthly comfort failed to do so, and they felt a security in knowing that their priest was always quite near—in fact, 'within gun-shot,' and ready to serve them."[13] This warm form of reciprocal combustion existed between Chaplain Corby and his regiment.

Chaplain Henry Clay Trumbull of the 10th Connecticut Infantry recorded this tribute to Chaplain Corby in his War Memories of an Army Chaplain.[14]

There were times when the very presence of the chaplain with his regiment on the eve of battle, or while already under fire, was inspiring to officers and men, who were encouraged to feel that they had God's blessing while one of God's representatives was immediately with them. Said a brave but rough officer in a New England regiment, with reference to this

---

[11] Robert Lacour-Gayet, *Everyday Life in the United States before the Civil War* (New York: Frederick Ungar Publishing Co., 1969) 210.

[12] Wm. Corby, *Memoirs of Chaplain Life* (Chicago: La Monte, O'Donnell & Co., 1893) 10.

[13] William Corby, *Memoirs of Chaplain Life* (Chicago: La Monte, O'Donnell & Co., 1893) 52.

[14] H. Clay Trumbull, *War Memories of an Army Chaplain* (New York: Charles Scribner's Sons, 1898) 5–8.

influence over the soldiers as soldiers, "We count our chaplain as good as a hundred men in a fight." That particular officer seemed, in his conduct, to care little for the chaplain as a public teacher of morals, or as setting a Christian example, but he did value his inspiring power over the men in the discharge of their duty as brave and faithful soldiers.

A notable illustration of the opportunity and power of a good regimental chaplain in the face of the enemy is furnished in the memorable service of Chaplain William Corby, of the Eighty-eighth New York Regiment, during the battle of Gettysburg. It was toward the close of the second day of that crisis conflict, while the Third Corps was being driven back, and the roar of battle was sounding on every side, that General Hancock called on General Caldwell to have his division ready to move into action. The Irish Brigade, under General Thomas Meagher, stood in column of regiments, closed in mass, awaiting the order to move forward. It was in that testing moment, of which the bravest soldier feels the oppressive solemnity, that Chaplain Corby proposed to give absolution to all the men before going into the fight. Most of the men in that brigade were Catholics, and those who were not were glad to share reverently in the benefits of the service. General St. Clair Mulholland, then a colonel in that brigade, has told of that service, and Father Corby, just before his death, in 1897, attested the accuracy of this narrative.

"Father Corby stood on a large rock in front of the brigade. Addressing the men, he explained what he was about to do, saying that each one could receive the benefit of the absolution by making a sincere Act of Contrition and firmly resolving to embrace the first opportunity of confessing his sins, urging them to do their duty, and reminding them of the high and sacred nature of their trust as soldiers, and the noble object for which they fought...The brigade was standing at 'Order arms!' As he closed his address, every man, Catholic and non-Catholic, fell on his knees, with his head bowed down. Then, stretching his right hand toward the brigade, Father Corby pronounced the words of the absolution:

"'Dominus noster Jesus Christus vos absolvat, et ego, auctoritate ipsius, vos absolvo ab omni vinculo, excommunicationis interdict, in quantum possum et vos indigetis deinde ego absolvo vos, a peccatis vestris, in nomine Patris, et Filii, et Spiritus Sancti, Amen.'

"The scene was more than impressive—it was awe-inspiring. Near by stood a brilliant throng of officers who had gathered to witness this very unusual occurrence, and while there was profound silence in the ranks of the

Second Corps, yet over to the left, out by the peach orchard and Little Round Top, where Weed and Vincent and Hazlitt were dying,[15] the roar of the battle rose and swelled and re-echoed through the woods, making music more sublime than ever sounded through cathedral aisle. The act seemed to be in harmony with the surroundings. I do not think there was a man in the brigade who did not offer up a heartfelt prayer. For some it was their last; they knelt there in their grave-clothes. In less than half an hour many of them were numbered with the dead of July 2. Who can doubt that their prayers were good? What was wanting in the eloquence of the priest to move them to repentance was supplied in the incidents of the fight. That heart would be incorrigible indeed that the scream of a Whitworth bolt, added to Father Corby's touching appeal, would not move to contrition."

Father Corby said of this scene: "In performing this ceremony I faced the army. My eye covered thousands of officers and men. I noticed that all, Catholic and non-Catholic, officers and private soldiers, showed a profound respect, wishing at this fatal crisis to receive every benefit of divine grace that could be imparted through the instrumentality of the Church ministry. Even Major-General Hancock removed his hat, and, as far as compatible with the situation, bowed in reverential devotion."

Who can doubt that the men of that brigade fought the better in that battle for their chaplain's presence and service for them?

Inevitably, courage was the standard in active army service. Every soldier must be ready to meet danger or death, and, if he failed in that supreme test of a soldier in time of war, he was every way a failure. A chaplain had a duty to inspire men for their service for their country. If he was himself a coward, or seemed unready to face a soldier's perils, no words from him could have weight with his men. His influence for good was destroyed among them. If, on the other hand, their chaplain shared their dangers bravely, his men gave him more than full credit for his courage and fidelity, and were the readier to do their duty under his direct appeals.

---

[15] Brig. Gen. Stephen H. Weed's brigade was in support of Hazlett's Battery at Little Round Top on 2 July 1863; Col. Strong Vincent commanded the 3rd Brigade of the 1st Division, V Corps.

Chaplain Corby was remembered not only for his service to the soldiers of the Irish Brigade, but also for his service to the students of Notre Dame University as their president. He died in 1897 at the age of 64.

"Chickamauga"

Chaplain William W. Lyle, 11th Ohio Volunteer Infantry

Born during 1825 in Paisley, Scotland, the Rev. W. W. Lyle came to America during 1848 and traveled over much of New York, Pennsylvania, and Ohio as a Congregational home missionary. He joined the 11th Ohio Volunteers at Point Pleasant on 31 January 1862 and served through the war until his unit was discharged from service on 22 June 1864. In his History of the Eleventh Regiment Ohio Volunteer Infantry *published in 1866, author Joshua H. Horton said that Lyle "held the idea that the chaplain's position was not strictly an ornamental one.... He attached himself to the medical department." At the regiment's 1894 reunion, Lyle was fondly remembered as always having been "seen well to the front in battle."*[1]

General Turchin's brigade of Reynolds's division, Thomas's corps, consisting of the Eleventh Ohio, Colonel Lane; the Thirty-sixth Ohio, Colonel Jones; the Ninety-second Ohio, Colonel Fearing, and the Eighteenth Kentucky, took position on a low spur of the ridge near the Chattanooga road, and in the rear of the tannery already spoken of.[2] Before the skirmishers were deployed, a scene occurred with the Eleventh, which, for sublimity and moving power, has been seldom surpassed. The chaplain rode up in front of the line, and the colonel gave an order which, on being executed, formed the regiment in two divisions, with the chaplain in the center. Without dismounting, he addressed the troops in a clear, loud voice, that sounded strangely amid the loud explosions of the artillery and the rattle of musketry. He spoke about the holy cause for which they were to

---

[1] William W. Lyle, *Lights and Shadows of Army Life: or Pen Pictures From the Battlefield, the Camp, and the Hospital* (Cincinnati: R. W. Carroll & Co. Publishers, 1865) 289–91. *Lights and Shadows of Army Life* is a compelling work that addresses many non-military topics while also competently reporting on the war. One of the book's images depicts a religious service on the Chickamauga battlefield.

[2] Brig. Gen. John B. Turchin (1822–1901), Maj. Gen. Joseph J. Reynolds (1822–1899), Maj. Gen. George H. Thomas (1816–1870), Col. Philander P. Lane, Col. William G. Jones was killed in action 19 September 1863 at Chickamauga; Col. Benjamin D. Fearing.

fight that day; that it was not for territory or revenge or military glory; but for home, and country, for liberty and truth, for GOD AND HUMANITY!

"It is but little I can do for you," said he, "in the hour of battle; but there is one thing I will do—I Will pray for you. And there are thousands all over the land praying for you this morning, and God will hear them. You must now pray, too; for God is a hearer of prayer. And if this is the last time I shall ever speak to you, or if these are the last words of Christian comfort you will ever hear, I want to tell you, dear comrades, that GOD LOVES YOU. I pray God to cover your heads today in the battle-storm. I pray that he may give you brave hearts and strong hand today. Be brave, be manly! Remember the dear old flag, and what it covers. And if any of you feel uncertain as to your future, O look to the Savior who died for you; and, if any of you fall this day in battle, may you not only die as brave soldiers for your country, but die as soldiers of the Lord Jesus Christ! Let us pray.

Instantly every head was uncovered and bowed in reverence, while hands were clasped on the rifles, the bayonets on which were gleaming in the morning sun. The flag, pierced and rent on a dozen battlefields, was drooped, and, strange but glorious sound on a battlefield, the voice of prayer was heard. The blessings of the Almighty were invoked upon the army, upon the generals, upon regimental officers, on our bleeding country, and upon the issues of that day. Loved ones at home were remembered, and God's blessing invoked upon all who might fall in battle. When the chaplain closed, he raised himself in his saddle, waved his hat two or three times around his head, exclaiming, "God bless you today, dear comrades, and make you strong and brave! Strike for Liberty and Union! Strike for God and Humanity! And may our battle-torn flag lead to victory this day! God's presence be with you, comrades!"

A low, murmuring Amen was heard from the ranks as the chaplain closed. Major General Reynolds and staff passed along the lines during the services, but halted when they came to the Eleventh. With uncovered head, the General rode up close to the regiment, and remained till the conclusion of the brief services. At the moment they were concluded, he uttered a hearty Amen, which had a thrilling effect. Grasping the chaplain's hand and shaking it warmly, while a tear glistened on his manly cheek, he was heard to exclaim, "Sir, I am glad I was here to join with you!" and instantly rode off, followed by his staff. This acknowledgment of religious principle, on the part of General Reynolds had a very happy effect.

Scarcely five minutes elapsed till the entire brigade moved forward and engaged the enemy.

Chickamauga[3]

The Sabbath's sun finally shone out clear and beautiful above the smoke that lay like a pall over the valley. It was expected the enemy would attack as soon as day dawned, but, with the exception of occasional picket firing, it was eight o'clock before the battle was renewed. The conflict of the day opened, as was expected, on the extreme left, and the determination of the rebels to overwhelm Thomas, who was holding the approaches to Chattanooga, was soon apparent, for they hurled their massed columns against him with the greatest fury and desperation. During the night, our troops had thrown up temporary breastworks of logs and stones, and as they kept behind these, or lay on the ground, rising up only to pour their volleys into the attacking columns, the rebel loss was very great. By ten o'clock, the fierce roar of battle was at its hight [sic], and the conflict raged with terrible fury along the whole lines, but on the left and left center the contest was the fiercest and most determined. Longstreet's men, as they came up in solid columns, flushed with the hope of crushing the Western troops, would exulting shout, "We are not conscripts!" to which the reply was given:

"You are not fighting Eastern store-clerks."

"We are Longstreet's troops!" shouted some of them, in front of the Eleventh and Thirty-sixth—to which our men replied, with a derisive yell:

"Who drove you at South Mountain? We are the boys that drove you there, and we'll do it again!"

At about midday, matters were so serious on the left and center, that division after division had to be sent to succor Thomas, who was contending against fearful odds. Indeed the army at large, in order to meet the massed columns of the enemy, which were being rapidly concentrated against Thomas, had to be continually closed up on the left. It was during one of those movements that a mistake occurred which came nigh resulting in the ruin of the Union army. "Orders were dispatched," says Rosecrans, in his clear report, "to General Wood to close up on Reynolds, and word was sent to General Thomas that he should be supported, even if it took away the whole corps of Crittenden and McCook." General Wood, overlooking the orders to close up on General Reynolds, passed to the rear of General Brannan, who was somewhat in the rear of Reynolds, which left a gap in the

---

[3] Lyle, *Lights and Shadows of Army Life*, 300–306.

battle line between Thomas and McCook. The right flank of Reynolds's division was thus exposed, as was, also, McCook's left. Through this open gap the rebels poured with deafening cheers, carrying all before them. The writer was close by at the time this scene occurred, and, assuredly, it looked forbidding enough. The first intimation that Reynolds had of the state of affairs, was a destructive cross-fire from the right, and, finally, solid shot and shell from the rear. All seemed to be lost; for the enemy, taking advantage of the gap made in the battle-front, had not only crushed Crittenden, and swept back the few brigades that were sent in to stay the torrent of disaster, but they were massing in the rear of Reynolds. The entire corps held its own bravely, but it could hardly be expected to continue to do so for any length of time, for the whole rebel army was now hurled fiercely and exultantly against it. Prompt, fearless, decided action was now necessary, or disaster would be inevitable. The ammunition and supply-trains were exposed, two of the gaps in the ridge were open to the Chattanooga road, on which our trains were now moving, and the rebel torrent must be stayed, at whatever cost. Reynolds was ordered to disperse the force massing in the rear. Their artillery was already in position, and was rapidly thinning our ranks. The sharp-shooters in the trees were picking off our men with impunity, insomuch that nearly one half of Company D, of the Eleventh, were killed or wounded in the space of half an hour. General Turchin's brigade, consisting of the Eleventh, Thirty-sixth, and Ninety-second Ohio, and the Eighteenth Kentucky, was formed for a charge on the massed forces in the rear, the infantry and cavalry of which could be distinctly seen advancing. The order was given to march by the rear rank—"about face"—and the brigade, starting on the double-quick, was hurled in a bayonet-charge against the enemy with almost as much precision and order as if it had been on dress parade, and all this, too, while the very air seemed darkened with the missiles of death, the ground shaking as if in the throes of an earthquake from the incessant roar and crash of artillery and the rolling rattle of musketry. As Colonel Lane remarked, it seemed as if the explosions "raised the hats off our heads." The concussion of the air was painful, the noise so deafening that orders could not be heard, and the smoke and dust in such dense clouds that objects at a distance could hardly be seen. General Reynolds, waving his sword, led the charge in person. Calm, reverent, and happy as a Christian, he joined us in our devotions on the morning the battle opened. A tear of religious emotion trickled down his weather-beaten cheek, while a fervent Amen! that thrilled every heart, burst from his lips, and now, bravely as a Christian soldier, he led his troops in that desperate charge—the most desperate made on that bloody field. On the left and front and rear the enemy was in massed line of battle; but away went the Ohio boys, charging bayonet back on the massed columns of the enemy, which had closed around them. Onward they rushed, like a resistless wave of gleaming steel, cheering and yelling as they charged on the dense masses of traitors who hoped to stay them. Their charge was irresistible—so thought the rebels—as onward and onward they rushed through one line of battle, a second, a third, and a part of a fourth, till they pierced the entire battle-line of seven deep, brought off a number of prisoners, charged on two batteries on their way out, brought off one gun, and gained a position on Mission Ridge.

But the work was not yet accomplished. In the terrible noise, and amid the smoke and dust, orders could not be heard, and, before reaching one of the spurs of Mission Ridge, the brigade got divided—one part following Turchin on the left, and the other Reynolds on the right, neither party being aware of the fate of the other. On coming to a halt, the party under Reynolds, comprising portions of the Eleventh, Thirty-sixth, and Ninety-second Ohio Regiments, was re-formed, and measures taken to reach the main body of the army. On marching forward—it was now nearly dusk—the junction of Ringgold and Rossville roads was reached. There was, at this point, a dense forest of heavy timber, rendered still more dense by a heavy undergrowth, which rendered any further movement very critical. General Reynolds, accompanied by two orderlies, went forward himself and reconnoitered the ground. He discovered a heavy force of the enemy in position there, and any further progress in that direction had to be abandoned. This portion of the brigade was marched back a little distance, to a log-house, which had been used as a hospital, and General Reynolds and Colonel Lane held a consultation, the result of which was, that it was thought better to halt a short time there and wait further developments. While performing the movements indicated, artillery had been frequently firing upon our brigade from the left, and it was thought that these being rebel guns, we were still surrounded.

The smoke was hanging heavily over the valley, and now the shades of evening were drawing on, and distant objects were getting more and more obscured. Presently, amid the rifted smoke, and away on a higher ridge, a flag is seen streaming in the wind, but its color can hardly be made out. A man is seen cautiously approaching, gun in hand. He is one of our men; for his uniform, although dusty and soiled, is "Union blue."

"Whose lines are those?"

"Ours!" is the welcome answer, which makes a hundred hearts leap with joy and pride.

In a few minutes the weary but dauntless band reach the outer picket-line, and there, clear, beautiful, glorious in the evening breeze, and amid the smoke and dust, floats the dear old flag! Here is the rest of the division, thought to have been captured! Cheer after cheer goes up, in welcome to the smaller band just come in, and who were also thought to have been either killed or captured. What a hearty shaking of hands! What a trickling of joyous tears over weather-beaten, powder-stained cheeks! What expressions of joy and gladness burst from manly bosoms! O, that was a moment and those were scenes that will never be forgotten!

Here were Granger's troops, that had come up to stay the rebel torrent, and prevent the enemy from overwhelming Thomas's right. The lines were again formed, Thomas presented an unbroken and defiant front, McCook and Crittenden had swept around between Mission Ridge and Lookout—McCook's troops, or part of them, had been thrown across the narrow valley to protect our trains sweeping around into Chattanooga—signal rockets were going up through and above the heavy clouds of smoke and dust, the last gun from Granger's batteries growled a fiercely defiant salute, and night—silent, solemn night—came down upon that battle-swept field, on which were lying twenty thousand bleeding men!

And so ended the battle of Chickamauga.

The rebel army had possession of the field, they largely outnumbered the Union forces, they fought upon ground of their own choosing, they had the advantage of a serious mistake on the part of a division commander, but, to all intents and purposes, they lost the objects for which they fought so desperately—the destruction of the Army of the Cumberland, and the possession of Chattanooga. Neither of these they gained; for Thomas, with his veteran troops, held the rebels in check, and, like a lion at bay, fought them, without giving an inch, till, on the Tuesday following, he fell back to the rest of the army, to an entrenched position around Chattanooga.

After the war, Chaplain Lyle stayed a term at Adrian College and then answered a call from Memorial Church in Seneca Falls, New York, followed by some years at Pilgrim's Church, Duxbury, Massachusetts. From 1880 through

1892 he led the First Congregational Church of Bay City, Michigan. Failing health induced him to seek warmer climes, and he made his way to Chattanooga, Tennessee, where he organized a Congregational mission church. Reverend Lyle died there on 31 December 1893, and his remains were placed in Forest Hill Cemetery.[4]

---

[4] Pension Case File of William W. Lyle, RG 15, Records of the Veterans Administration, National Archives, Washington DC.

From Shiloh to Atlanta

Chaplain Milton L. Haney, 55th Illinois Infantry Regiment, USV
(Medal of Honor, 1896)

The Reverend Milton Lorenzo Haney was the pastor of the Methodist Episcopal Church in Bushnell, Illinois, when the war began.[1] As a patriot and an abolitionist, he helped recruit "above one hundred men" for the army, under the assumption that they would march to war while he remained in his home parish. The men, however, elected Haney as the captain of Company F, 55th Illinois Infantry Regiment on 11 October 1861. After prayer and consultation with his family, Haney accepted the commission and reported for duty. The regiment moved to Paducah, Kentucky, where Haney saw Confederate troops for the first time, the prisoners from Forts Donelson and Henry held under guard. On 6 March 1862, Haney resigned his company command to accept the position of regimental chaplain.[2] Nine days later, on 15 March 1862, the 55th Illinois reached Pittsburg Landing, Tennessee, as part of Brigadier General William T. Sherman's command. Haney received his baptism by fire at Shiloh, then continued to serve as a combat chaplain with Sherman's armies at Vicksburg, Chattanooga, Missionary Ridge, Kennesaw Mountain, Atlanta, and Ezra Church. For heroism at the Battle of Atlanta on 22 July 1864, Chaplain Haney received the Medal of Honor, one of only four chaplains in the Civil War to be given the award.

In 1904, Reverend Haney wrote his memoirs and had them privately printed under the title The Story of My Life, *a copy of which resides in the US Army Chaplain Museum, Fort Jackson, South Carolina. In comparison with the* Official Records of the War of the Rebellion *and memoirs from other veterans of the 55th Illinois Infantry, Haney's memories of military operations are accurate and include details not available elsewhere. The selected narratives below, including spiritual insights and chapter divisions, are his own.*

---

[1] Milton L. Haney (1825–1922) was the son of the Rev. James Haney (b. 1776), a Methodist local preacher and a former Ohio legislator who moved to Illinois in 1834. Milton and three of his brothers became Methodist ministers. His older brother, Richard, served as chaplain of the 16th Illinois Infantry from 24 May 1861 to 18 June 1862 when he resigned due to poor health.

[2] Haney succeeded Chaplain Lewis P. Crouch who resigned 1 March 1862.

The Battle of Pittsburg Landing

We left Paducah for Pittsburg Landing on the steamer Hannibal on the morning of the 8th of March, 1862. Reaching Savannah March 11, we were ordered on an expedition to destroy the Memphis & Charleston R.R., which failed because of high water, and our fleet returned to Pittsburg Landing March 15, knowing little of what was before us.[3] The location of the troops involved sad blunders, which afterwards were made plain by sadder experience. We were so disconnected as to give any wily foe fearful advantages over us. The officers, including two great generals, Grant and Sherman, were in need of experience. Had this battle occurred two years later we would not have sustained one-half of the loss. If it had occurred later in the war we could not have been surprised. As it was, we were, and utterly unprepared to meet such a foe. The army of Sidney Johnston was within six miles of Shiloh Church on Saturday and a large proportion of it much nearer.[4] Generals Johnston, Beauregard, Bragg, Hardee, Polk and Breckinridge held a counsel [sic] within two miles of General Sherman's tent, with lines of battle to their right and left and a heavy reserve force behind them, almost at the same hour our great commanders were giving assurance that no battle would occur at Pittsburg Landing.[5]

When in camp an army is usually inspected each Sabbath morning, and each soldier is required to appear as neat as possible, with attire in as perfect a condition as circumstances permit. On Saturday night I had preached to a Michigan regiment in General Prentiss' division on the very ground where many of them met death on Sunday morning.[6] It was a mile away, and, returning to camp in the night, my boots sank into a white clay in crossing the creek. Having had breakfast, these boots had to be prepared for

---

[3] Savannah is on the Tennessee River approximately twelve miles north of Pittsburg Landing. Shiloh Methodist Church, two and a half miles west of Pittsburg Landing, and the site of heavy fighting, provided the modern name of the battlefield.

[4] Gen. Albert Sidney Johnston (1803–1862), former secretary of war for the Republic of Texas, and appointed general in the Provisional Army of the Confederate States by Jefferson Davis. Gen. Johnston was mortally wounded at Shiloh.

[5] Gens. Albert Sidney Johnston, P. G. T. Beauregard, Braxton Bragg, William J. Hardee, Leonidas Polk, and John C. Breckinridge.

[6] The 12th Michigan Infantry in Brig. Gen. Benjamin M. Prentiss's 6th division.

inspection. One of them was nicely cleaned and shined, when the long roll was sounded and a wild rush for arms and a place in the line instantly followed. One boot was black and the other white. Having almost unbounded confidence in an army and its commanders, I said audibly to myself: "You will not catch me out to war looking this way," and I blacked the white boot. I could not definitely testify, however, that it was polished equal to the other. Then I had sufficient time to get my trunk into a wagon to prevent its being captured.

The regiment moved a quarter of a mile east, and was formed into a line of battle. Looking southward across a little creek I saw two heavy lines of Confederate infantry moving down the ridge in an easterly direction, evidently intending to flank our left.

The skirmishers of both armies had then met in the ravine, and a severe contest had opened. Our Brigade Surgon [sic], Dr. Roller, came just then, and with much earnestness requested me to take charge of the ambulances during the battle, which I did.[7] Just after I left to get my ambulances in place the Confederates, having planted a battery in full view, opened upon our poor boys, and the Colonel, in order to have them all killed at once, ordered the regiment to form square. Behind us the way was open for Johnston to reach the landing if these eight hundred men had not stood in his way, and I shall go to the judgment believing that their valor saved the day.[8]

New soldiers are especially affected by artillery, and old soldiers by musketry. The Confederates opened on this body of new soldiers with fuse shells. It was the scream and crash of these which gave wings to the 71st Ohio and select portions of the other two regiments. The two regiments left must have been annihilated had they remained where they began. The 55th Ills. were well nigh panic stricken, and went wildly for some rods, but when they reached a ridge they halted, and with the 54th Ohio held that ground till their ammunition gave out, at 2 o'clock in the afternoon! But nearly one-half of that fighting force were then either dead or bleeding!

I found difficulty in locating my ambulances, and when located I was not sure I could get them out. Wounded men are borne on litters to the

---

[7] Dr. Edward O. F. Roller of Chicago, acting brigade surgeon, March 1862 to August 1863.

[8] Brig. Gen. John K. Jackson's 3rd Brigade of Bragg's 2nd Corps attacked the 55th Illinois Infantry and the 54th Ohio Infantry Regiments in Larkin Bell Field—six regiments in a quarter mile front.

ambulances in such cases and then carried by the latter to the hospital. A regimental surgeon is expected to do nothing of a permanent character, but to stop blood or temporarily bind up wounds and send them right on. Having no horse, I was nearly overcome with the heat, and there all alone stood a horse with a saddle and a bridle, loose in the woods. I never learned whose he was, or how he came there. The presumption was his master was shot. So I mounted and hastened back to my post.

Reaching a point in front of the ambulances, I saw the wounded who came down the hill had to pass a point where for rods they were under fire, but by going down the bed of the creek this would be avoided. So the best I could do for them was to stand there and direct them. I took shelter behind a tree, which was not quite as large as my body, and I tried to make myself smaller, but the gentlemen I had met at the summit had a clear intention to move me from that tree. If it is yet standing I suppose forty bullets could be found in it today. A large number of the wounded went direct to the landing across the hills, which was less than one mile, while it was three miles by road.

When my ambulances were filled, mounting my captured charger, I led them to the landing. I had some fear as to my ambulances, but I saw them all in procession. On arriving at the landing I found one was missing. The rear driver, when he came to the place of exposure, cut his mules loose from the ambulance, mounted one of them and made a direct line across the hills for the landing! Providentially, all who were in the ambulances were able to walk, and some less hurt helped others, going down a ravine till they reached our gunboats and were saved.

Having reached the landing a little after two o'clock, I found the hills covered with stragglers and the woods strewn with men, wildly coming that way. I knew at the front the sifted braves were holding the line against fearful odds. I saw across the Tennessee the head of Buell's army protruding from the woods, and shouted for joy.[9] If the enemy could be held at bay for two hours we would have twenty thousand fresh troops on the field and the day would be saved. I was faint from the tremendous strain of the day, but met Grant's Medical Director with a lot of canteens filled with brandy strung around his neck. I said: "Doctor, give me some brandy!" And I took a

---

[9] Maj. Gen. Don Carlos Buell (1818–1898) was a veteran of the Seminole Wars and the Mexican War and commanded the Army of the Ohio 1861–1862.

small quantity on an empty stomach, and living wholly without stimulants as I did, it gave me immediate strength.

Twenty-two hundred men were rallied and gotten into the last line which was formed on Sunday at Pittsburg Landing. This last line was not one-fifth as long as the first in the morning, but it was well organized and near the landing. We had much artillery, and it was located so that the gunboats could assist. I wept for joy when our artillery opened and thanked God as I have rarely thanked him, and the day was won. The Confederate army was practically beaten before sunset Sunday night, and only fought on the defensive from that time till driven back to Corinth.[10] General Buell's troops were over in the morning and aided in the fight Monday. It was years before I could respect General Buell, because of his dallying at Pittsburg Landing.

The horrors of war are not fully seen in the battle, but in the harvest of agonies which result. Our wounded on that Sabbath, by the hundred, were dumped out on the ground without any cover. There was some relief from the boats, which received many and soon carried them to hospitals beyond, but I was shut in with the sufferers on the hill above the landing. I saw the camp of some regiment not far away, and hastened to procure their tents. The regiment was not there, but the camp was guarded, and they would not let me have a tent at any price. I still wore my Captain's suit and it was valuable that day. I got a sword and went among the stragglers and to each man I met who was armed I said: "Fall in here, sir." till I had a troop of my own, and marched on that camp. In my new command there was a little Dutch Sergeant, and as I came near a tent I sad [sic]: "Sergeant, take down that tent, sir." Those tents were all up among the wounded on that ridge and filled with suffering men before the guard could fully realize that they had nothing left to guard! Their camp kettles came with us also, twelve of them, and while my men were building fires I was down at the landing on horseback with two sacks and filled them with hams and potatoes, and we had hams, potatoes, and potato soup, giving ham after ham. When men bleed they must have food or die. I think wounded men did die at Pittsburg Landing who would not have died had food been furnished in time. There were sixty in one group I remember, and during the night we had to carry out their dead. Dear Doctor E. O. F. Roller, though weak in body, went through that terrible night, doing his utmost to save life and alleviate pain.

---

[10] Corinth MS.

I did not hear from my regiment, but found by sunrise the next morning where it was located. I had strong fears that the men were left without food, and supposed they would be ordered early into battle line again. I seemed impelled to do something for them, and hastened with an empty sack to the supply boat as before, and filled the sack with hams. Just as I came in sight with them they were ordered to march. I rode in advance of them, and dropped a ham here and there, asking them to divide, and dismounted and cut the last ham in slices and gave it to them as they marched. Some of them had not had breakfast Sabbath morning, and all of them had fought all day Sunday and lay on their arms all night without food! They were now going out for a second day's battle, with no prospect of food for twelve hours to come.

Many of the wounded were taken to the boats on Monday and more help had rallied, so I was relieved of my tasks somewhat, though our cooking had to go on all the same. I had noticed that men who bled suffered with thirst, and, procuring a lot of canteens, I filled them with spring water and rode over the field behind the army. O, I was so glad to be able to satisfy the thirst of those wounded men. One of our boys had been shot and captured on Sabbath, and the Confederates left him in one of our tents behind them as they advanced and we retreated on Sunday. Now, as they retreated and we advanced a battle was fought over his head and the enemy was driven beyond him. Our artillerymen were harassed by sharpshooters, and the Captain fancied the missiles came from behind that tent where this boy was lying, so he ordered the tent destroyed. The Confederates had run over him twice, two battles were fought over him, and now our artillery let loose upon him! In the recital of his experiences of those two days he came to the destruction of the tent over his head by our own men, and said: "Chaplain, when I saw that tent going to pieces over my head you may depend if I ever prayed I prayed then!" God covered him and he lived to tell the story.

After the battle of Shiloh, the 55th Illinois Infantry moved against Corinth, Mississippi, and thence to Memphis where the regiment remained until November 26, 1862 when the Vicksburg campaign began.

Before Vicksburg

The Mississippi River being cleared to Vicksburg, everything now centered in taking that stronghold. Sherman's force was to reach the mouth of the Yazoo, above the city, and await the arrival of Grant's force across the country, but the latter was compelled to return to Memphis.[11] After Sherman affected a landing on the Yazoo River it leaked out some way that he was to wait till General McClernand arrived, who was the ranking officer and would assume command.[12] This angered Sherman's officers and was displeasing to Sherman as well. A council of war was held and the decision arrived that "we would be in Vicksburg or in hell" before General McC. Arrived. Many I fear, reached the latter place, but we did not get into Vicksburg.

Arkansas Post was an old Government fort and there stood out a very old United States gun, which the rebels loaded with grape shot and let them loose on us.[13] There were three successive shots, which came directly over my bed. Either of them would have cut me in two if I had been standing. The gun was so large and so near that those grape shot came with awful force. The next day we were idle for a time and the gunboats were playing fearfully on the fort.

While standing there idle I felt a strong inclination to go around to the right, and somehow feared the wounded were being neglected. On reaching the rear of the hottest fire I found no ambulances, and many wounded men were staggering about in the woods. On inquiry it was plain the commander of the ambulances was frightened by the bullets in those woods, and hastening to General McClernand's headquarters I complained to the Medical Director, who gave me authority to bring them up. About the time the wounded were sent away those brave Texans hoisted the white flag, and such a shout I have never heard before or since as went up from the Union army. After seeing the capture I hastened to the boats to see what was done with the wounded. A large Southern Mississippi steamer lay near, which they said was filled with the wounded. On reaching her cabin I found two rows of men lying side by side, the whole length of the cabin, and apparently wholly neglected. There were doctors on board, and I asked what this could mean. They said the doctor in charge was drunk and they could do nothing without orders. "Orders," said I, and found myself nearly wild with the spectacle before me. There was not a dish in the cabin that could be used to

---

[11] Maj. Gen. William T. Sherman (1820–1891), Maj. Gen. U. S. Grant (1822–1885).

[12] Maj. Gen. John A. McClernand (1812–1900), US Congressman (D-Ill.) 1843–1851 and 1859–1861.

[13] Arkansas Post was fifty miles north of Vicksburg on the Arkansas River and was held by five thousand Confederate troops, the majority from Texas regiments.

wet their wounds. Flannel clothing, when wet with blood and dried in the sun, becomes nearly as hard as a board, and inflammation was coming up in every wound. Finding a large wash dish below, I went the whole round and wet every wound with cold water. In this round I marked many who would die, and made a second round, leaving a tract to be read to the dying man by his comrade near him who was stronger, giving words of cheer as I went.

I went to my Brigadier General to induce him at once to go to Sherman with this outrage.[14] He higgled about it, and after I had pressed it till my heart was sick he said he would. As I turned away I felt he would not. So I turned toward Sherman's headquarters myself and found him standing by his tent. Saluting him, I laid the thing before him. Sherman was a very nervous man, and when excited strongly he would turn clear round on one foot. He was evidently angry and much excited, as he said "D—n it, Chaplain, I am not responsible for the neglect of the doctors." To this I responded "General Sherman, I am aware, sir, your not responsible for their neglect, but you command all the doctors in this realm, and if this matter is not righted I will publish it if it costs my head!" It seemed but a few minutes till the doctors were in commotion, and I think in less than three hours all those dear boys were on nice cots with clean, white pillows, their wounds dressed and they nicely cared for.

The next time I met General Sherman was in front of Vicksburg when the regiment wanted to send me home for sanitary goods for our sick, and the papers had to have General Sherman's signature. I went to his tent for that purpose, and he met me very cordially. I said: "General Sherman, if it please you, I would like to get your signature to this paper," and turning to his Adjutant, he said: "Adjutant, sign that paper," and remarked to me that to the end of the war he would be glad to do anything he could to accommodate me. Sherman was a great man, and, of course, knew my course was erratic and not in accord with military usage, but his great soul knew it was right.

The Mississippi River had been thoroughly blockaded at Vicksburg and a fearful array of artillery overlooked the river from its hills for nearly five miles. If supplies for an army could run this blockade then an army could reach and cross the river below the city, and Vicksburg could be put into a

---

[14] Brig. Gen. Joseph Andrew Jackson Lightburn (1824–1901), soldier, legislator, and Baptist minister in the Broad Run West Virginia Baptist Association. A year later, Lightburn personally led a counterattack against Manigault's Brigade at the Troup Hurt House during the Battle of Atlanta, 22 July 1864.

siege. One morning a wooden gunboat ran the gauntlet and came out unhurt, and Grant called for volunteers to man the transports, which were to run the blockade, and soon had to place a guard on each vessel to prevent it from being overrun. The old steamboat officers would not run the risk, and each boat had to be officered with soldiers. Hence for days these beginners were maneuvering those great vessels on the river at Milliken's Bend. Governor Yates came down for the occasion, and invited me to go on his staff, so I could be on Grant's boat of observation.[15] So I was greatly favored. Grant's boat was anchored at a point in the river where he could see the whole movement. At a sign three large steamers laden with army stores left for the blockade. On the point of land west of the river and nearest the city there was a cluster of houses, which the rebels were to set on fire in case boats should undertake to pass in the night. So by the blaze of the burning buildings Grant's boats were clearly visible. The roar of artillery was grand and fearful, but those braves made the entire circuit without injury. General Grant rarely showed much emotion or acted nervously, but that night he walked the boat backwards and forwards, indicating a deep solicitude for the men who had volunteered to face death as these had done. That was one of the most striking scenes I ever witnessed, but the daring of those men gave us Vicksburg.

Three large Mississippi steamboats laden with army supplies were now below the city and under our control. So Grant was ready to move, and leaving Millikens Bend in April, the Union forces were on their way to Grand Gulf, on the Louisiana side of the river. It was of the highest importance, on reaching Grand Gulf, that the crossing be effected with the least possible opposition. So the army of Sherman was sent up the Yazoo River to attack Gain's Bluff [sic].[16] So, unexpectedly to the enemy, two heavy lines of infantry, with artillery, were landed in front of Gains' Bluff [sic] with a gunboat or two to back them, as though we were going up that bluff at any cost. This drew from Vicksburg and below a heavy army to reinforce Gaines' Bluff [sic] and diverted the attention of the Confederate commander from Grand Gulf till Grant's army was on the Vicksburg side of the river, and Sherman retired from Gaines' Bluff [sic] like a gentleman, without any serious loss to his army, and hastened to join Grant.

---

[15] The Hon. Richard Yates (1815–1873), Civil War governor of Illinois. He gave U. S. Grant his first Civil War commission as colonel of the 21st Illinois Volunteer Infantry Regiment in June 1861.

[16] Haynes Bluff.

The Siege of Vicksburg

Coming into Vicksburg from Black River brought great consternation to the natives, and there was a rush for the hills of the Yazoo. The slaveholders forced their slaves to go with them, though many, when they got into the hills, stole away and ran for protection to the Union army. There were clusters of slave cabins, and as they returned, bringing what little they could, they entered these cabins. The soldiers all expected a siege, and there was a scrambling for cooking utensils for camp. A black man was carrying a frying pan and a mounted soldier ordered him to give it to him. The slave answered: "Lord, Massa, I borrowed it, and promised to take it back, sir." He cursed him, but the man ran with the pan and threw it into the door of the cabin where it belonged. The soldier followed quickly and ordered the woman to give it up. She pleaded it was all she had and she could not spare it and closed the door. He deliberately got off his horse, put his musket through a crack in the cabin and fired it at her. She fell like a beef and he walked in and got the frying pan and went away! Her left limb was broken above the knee, and the musket being so close the bone was badly shattered. Dr. Roller amputated the limb and cared for her till he was overtaxed with the sick and wounded and begged me to take charge of her. I brought soup and other nourishment and dressed her wound for thirty days. During that time I made use of every means I thought of to inspire courage and bring cheer to her soul, but in no case could I produce a smile. Her heart had died! She was a slave from infancy, had a child when fifteen years old, and her life had been a horror to her. When we came she, with all others slaves, recognized us as her city of refuge and at the risk of her life ran into our arms for safety, to be shot down like a beast!

One morning I went in and saw there was gangrene in her wound, and promptly told her she must die. Her face lighted up as I told her, for the first time in thirty days she smiled! It comforts me now to remember the care I took of that desolate soul. O, what wailing there will be at the judgment seat of Christ!

In the first assault we made upon the works many were killed and wounded, and it was a day of great sadness.[17] The second assault on the works at Vicksburg was made in columns by divisions, and not in battle line, as before. In the long line of rebel breastworks there was a fort here and

---

[17] On 19 May 1863, Sherman's troops attacked Stockade Redan northeast of Vicksburg.

there, perhaps a mile apart. Our attack was now made upon each of these forts, and each division had to have a scaling party to precede it and prepare the way by removing any barriers which might be found when they got there.[18] These were not coerced, but so many from each regiment were allowed to volunteer. It was known to be a very hazardous undertaking and meant death to a large proportion of those who volunteered. The 55th Ills. was drawn into line and the statement made that so many men were wanted, and the first who stepped out would be taken. More than the number stepped out, and my brother's son was among the first. There were about sixty to each division. We had two ridges to pass before reaching the part which exposed the men to the fire of the enemy. The scaling party was to go right through to the fort and the column was to follow and support them. The fire was heavy when they reached the second ridge, but the scaling party passed and hastened forward to the fort; but the head of the column, on reaching the ridge, lay down! This left the sixty boys alone with nothing but the breastworks between them and the enemy, and brought on a hand to hand fight. At first the rebels undertook to put their muskets over the works with nothing but their hands visible, and our boys would shoot their hands. Then they threw hand grenades, which were little fuse shells. They cut the fuse so they would explode immediately, and tossed them over among the boys. Their only chance was to catch them like a ball and throw them back before the explosion, and have them kill rebels instead of them! This they did in so many cases. My regiment was half way back in the column and the 8th Missouri at the head. The latter sent word back that if the 55th Illinois could come forward and support them they would go over the works. So the 55th was brought forward in line of battle and provision was made when they came to the first ridge the artillery would open fire over their heads to prevent their receiving the fire of the whole rebel line before them. I started with them, but both officers and men insisted I must not go, so I got at the root of a tree, where I could see them through. They came to the ridge and the artillery was a few seconds late and the whole rebel volley was poured into them. They reeled and fell to the ground, and to me it looked as though they were nearly all slaughtered. That was the supreme moment of my

---

[18] Gen. Grant attempted a second frontal attack on the Vicksburg line on 22 May 1863, which was repulsed with serious losses. Sherman's XV Corps attacked the northern part of the line from Stockade Redan to Fort Hill. Two enlisted men from the 55th Illinois Infantry were subsequently awarded Medals of Honor for their bravery during this action.

whole life. It seemed unbearable! Then came instantly the fire of our artillery, which made every rebel hide his head, and my braves sprang to their feet and dashed beyond the ridge, very few of them being hurt at all! They were veterans and knew how to dodge even musket balls, and I thought they were all killed!

When they reached the front even then the 8th Missouri would not undertake the fearful task of scaling the works. One of our men was shot through the brain on the heights before the regiment started, and was writhing and liable to fall down a hill.

All this time that scaling party was in a hand to hand conflict with a host of Confederate soldiers and no support behind them. They could not get away without utter slaughter, so they fought with death till the darkness of the night furnished a way of escape to those who yet survived. My brother's son fought desperately till nearly sunset, when a hand grenade exploded when it reached him and he was instantly killed.[19] He was a namesake of his uncle Dick, loved me as I have rarely been loved, and his death was to me as the burial of a child.

During this siege there came much sickness to the new recruits. The 127th Ils. Was the finest looking body of young men I saw come into the service, but they had been painfully exposed, and their chaplain had left them.[20] They were kept in an unhealthy ravine till nearly all of them were diseased. They got to dying till every man who became sick expected to die. Their surgeon was a good man, but some way they got set against him.[21] I was so moved at this condition that I had to take them on my soul in addition to my own regiment, and the hospital. They seemed to have lost all heart and death was in sight of them all. The attempt to rally them was among the most difficult undertakings of my life. I made fun, told witty stories, laughed, sang, ridiculed, prayed and shouted! The final record may show that above one hundred lives were thus rescued, but it nearly cost my own!

Sickness and Rest

---

[19] Sgt. Richard Haney, Co. F, 55th Illinois Infantry, killed 22 May 1863. *The Story of the 55th Regiment Illinois Volunteer Infantry in the Civil War 1861–1865* (Clinton MA: W. J. Coulter, 1887) 494.

[20] Chaplain Jonathan C. Stoughton, 127th Illinois Volunteers, was mustered 6 September 1862 and resigned 10 August 1863.

[21] Surgeon Joel R. Gore, 127th Illinois Volunteers, was commissioned 6 September 1862 and mustered out 31 May 1865.

When Vicksburg fell I had strength enough to hold myself up by clinging to the limb of a tree till I witnessed the surrender, and then passed through the most serious sickness of my life. My regiment had gone with Sherman to East Mississippi in pursuit of Johnston, and returned to Black River, where they went into camp during the hot weather.[22] I was weak when disease left me, but was anxious to rejoin the 55th. So I began riding a little each day, preparatory to the longer ride. The day before leaving I rode down into a valley, where I watered my horse, and to the right of me saw a slave woman washing clothes.

She was, I suppose, short of fifty years old. I accosted her and she responded, but looked a little confused, as I was a stranger. To relieve her of all fear, I asked: "Aunty, what church have you where you live?" "There was no church, sir." Thinking the dear soul did not understand me, I asked: "Were they Baptists or Methodists where you lived?" "There was neither, sir. No, sir, I don't belong to no church on dis here lower erf, but I do belong to de church of de First Born in heaven!"

The whole story is this: Her first master was a good man and gave his slaves opportunities to be religious, but they were all sold when she was either nine or eleven years old. She had never known a letter of the alphabet, nor read a syllable of God's word, and since she was eleven years old, at the farthest, she had not seen the face of a minister, heard the gospel preached nor been in a gathering for prayer. Her last master had prohibited all religious people and religious service on his immense plantation. "Well," I said, as I was bewildered with her knowledge of God, "how did you find out you were a member of the church of the First Born?" "O, sir," she responded, "seven years ago I was in de cotton field and dere was a great load of sin on my soul, and I prayed and prayed! One day I went down into a deep holler and got down by the side of an old log and prayed and prayed! De load on my soul was so great that I thought I would die. But sir, dere came a great light and wid dat light dere came a voice, and dat voice told me I was a member of the church of the First Born! Since dat time, sir, wheneber dere's great trouble and I feel I can't go through, dat voice come back and tell me, 'You are a member of de church of de First Born!'" I found by after inquiries and talk that she had stumbled into the experience of heart holiness, and was reveling in the joy of perfect love. There are millions of

---

[22] At Big Black River Bridge on the railroad from Jackson to Vicksburg. Sherman's opponent was Gen. Joseph E. Johnston (1807–1891), department commander and twice commander of the Army of Tennessee, CSA.

intelligent Christians who claim they have not sufficient light to get wholly sanctified; but this slave woman had! She had no learning, no Sunday School, no Bible, no preacher, no church, but she found God!

The next day I had a joyful meeting with my boys of the regiment in Camp Sherman on Black River. Here we had rest from the burdens of war for a time, and God was with us. During our stay the boys arranged a large seating for Divine service, and we had glorious times. For some days we had a protracted meeting, where forty sinners were converted and a number of Christians were beautifully sanctified. At least three preachers came out of that soldiers' revival. Had I been an infidel myself, and seen the triumphs of the cross which I saw in the army, it seems to me it would have made me a Christian.

Chattanooga

We came by transports from Vicksburg to Memphis, and then across the country to Chattanooga, taking dinner under the guns of the enemy at Lookout Mountain. We camped above the city, near the mouth of the little Chicakmauga [sic], which comes down from the north. General Bragg had the Union troops shut in, and his two flanks were on the Tennessee River. Hooker had effected a crossing below the city, on Bragg's left flank, and Sherman was to cross on his right under cover of the night. Our brigade was selected to perform that hazardous task.[23] Before entering the pontoon boats we had in our regiment a season of prayer, in which was given gracious assurance of protection in what seemed to be among the most dangerous undertakings of the war. The boats were lying in the Chickamauga, and when this right night had come we went quietly on board and as quietly drifted into the river. On reaching the river we were to drift down three miles, clinging closely to our side, till a signal was given, when all were to cross and effect a landing at any cost. The Confederate pickets were stationed all along on the south bank and their fires were burning.

A surgeon who had just come from the North to serve in the army happened to be in the same boat with me. As we neared the river I noticed him shivering like a man with the ague as he said in a whisper: "When we come out into the river we will be torn to pieces," and he sank down in the boat till his face was on the bottom! His fears attracted the whole crew in

---

[23] Brig. Gen. Morgan L. Smith's brigade of Maj. Gen. John E. Smith's division, XV Corps.

such a measure as to turn us all away from thoughts of danger. Our boats would jostle against each other and against the willows, making a noise which was evidently heard by the rebel pickets, as I saw, by the light of their fire, some of them rise and look toward us. At one post the picket squinted with his hand above his eyes, as though determined to see us, and I heard him say with an oath: "There is a boat, —— ——!" But we went right on. When the signal came, those in front turned squarely across [t]he river and went up its bank. God had put the picket post there asleep and the poor fellows were in our hands before they waked.

A rebel Lieutenant, with a group of men, hearing the noise of this rush among the dry corn stalks, came hurriedly through the darkness right into our hands, and, throwing up his hands, said he was in the wrong place, but the boys told him he was all right, to come around to the rear and he would be cared for. All this without firing a gun! Behind where we landed, on high ground, we had artillery, which was to open fire over our heads as we were landing, giving a chance for us to get up the bank, and in case we were met at the brink by the enemy we were to go up at the point of the bayonet. Not a musket was loaded, as in the confusion of ascending the bank if we had fired our own men would have been in great danger. The landing had been effected before our boat reached the shore, and our new doctor hearing it, arose and yawned as though awakening from sleep, declaring he had quite a nap. The men who rowed our brigade down and across hurriedly recrossed and took in the other brigade of our division, then Gen. John E. Smith's division. So in a brief time two divisions were ready for battle, had the enemy come at us. By daylight we had lines of breastworks, and in a few hours the army of Sherman was tramping over on a pontoon bridge made of the boats we had been using. The enemy had no heart to come down from the mountain to attack us and we had things our own way. To this day I have not doubted that God interposed on our behalf, putting a deep sleep on the rebel watchmen, and thus opening the way to the right flank of Bragg's army. When ready, Sherman moved up the river on the south side to reach the enemy's works, having some severe skirmishing. In one of these I met Gen. M. L. Smith, our brigade commander, who said: "Chaplain, I would not go into that brush; it is filled with bullets." So I halted. The General stepped back five rods or more and turned toward the enemy. In less than five minutes he was seriously wounded. From that wound he really never recovered. He was a splendid soldier, a first class officer and a thorough gentleman.

We had taken the first mountain and were ordered down to the base of the second. Each regiment came down by itself. When nearly half way down the rebel artillery opened on us and the old Colonel became confused and ordered the men to lie down, and shell after shell struck among us, and their explosion filled the heavens with dust and smoke. It was very plain, if we were lower down, the artillery could not reach us, but the men were kept at the best point for slaughter till it looked as if not many would be left. It was an agony to endure it, and I cried out: "Colonel, why don't you take the men to the bottom of the hill?" We were then ordered down. I supposed numbers would be left on the hillside, but when our casualties were summed up one Irishman's finger was scratched, the face of another was slightly scorched with powder, and a third was slightly injured! A regiment which followed was passing a tree when a shell struck it and exploded, making a gap in the column (four men abreast) which looked to be 12 to 15 feet. They all sprang up, and I think none were hurt.

An effort was made to storm the next mountain, whose sides were very steep. The men climbed nearly to the summit, but were forced to retreat, leaving the wounded and dead on the mountain.[24] The enemy seeing we would take their works the next day, retreated in the night, leaving our dead largely stripped of their clothing. The next day there was a general rout of the whole Confederate army, and the battle of Missionary Ridge was ended.

Sherman then went to the relief of Burnside at Knoxville, but the enemy left before we reached the city. We followed them down to Jellico Plains through a beautiful country of hills and valleys, crossing Jellico River, which comes out of the mountains.[25] Our men plunged right in and waded across, though it was nearly waist deep. I saw a group of Confederate prisoners, most of whom had voluntarily surrendered because of being sick. They looked so pale and feeble that it was trying for them to wade the stream. I said to one of them: "Put that sick man up behind me and I will take him over." When over those other pale faces haunted me, and I returned for another, and then another, till the one who had helped the others was alone. So I said: "You wait and I will come for you, too." The dear man had heard everything that was evil about the "Yanks," and was

---

[24] On the extreme right flank of Gen. Bragg's position on Missionary Ridge. The National Park Service named the site the Sherman Reservation on modern maps. There is a monument there to the 55th Illinois Infantry.

[25] Tellico Plains, south of Knoxville on the edge of the Cherokee National Forest.

really confounded at my treatment of them. He piled up adjectives in my favor, and when he had exhausted his vocabulary he said as he got off the horse: "Sir, I have a beautiful sister at my home, and if you will come down after the war is over you shall have her, by all that is good and great!"

We were cut off from our supplies and compelled to live on the country for a time. The Colonel was notional and appointed forage parties who failed to supply the wants of the men. Having halted for the night, I went from headquarters to see the men and met the line officers in a body, which was very unusual. Asking what it meant, their spokesman said: "Many of the men have marched all day without a mouthful to eat, and we are going to settle with that—old Swede!" I begged of them to let me handle the Colonel, and if I failed they could then come at him.[26] Coming to the Colonel I said: "A large number of men have marched all day without a mouthful to eat." "Is dot so, Chaplain?" "Yes, it is lamentably true, and the foraging party don't seem to succeed." "Well, Chaplain, I will do whatever you tink best." I told him if he would let me chose [sic] my men I would see that the boys had something by noon the next day, and he was pleased with the proposition. I reported to the officers and their wrath cooled down. I chose Joe Presson as my Sergeant and a company of spirited men, and we struck the column with supplies before noon.[27]

Riding up to a nice looking home, the husband, wife and two girls met us at the gate, but Joe marched right into the house without ceremony. They were Union people, as they claimed, and had three sons in the Union army. Many rank secessionists, when we came, were good, loyal folks, so I was questioning them pretty closely when one of the girls ran into the house and brought out a pile of letters from her three brothers and their photographs in our uniform: "There," said she, "if you don't believe we are Union folks and that my brothers are in the army, read those letters!" And the tears gushed out of her eyes. Just then Joe came out saying: "Chaplain, there is a pile of meat here." I answered: "These are real Union people and have suffered much, Joe, and we will not take anything here." There were

---

[26] Col. Oscar Maumberg, 55th Illinois Infantry, formerly an engineer from Sweden. Lt. Col. James Augustine replaced Maumberg as the regimental commander after Chattanooga was taken.

[27] Qm. Sgt. Joseph H. Presson, 55th Illinois Infantry, had joined the unit as a corporal in Company A. Presson became a Methodist minister after the war and served as chaplain of the Nebraska legislature.

also some turkeys on the fence, and as Joe looked at those turkeys and thought of the meat he gave me a look which stays with me till this day!

As we came down into a valley I heard a boy say to his mother: "There are more coming; get ready." I found he had been going down to the road and back all day as the army was passing and bringing soldiers up, that his mother could give them a warm meal and send them happy on their way. I informed her of my errand and she asked what I wanted. I said: "Some meat, if you have it to spare." "Well, how many pieces would you want?" I said two or three, and the bacon was in Joe's hands at once. I said to him: "You go across the valley there and get what you can, but be sure and do no wrong." I went in to talk and pray with the family. There was an old lady on her bed who was exceedingly feeble, looking as though eternity was at the door. I said to the woman of the house: "It may seem singular to you, being at the head of a foraging party, but I am a Methodist preacher and I came in to talk to you about the Lord." The old lady sprang up in the bed and shouted aloud the praise of God. She had not seen a minister for about three years nor heard the voice of prayer outside their home. They were Southern Methodists, but had been cut off from the church because they were loyal to the Government. Having prayers with them, we all had a Pentecost together, which was glorious. The memories of holy fellowship in those days of war, with such Southern saints, thrill me to-day with the gladness of the Lord!

Diverse Experiences

Those who "veteranized" were promised a furlough, and we were all subsequently sent home.[28] The treatment we received on the way, in Chicago and at our homes, was flattering beyond expectation, and, of course, it was a great feast to us all. My wife and little folks accompanied the regiment to Chicago.[29] Her heroic spirit never faltered during the war. When I was reported killed again and again she insisted I was alive and

---

[28] A War Department General Order, issued 25 June 1863, granted a furlough of at least thirty days and a bounty of $400 to volunteers of at least nine months' service who re-enlisted. When a large proportion re-enlisted, the regiment was sent home as a body at government expense, and the "veteran volunteers" were allowed to elect new officers as well as recruit new members.

[29] Mrs. Sarah C. Huntsinger Haney (1831–1920), known as "Katey" to her husband. Two of the Haney's children predeceased their parents. One son, Conrad A. Haney (1855–1931) survived them.

would come through unscathed. She came to me at Larkins Landing when not one woman in a hundred could have gotten through. Orders had been issued against women coming to the front, and when she reached Louisville the commander of the post refused to give her a pass. She answered it was too bad; she ought to have provided for this before leaving home. To this he replied with a distinctively military air: "You could not get through without a pass from me!" She answered: "Would not an order from General Grant suffice without your signature?" And with her lady friend she went to a hotel and had a telegram sent to General Grant that the wife of Chaplain Haney, with a lady friend, wished to come to the front, and immediately came an order from the General, signed by his own hand, to pass them. The next morning she, with her friend, was at the depot in due time, where at the car entrance she was met by his lordship, the commander of the post. He objected to their taking the cars. She replied that they were expecting to go, and after sufficient satisfaction for his impudence she showed him her order. This occurred before my wife was sanctified.

We rejoined Sherman's command after our furlough, at Big Shanty, north of Mount Kennesaw.[30] Sherman had maneuvred [sic] and fought his way through from Chattanooga to Kennesaw Mountain. There were some hidden works of the enemy around the base of the mountain which Sherman wanted discovered. The railroad track had not been taken up, so the General suggested to a soldier engineer that he would like a reconnaissance of that unseen locality. The soldier mounted an engine alone, ran around the point under fire, got the desired information and returned unhurt! When he alighted from the engine he walked up alongside of it and patted it like a man would a pet horse, and calling it by name said: "Good old girl," and walked off to his tent as though no extraordinary thing had occurred. There are countless thousands who would not have taken the risk he did for a millions [sic] dollars!

It was soon understood that we were to assault the enemy in this stronghold. Sherman was doubtful about it, but called a council of war, and some of his generals, Logan especially, strongly favored it, and Sherman was overruled. It afterward proved he was right and they wrong. Our troops were to go around to the west side, but were lying to the north on their arms for quite a time. One of the boys, who was a brave soldier, came to tell me that he had a strong conviction if he went into this battle he would be killed,

---

[30] Now Kennesaw GA.

and asked me what to do. He had been clearly converted, but had let go his hold on Christ. After reflection, I said: "You go down into that ravine and pray till you get tremendously blessed, and come to me again, and if you then want to be excused I will see your Captain and get you off." I knew we were to be there yet for a time. He obeyed orders and disappeared for an hour, perhaps, but when he reappeared his face was aglow with glory, and coming to me, he said: "Chaplain, you need not speak to the Captain now. I am all right," and went into the battle and came out without a scratch.

A deep cloud hung over my soul as to this battle, and I was pressed with the thought of disaster. My heart friend, Captain Augustine, was commanding the regiment, and it was plain to me that he expected to die that day.[31] A few minutes before orders to charge had come he turned his back on the regiment and faced me with a steady, long, last look, with feelings between us too big for utterance. To me it was as though he said "I will see you no more!" God had, as I believed, used me in pulling him away from the vortex of infidelity, and I trust his soul had so apprehended Christ that I shall see him again. Our dead were left in the hands of the enemy, and that night Lieut. Henry Augustine, the Captain's brother, and myself undertook to secure his body. Their picket line was this side of where the body lay, and we were halted before we reached it. We both stepped behind a large tree for protection from bullets, and I promptly told the picket the object of my coming, and plead the case thus: "His mother is old and feeble and has lost one son in battle, and we fear the death of the Captain will take her life; so we want to send the body home, which will be a great relief to her." To this he responded, "Where is General Sherman?" I said: "I supose [sic] he is at his headquarters." "Well," he answered, "General Sherman can get this body and all those bodies." So in the morning we went to see the General and laid the case before him. He was much moved, but said: "Chaplain, it is a great humiliation to me to ask any favors of those rebels!" I quickly responded: "General Sherman, we will not ask you to do it, sir."

Young Putnam was a boy of twenty summers and was converted in Camp Douglas.[32] He had been true and faithful to his vows and a good

---

[31] Lt. Col. Jacob M. Augustine, 55th Illinois Infantry, enlisted at Canton on 30 July 1861 as first lieutenant of Co. A and was promoted to captain in early 1862. Elected lieutenant-colonel by veterans, he was killed 27 June 1864 while leading the regiment in an attack at Pigeon Hill on the flank of Little Kennesaw Mountain.

[32] Pvt. George W. Putnam, Co. C, 55th Illinois Infantry. Camp Douglas was in Illinois where the regiment mustered.

soldier. In helping to remove the Captain's body nearer the base of the hill his thigh was broken and the largest artery cut. Taking his canteen strap, he bound it tightly around the limb and restrained the bleeding, but could not stop it. Having rolled himself down to a stream of spring water at the bottom of the hill, he quenched his thirst, and seeing he must die, he sang the hymn with the chorus: "I'm going home, I'm going home to die no more, To die no more, to die no more, I'm going home to die no more."

His notes of victory rang out amid the thunder of shot and shell while dying under the guns of the enemy. Dear, modest, beautiful Christian boy! I helped bury his remains with others who had lain for days in that hot sun, till I only knew him by the canteen strap about his limb! Luther said "O, God! How dreadful is this world!"

After this battle Sherman flanked the enemy and forced retreat, which ought to have been done without the battle; and Johnston's army fell back to Atlanta. President Davis came to Atlanta to hold a council of war, and General Johnston told him plainly he could not hold the city against the force of Sherman's army. Jefferson Davis insisted it should be done and General Hood said it could.[33] So Johnston was superceded by General Hood, and we all heard about it in a few days. Our men rejoiced in the change, though they knew it meant more fighting. Johnston was a skillful general and saved his army by retreating. Hood was full of fight, but greatly lacked in caution. Under Johnston's command he was pre-eminently useful, but when he came to command himself he ruined his army. On the 22d of July, 1864, he ordered whiskey barrels to be opened, that the boys might fill their canteens, for this was their last battle, and they would drive the Yanks out of the country. It was the last battle for many of them, but the Yanks went the other way.

Hood massed his forces and threw them against our left wing, got into our rear and attacked us from both sides.[34] There was a division of our Seventeenth Army Corps who changed sides of the ditch six times in the fight and repulsed the enemy each time. We were near the center and had naught to do but look and hear. The musketry was simply terrific. General McPherson was to our rear nearby, and to succor the men on the left he

---

[33] John Bell Hood (1831–1879), succeeded Gen. Joseph E. Johnston as commanding general of the Army of Tennessee during the latter phases of the Atlanta Campaign. Hood was Maj. Gen. James B. McPherson's classmate at West Point.

[34] The Battle of Atlanta, 22 July 1864.

rode over, not knowing the enemy was inside his lines, and rode right into a rebel troop, and they killed him. He was a great man and a splendid officer.[35]

Hood being repulsed on our left, threw his troops around our center. It was a woodland and we could not see far. As the order came for battle against three lines of rebel soldiers, six men deep, it looked as though a fearful conflict was before us. Seeing somebody's musket lying there, I thought it ought to be used, and went into our left company with Lieut. Eichelberger in command.[36] For the first time in the war we were behind breastworks and the men had an idea that no force could drive them. When the enemy came in sight a terrible fire of musketry scattered them at once and they were forced to disappear. The 57th Ohio was to our right and their right rested on the railroad coming out from the city, where we also had a battery. When the enemy disappeared an order came to fire "right oblique," so we kept up an incessant fire. While one man stepped up on the step and fired his mate stepped into the ditch and loaded. When loading my gun I faced northward, and to my surprise the right of the 57th Ohio was retreating. The breach had been closed to our rear for about twenty steps and they dashed into the brush. The next time I loaded more were going and I thought when that comes down to the right of my regiment it will stop; but lo, when they were gone our right beyond it gave way, and I began to command them to stand. This continued from right to left till Captain Eichelberger and one man with myself were all that were left. That one said to me: "Chaplain, don't let us go!" Eichelberger raved like a wild man. He thought we were utterly disgraced. Neither of us saw a rebel anywhere. As we walked back the bullets appeared thick, but we did not seem to care for them. The Lieutenant broke into tears and wept like a child. Having gone through the brush perhaps thirty rods, a group of the scattered men began to gather around us and Eichelberger insisted that we return and retake the works. I said it would be foolish with these forty men to undertake that when the whole regiment had been driven from them so wildly. But a soldier came to me, saying: "Our men are still in the line, holding it against fearful odds!" I said that was impossible, as I had seen the last man out before I left. But he insisted they were and asked me to listen to the muskets. A musket

---

[35] Maj. Gen. James B. McPherson (1828–1864), commander of the federal Army of Tennessee.

[36] 1st Lt. George W. Eichelberger, Co. B, 55th Illinois Infantry, enlisted 7 October 1861 at Fulton IL as a private.

fired toward you has a sharp, short sound; fired from you, a light, prolonged sound, and I was persuaded they were our muskets, and that men, having seen their foolishness in retreating, had run back and re-entered the works and were holding them against a great force. Now, we were the cowards and they the heroes; so it was our duty to reach them in the shortest possible time, whatever it might cost!

The men had said they would not go unless I sanctioned it, and now our duty seemed plain. We fell into a thin line and the farther we went the faster, till suddenly coming into the clearing, we were face to face with a thousand rebels between us and our works, only about twenty steps away! A rebel seeing me before I saw him, had his musket drawn on my breast. My musket was down at "trail arms," but was changed to a make ready, take aim, fire! In amazing quick time, and all that could retreated, as the only thing but capture or death! The mystery was now made plain. When they were repulsed with slaughter in our front they turned northward and one column came down the railroad cut and filed to the right and behind the 57th Ohio, and the right company, seeing them, fell back to keep from being captured, and as the retreat of the two regiments was brought about as above described. We on the extreme left did not see the rebels at all and some of us only left because all the rest had gone! The rebel column which came down the railroad cut and was in the brush on our side of the line when we retired was now between us and our works.

The right command given those two regiments as the column came through the cut would have sent them back in confusion with but little loss, but that right command was wanting. But the gentlemen did go out in haste before the sun went down, and we were again in possession. Lieut. Eichelberger was shot through the head a few feet from where I stood, others were killed and some wounded, and a part of our group captured and taken to prison. As I turned after firing, it was said by a cool-headed sergeant who was looking on, that one hundred muskets were fired at my person. It may have been less, but the brush was mowed to the right and left by rebel bullets, and by a miracle my life was preserved. A voice went through me, assuring me that no rebel bullet should touch me, and I praised God till two o'clock that night that he had carried my head in time of battle and enabled me to "run through a troop and leap over a wall." (Psalm 18:29)[37]

At Atlanta

On the 29th of July we were thrown around to the northwest of Atlanta, and General Hood made a desperate effort to break the Union line at the point where we were situated. We were approaching the enemy in two lines and that day our brigade was in the reserve line some rods to the rear.[38] The front line had ascended a long hill to near the summit with skirmishers in front. The latter had passed an open spot of ground and entered a woodland, where the enemy rose up in full force right before them. Nothing could save them from capture or death but retreat, and as they turned and ran the storm of bullets was fearful. The bravest men can be made wild when running if a hailstorm of bullets is pursuing them! It was plain a battle had opened, and I had promised my wife not to epose [sic] myself as before, unless there was great need; so I turned to find my place with our doctor, to help care for the wounded. I had crossed a deep little ravine with steep banks, and gone some distance, when I turned and a host of men were coming down the hill onto my boys like a herd of wild buffalo! I saw at a glance if our lines were broken and we forced to retreat we would have to pass over an open field with the probable loss of a thousand men; and the time of "great need" had come! I shouted to my men to close the works and not alow [sic] a man to pass if they had to take his life, and turned to join them. I had no weapon and sought for a club, but found none.

Dr. Smith, seeing the terrible conflict, came to the rescue and met a big Indianian.[39] He seized the giant and the doctor was small of stature. The Indiana soldier did not seem to know he had any opposition and went off with the doctor like an ox would with a fly on his horn! It would be rare to find a bantam rooster more plucky than Doctor Smith. The skirmishers in front had gotten such momentum as they reached the front line that instead of stopping or being stopped, they dashed through, bringing many others with them, making a gap in the ranks, and we filled that gap.

---

[37] The Medal of Honor was issued to Haney on 3 November 1896 for voluntarily carrying a musket in the ranks of his regiment and rendering heroic service in retaking the federal works which had been captured by the enemy. He does not mention the medal in his autobiographical manuscript.

[38] Haney is referring to the Battle of Ezra Church, 28 July 1864.

[39] Dr. John T. Smith, surgeon, 55th Illinois Infantry.

The enemy made three distinct assaults on us at that point during the afternoon. To break the line they had to take a battery on our right. My regiment was broken in two by the abruptness of the hill, and I had taken up a musket which one of the raiders had left and stood with two companions. The second assault was furious and my two companions commanded the open space to our right and front which had to be passed to reach our battery. The weather was hot and my musket being fired so rapidly, seemed as though it would burn me and was in danger of exploding. So I buried it in the sand to cool it off as we waited for the third assault, which was led by a young Colonel, who as we were told, was Captain of the company who killed General McPherson a week before, and was promoted to the colonelcy on that account. He brought his men to the death line where two preceding parties had given way, and they halted. He urged and roared at them, but they did not move. I think the dead of the previous parties were lying there before them, and the fire of our men was fearful. Having failed to drive them, he dashed through and lead them. This colonel had to pass a lengthened open ground, in passing which his death rate was fearful. Their flag came down at least three times, and would be seized by another, till they were only fifty yards from the battery, which is much too near for safety. Attention was called to the colonel, and when he was buried the next day we found fifteen bullets had pierced his body!

Between these three attacks I hastened to help the doctor with those who were hurt. He was sheltered by high rocks not far away, and the last time I went I saw one lone man up to my left on an elevated spot of ground, lying on his back and beckoning me to come. I hastened and knelt by his side. A musket ball had gone clear through his body near the stomach. His eyes were badly sunken and he was breathing heavily. He looked me piercingly in the eyes in silence till I had felt his pulse, when he said "Chaplain, I suppose I have but a few minutes to live, and I feel that I am unprepared for eternity. I hoped you might tell me words whereby I could be saved!" It seems now to me that in all this ministry I never was so empowered from God to bring a soul so quickly and so thoroughly to Christ as in this case. I had an inner sense that he saw and would with his whole heart take hold of Christ as his present, Almighty Savior, and I struck up to sing:

Grace's store is always free, Drooping souls to gladden
Jesus calls, come unto me, weary, heavy laden

Though your sins like mountains rise, Rise and reach to heaven
Soon as you on him rely, All shall be forgiven.
Jesus' blood hath healed my wounds, O, the wondrous story
I was lost, but now I'm found
Glory, glory, glory!

He had closed his eyes while I was singing, but when I was half way through the last verse he opened those eyes now beaming with God light, and said: "Chaplain, I have found him," and his spirit went up to God.

After the third assault that afternoon the enemy retired, leaving their wounded on our hands. I hastened to the front. At the root of a tree nearby lay three wounded and two dead Confederates. The wounded boys looked wildly at me as I approached them, having heard terrible things about the "Yanks;" but I quieted their fears by assuring them of the best care we could give them. At this stage of the war they died from wounds through which our men would live. Their food was insufficient and their power of endurance crippled by it. I wept more than once when burying the brave boys, on finding nothing in their haversacks but a little unbolted corn meal, and in a few cases ground with the cob, as we grind it for cattle! Then they were disheartened and felt their cause was practically lost before the end of the war. But few of them, with the best of care that could be given, now survived a thigh breach. The thigh of one of these was badly broken, and before leaving him I asked about his soul. He said he had really opposed the war, but was shut in to either be drafted or volunteer, and he finally volunteered. Up to that time he was a Christian and a Methodist class leader, but from the day he entered the army until now God had seemed to have left him. I told him I was a Methodist preacher, and we both wept, I giving him what encouragement I could, duty called me. The next day I was at the general hospital, and some distance away I saw a Confederate holding up his hand and beckoning to me, and on reaching him he asked if I was not the man who talked with him at the tree where he was wounded. I said, "Yes." He expressed a strong desire that I talk and pray with him, which I did, and while praying the Lord saved him. He was wondrously blessed from that hour till his death three days later! So great was the triumph of his soul and so glorious the manifestations of God in him that the Christian soldiers in the hospital felt the ground was hallowed where he gave his spirit up to God, and after his body was removed they held their prayer meetings on that spot.

Mustered Out
From Atlanta I went home as a recruiting officer, and was to report to Governor Yates. It was arranged by request that I be sent home to recruit my regiment. We were so small that a full corps of officers could not be mustered in. The Governor counselled with the Republican Central Committee and all agreed that it was dangerous to have any more loyal men taken from the state till after the election, and proposed, if I would not actively work as a recruiting officer till after election and would make war speeches in two doubtful districts, that the Governor and Central Committee would arrange with the Secretary of War to give me two hundred men from the draft.

So I made war speeches till after Mr. Lincoln was elected, and a large number of recruits were secured and sent to Springfield to report and be forwarded to the 55th Ills., but, to my utter dismay, I found afterwards a large majority of them were sent to other regiments, and the draft in Illinois was an utter failure. After waiting till the time of promise had come and gone, the Secretary of War[40] addressed me an earnest note, expressing regret that he was utterly unable to fulfill his promise to me, as the draft had failed, and I was persuaded that my recruits sent to Springfield had been sold to other parties for money. General Sherman had gone to the sea, and I asked the Secretary of War to muster me out, which he did.[41]

In the fall 1865 Reverend Milton L. Haney took a pastorate in La Salle, Illinois, and continued to serve as a pastor and evangelist for the next thirty-one years. It was said that he led not less than 20,000 people to a profession of faith during his evangelistic missions in ten states. Haney died in Pasadena, California, in January 1922 at age ninety-seven.

---

[40] Edwin M. Stanton (1814–1869).

[41] The veteran volunteers of the regiment elected Haney as their colonel on 6 April 1864, but he had to accept lieutenant-colonel's rank due to the unit's small size. He left the regiment 24 August 1864 on recruiting duty. He resigned 2 December 1864 and was mustered out 20 December 1864.

"March of a Day"

Chaplain Randall Ross, 15th Ohio Volunteer Infantry

Born 9 January 1818 in West Newton, Pennsylvania, Randal Ross was ordained a Presbyterian minister in 1847. He led congregations at Cumberland and Sharon, Ohio, through 1860 when he became president of Sharon College. He was a mature forty-three and a father of four when he joined the 62nd Ohio Volunteers during October 1861, as a corporal in Company I. Ross was an 1844 graduate of Franklin College in Athens, Ohio, and his academic skills got him detailed as commissary clerk and regimental mailman. He also possessed a divinity degree from Allegheny Seminary in Pennsylvania, which led to his being mustered as chaplain of the 15th Ohio on 6 July 1863.

Gaylesville, Ala.[1]

By the above you will see that I am no longer in the "State of Georgy." We are "into Alabamy" about seven miles; and after about three weeks' hard marching hither and thither, as the rebels see fit to lead, we have at length halted. For how long, I know not.[2]

Feeling somewhat in a mood for writing, however, let our halt be long or short, I will endeavor to improve the time, in part at least, by holding intercourse with the civilized world through the medium of my pen. But of what shall I write? A thousand subjects crowd upon the mind with claims of interest; but which would be most interesting is difficult to decide. There is Southern Scenery, Southern Fertility, Southern Agriculture, Southern Climate, Southern Treason, Southern Suffering, Southern—a great many things that might afford themes for interesting letters. And then there is the Evening Camp Scene, that no painter can portray; the "Thousand and One" "Grape-vines," too, that we hear passing through camp daily, when we get cut loose from the outer world, as we have been for the last three weeks.

---

[1] Randal Ross, "A Day's March," *The United States Service Magazine* (February 1865): 180–83.

[2] This letter was most likely to have been written during the middle of October 1864. Gen. Sherman broke off his pursuit of Gen. Hood's Army of Tennessee at Gaylesville. Sherman then began his March to the Sea, leaving Tennessee in the hands of IV, XVI, and XXIII Corps under Gen. George H. Thomas. The 15th Ohio was in the 1st Brigade, 3rd Division, IV Corps.

The "March of a Day," too, might afford sufficient inspiration for one letter. The "March of a Day!" What a conglomeration of ideas is contained in that short phrase! True, most folks, except those who are actively engaged in it, associate nothing more with the phrase than the simple change of location by the army, or a part of the army, for a distance of perhaps eight or ten miles. But what a faint idea does this present of the reality! Perhaps after dark, the evening before, an orderly rides rapidly up to regimental headquarters, with a paper in a large yellow envelope. He hands it in to the colonel in his tent. Orders to move! The adjutant is ordered to notify company commanders to be ready to move by daylight tomorrow morning. Company commanders notify their men. This requires the men in the regiment and the cooks to be up at least two hours before daylight.

So at about 3 A.M., all over the camp, men are chopping and splitting up rails with which to make fires. Then you can hear the men pounding their coffee in their tin cups with the butts of their bayonets. All over the camp, too, is a continual gabble: talking, shouting, singing, swearing—a perfect Babel! Who can sleep in such a place? There is no use trying. Before I get accustomed to the noise and confusion now in camp sufficiently to enable me to sleep, Green, the colored cook, thrusts his black face and curly head in at the tent door, and announces: "Breckfas' ready, gemmen. De sun looks mos' bu'ful comin' up ova dat ar' mounting." So we have to practice upon one part of *Poor Richard's* maxim, "early to rise," willing or unwilling. We roll over, yawn, slowly rise; wash, dress, comb hastily; gather round half a dozen tin cups, tin plates, knives, forks, and spoons, spread out upon an oil-cloth, which is spread out upon the ground. For breakfast we have *coffee, crackers*, and *salt pork*.

Breakfast is scarcely over when the bugle at brigade headquarters sounds "*Strike tents.*" In a moment all the regimental bugles catch up "the joyful sound" and all blow, "Strike tents!" "Strike tents!" "Strike tents!" too. A regular shout now rises from the men, and in a moment you can see acres of tents melt away like April snow. Soon all these tents and blankets are seen only in little bundles, tied up ready, at the proper signal, to be shouldered by the men. The field that a moment ago was covered white with tents, is now seen covered with armed men, standing among their smoking camp-fires, and the little poles and forks upon which their tents were lately stretched.

After an hour, or perhaps two, spent waiting on somebody, the proper signal is given by the bugle (for every movement is made in obedience to the sound of the bugle); cartridge-boxes, haversacks, canteens, knapsacks, shelter-tents, and blankets are put on, and arms are shouldered. At the proper signal, also, every man takes his proper place, and, with arms at "right shoulder," all move off. But we don't move far. We get out to the road, perhaps, to find that somebody else occupies it, or that somebody that precedes us in the march is not yet ready to occupy it. "Halt" is blown by the bugler. Arms are stacked. We lie round for an hour or more, perhaps. Again the bugle sounds, "Attention." The men all gather up to move, perhaps, only a mile or two when we run against somebody's wagon-train, blocking up the road. Again we stop; stack arms; lounge round perhaps for an hour or two. We move again. Soon, however, we again overtake the blockading train; a team of mules are down in the mud—mules, mud, harness, chains, all in one promiscuous mass! Drivers are whipping and cursing; wagon-masters and guards are, some with rails prying, and others grunting and going through the motions of pushing at the wheels; and all cursing and swearing at the drivers and the mules. But "it is no go!" It is useless to wait here. So we take through the fields and bushes on either side of the train, and push forward.

It is now past noon, and we have made but two or three miles of the twenty to be traveled today. Lost time must now be redeemed, if possible. There is no time now to stop for dinner; so on we move with rapid steps. We have but few "halts" for rest. We are now sweeping up through a level fertile valley; now straggling through the brushy woods; now passing through the deep and winding mountain pass; now climbing the steep and rugged mountain side; now wandering along its rocky ridge; and again we descend the other slope into the neighboring valley. Thus we go "marching along," while many a witty remark is made, and many a laughable scene is witnessed. Shoes frequently give out, and leave the soldier to make his march in his bare feet. As I made the march today with the rest, I noticed a soldier with but one shoe on, and with his other foot tied up in a piece of cloth. Supposing that there was something the matter with his foot that he could not wear his shoe on it, I inquired. "Oh, there is nothing the matter with the foot," said he; "the matter is all with the shoe. It gave out, and I threw it away."

Passing a large frame-house, or rather what had been a large frame-house, now stripped of the weather-boarding and every thing except the roof standing upon the bare studding, I noticed that some soldiers had placed a large board over where the door had been, with "ADMITTANCE NIX," written in large letters with chalk. On another board, on the studding where the hall had been, was written, "ROOMS TO LET HERE."

At another time we were passing a large, deserted plantation, and in the gateway that opened into the yard, in front of a little old negro-cabin, some soldier had placed the bed of an old buggy, and had set on it a little wood stove, in which he had kindled a fire; and on a board stuck up on the gate-post was written with chalk, in large letters, "HOT COFFEE HERE AT ALL HOURS." On the side of the old cabin was written, in like manner: "PIG'S FEET," "FRESH OYSTERS," "HOT COFFEE," "WARM MEALS AT ALL HOURS," "HAM AND EGGS," "FRESH SAUSAGE," "TURTLE SOUP," &c., &c. The novelty, or rather the ridiculousness, of these things, here, where the like had not been seen perhaps since the war commenced, or perhaps never, called forth from the soldiers, as they went trudging by, one continued stream of witty remarks. One would, perhaps, cry out, "And how are *you*, restaurant?" Another, "Bully for the restaurant!" Another, "And how are *you*, cooking-stove?" Another, "Bully for the cooking-stove!" Another, "Cooking-stoves are played out!" Says another, as he comes waddling along, almost "played out" himself, "I'll take the ham and eggs, just now." Another, "I'll take a dish of oysters, waiter." The next calls out, "Waiter, bring me a cup of hot coffee!" Another, "I'll take some chicken, waiter; fetch along enough for the chaplain, too." Another, "Fetch on your pig's feet, waiter." Thus it went while the whole column was passing. Thus these Union soldiers passed the time in jollity and mirth, scarcely seeming to realize the fatigue and labor of the march.

General Sherman has broken loose from his base of supplies, and, it is said, has given liberty to live off the country. At least that is the understanding with the men; and they are not slow in understanding such permission to mean, "Go for it, boys! Don't starve in a plentiful country! Forage liberally; for what *we* don't take, *Hood's men* will get."

Hence towards evening there are about as many chickens, turkeys, pigs, and geese in the regiment as there are men. And, oh, what loads of fresh pork, mutton, veal, and sweet potatoes some men carry in addition to their warlike equipments! In the rear of each brigade what a caravan of poor mules and old worn-out horses! Some with bridles on, some with only ropes round their necks. All are, however, loaded with immense bundles of all kinds of "*traps:*" camp-kettles, large and small; coffee-pots and frying-pans, of all sorts and sizes. On the top of all these, some have bags of sweet potatoes, chickens, turkeys, geese, parts of sheep, hogs, calves, &c., &c.

Well is it for the man whose mule or horse does not "*get down*" under his load. When such is the case, it requires a large amount of labor and swearing to get the "traps" off, and the mule up, and the "traps" all on again, and then get up again to his proper place in the grand cavalcade. And happier still is the mule-driver, or rather mule-*leader*, whose mule is able, when he gets down, to get up again when the "traps" are removed from his back. A good-natured, honest Dutchman had got an old horse and an old buggy, and put his "traps" into it, and was getting along swimmingly, till we came to one of those places, often found in this Southern world, where the surface of the earth lies upon a foundation that very obligingly yields to downward pressure, and when a wagon-wheel gets through the surface into it, the longer it stays in one position, the deeper it sinks into the mire. Here the Dutchman's horse sank, floundered, fell, stuck fast in the mud. The buggy, too, sinks in the mud, sticks fast, and is likely there to stick. In a cavalcade like this there are more Priests and Levites than good Samaritans, and each feeling that to help the Dutchman in distress was none of his business, and that he had enough to do to get along himself, all pass by on the other side of the Dutchman in his calamity. It is now dark, and I happen to come along that way; so he comes running to me, calling out, "Shaplein! Shaplein! mine horse ish entire gone up,—complete pegged out!" And sure enough there the old horse was, but I thought, from the fix he was in, he looked more like being "entire" gone *down*, or *under*, than "gone up"—completely swamped in the mire, and the buggy up to the axles in the mud. There is no use in trying to get this "rig" along any farther. It must be accounted for now as "expended," or "lost in the service." So I take a bundle of hay out of the buggy and lay it by the old horse's head, helped Shake to get his "traps" along, and we leave the poor old horse to his fate.

As evening approaches, we find here and there men sitting or lying by the roadside, waiting for the ambulances, They have given out on the march. On we move, but the camp, though anxiously looked for by all, is not yet reached. The shades of evening close in round us. It is now dark, and still we trudge along. We meet a man on horseback. "How far to camp?" "How far to camp?" rings out all along the line, as he passes. "Two miles and a half," "two miles and a half," he answers as fast as he can utter it, to keep up with the inquiries put to him. So on we move to overcome the "two miles and a half." But, oh, how long they seem tonight! Every hill we ascend, and every bend in the road we pass, we anxiously look to see the campfires. But we are often disappointed. At length we descry the glimmer of the distant campfires. The sight calls forth a shout from the men all along the line. After sundry and patience-trying stops we finally reach camp. And, oh, what a camp! Upon a steep hill-side, while there is plenty of level land in the neighborhood; rocky, too, and a perfect thicket, while there is plenty of clear, smooth land all around. Who made such a selection of a camp as this? No difference. It has been made by the proper authority, and our duty is simply to submit. We march by faith. We fight by faith. We crawl up this hillside, and in among these rocks and bushes, in the dark, to camp for the night, by faith. We have not faith, however, to believe that the officer who selected such a place in which for us to camp, camps tonight himself in just such a place. There are more curses than prayers among the men in the bushes just now. We have had no dinner today. We have made a march of over twenty miles. We cannot do without supper also. But what a place this is in which to get supper! No wonder the cooks grumble, and some of them even swear. The brush is rid off sufficient space on which to build fires. Fires are kindled—a little coffee is made—a little meat is fried. With salt pork, coffee, and crackers we make our supper. We spread down our blankets among the bushes, retire to rest, and are soon oblivious to the toils, and trials, and dangers of "this cruel war."

Such is a brief sketch of "The March of a Day"—a long and toilsome day. But it, with all its toils, and labors, and dangers, is gone—gone forever! All its thoughts, and words, and deeds are recorded in God's book of remembrance, to stand in uneffaceable record till the day of final accounts. Ah, and are all these foolish and wicked oaths I have heard uttered this day, by both officers and men, recorded there, to be remembered on that great day, for which all other days were made, against those who uttered them? Uttered perhaps in anger, perhaps in jest, perhaps in simple thoughtlessness. But there they are, and all other thoughts, and words, and deeds, whether good or bad; and with this record against us, we are one day nigher eternity,—one day nigher death, the resurrection, and final judgment. Oh, that we could all improve by the past; and that our noble soldiers, while they each day make "A Day's March" in the discharge of their duty in our country's cause, may make also "The March of a Day" towards that better country where wars, and fightings, and wearisome marchings are unknown, is the earnest wish of him who writes.

Randal Ross,
Chaplain 15th Regt., O. V. V. I.

Mustered out 21 November 1865 at San Antonio, Texas, Chaplain Ross returned to his family in New Concord. Ross was on the move through the west as a home missionary through 1866. He settled in Greenwood, Missouri, during the early part of 1867 and was involved in the founding of Lincoln College. Reverend Ross spent three hard years seeking out donations for the college. His health broke during 1874, and he died 20 April 1877 at his Greenwood home.[3]

---

[3] Service File of Randall Ross, RGs 94, Records of the Veterans Administration, National Archives, Washington DC.

Petersburg and Appomattox

Reverend Henry Rinker, 11th New Jersey Volunteers

Henry Rinker thought he was lucky to survive a few months as a private, but he was still hopeful of receiving a commission before the war ended. On 3 June 1865 he was in fact commissioned chaplain in the 86th New York Veteran Volunteers three weeks before they were mustered out of service. Rinker may have been the last chaplain to be commissioned in the war, but at the time he wrote these letters to his wife, Mary, about the fighting at Petersburg and surrender at Appomattox, he was still an enlisted soldier.

11th Regt. N. J. Vols. March 26, 65[1]
My Deary Mary
You know it is not my custom to write on Sabbath. But I think on this occasion I am excusable. The news of the battle yesterday may reach you and make you uneasy unless you hear in season. Yesterday morning quite early we heard heavy and rapid cannonading & musket firing far up on our right toward Petersburg & Richmond.

The rebels made an attack upon our works there & at first succeeded but were driven back at last with heavy loss.[2] The orders soon came to pack up and strike tents. At length our regiment was ordered to leave knapsacks and fall into ranks. We marched out against the rebel works about 9 A.M. Our regiment was put forward as skirmishers. Regiment after regiment, Brigade after Brigade was drawn out, until along the whole line perhaps over sixty thousand troops on our side were engaged. The fighting in some parts was terrific. It was uninterrupted until after dark. For about fourteen hours my muskit was not out of my hands. Our regiment lost sixty-four men—though strange to say my company had not a man even scratched. We were all day scouring the woods as skirmisher in regular indian [sic] style—dodging from tree to tree, from ravine to ravine, creeping behind old fences & logs—running & yelling occasionally like demons.

---

[1] 11th Regiment, New Jersey Volunteer Infantry.

[2] Maj. Gen. John B. Gordon's Confederate attack against Ft. Stedman on the eastern side of the Petersburg defenses was an initial success. Later in the day, counterattacking Union soldiers regained their lines. There were approximately four thousand Confederate casualties, many of whom were captured.

About four o'clock we came to an open field where a severe fight was raging—the 12th N. J. was charging upon the enemies' rifle pits. A more exciting scene I never witnessed. The yelling, screaming, running & firing were awful. Officers on horseback were galloping back & forth like mad. Squads of rebel prisoners were conducted back through the field—and we could distinctly see our boys charging into the pits. As skirmishers it was not our business to charge & we were marched down on the right of the pits in a ravine to prevent a flank movement of the rebs. I was perfectly cool & collected all day & even in the advance of our skirmish line. But I can tell you my senses were all about me. There was not a leaf on a bush moved without my seeing it. I realized no special fatigue until after we returned to camp past midnight. The boys manifested no little surprise at my coolness. Some of our officers are cowards. Today all is quiet. We have again put up our tents. But how long we shall remain it is of course impossible to tell. Our loss is heavy and I do not think that any great advantage has been gained though we have advanced our picket line about a quarter of a mile. I have thus given you a brief account of my first battle.

Of course I feel very thankful that I have escaped uninjured. A man that is sober and keeps perfectly cool and collected can avoid many dangers in a battle. But of course God alone can keep him in perfect safety. You say that you cannot bear to have me remain through in the ranks as a private. If I live I shall have a commission without fail. I should prefer a chaplaincy, though perhaps in some respects a Lieutenancy would be quite as desirable.

You must excuse any thing further just now as the mail is about to close & I desire to get this off to-night.

Love and kisses from papa to the dear children. God bless and keep you all in safety & in peace. I send you a leaf & a sprig of peach from the battlefield.

Your own H. Rinker

Army Potomac—near Appomatox [sic] Court House
April 9th, 1865
My Dear Mary—

This has been the most exciting & glorious day that I have ever been permitted to behold. We have just bagged Gen. Lee & all his Army. The scenes in the Army today beggar all description. Thousands of men & officers cried & laughed as if crazy & jumped & shouted till they were literally exhausted. Since I wrote to you last very hastily near Petersburg we

have been intensely on the chase. Such excitement & fighting were never before seen. I shall have very much to tell when I get home—which I hope will be before many months. I write now in haste as we expect a mail to go out early in the morning. We have had no mail either way since leaving Petersburg. We left there a few moments after my last letter was written. We shall have mails now I trust more regularly. But you must not be worried should there be a delay at any time. I am well and unharmed—though I have witnessed strange scenes & had escapes. What the next step will be we cannot tell. We may have to go in pursuit of Johnston. I will write you soon again. I am sorry those painters & Smithy have given you trouble. You did right to consult Coult. Take his advice at any time, and get him to render you whatever assistance you need. Use what money you need & draw two or three hundred from bank. I will send a note. But should you not get it in season, you can write the note with your signature getting Moose or Coult as endorser. I do not think we shall be needed long. God bless you my wife.
    Yours,
    H. Rinker[3]

---

[3] From the Civil War collection at the Military History Institute, Carlisle PA.

Chapter 4

Ministry in Prisons and Hospitals

"Where the grapes of wrath are stored..."
—Julia Ward Howe

During the Civil War there were not many examples of chaplains ministering to prisoners from the opposing army unless the prisoners were wounded. As soon as possible, prisoners were segregated into groups of enlisted men and groups of commissioned officers and sent to different military prisons or different parts of the same prison camp. The largest prison for Union enlisted soldiers was at Andersonville, Georgia, while the largest facility for Union officers was at Libby Prison in Richmond, Virginia.[1]

Whether Confederate prison camps were more deadly than Union prison camps was a question debated for more than 120 years. Jefferson Davis alleged in his *Rise and Fall of the Confederate Government,* published in 1881, that fewer Union prisoners died in Confederate prison camps than vice versa. Of the 270,000 Union prisoners held by the South, 22,000 died, for a death rate of less than 9 percent. Of the 270,000 Confederate prisoners held by the North, 26,000 died, for a death rate of 12 percent.[2]

Within the past ten years new evidence suggests that Davis may have been right. Of the forty-five thousand captives at Andersonville, thirteen thousand prisoners died, for a death rate of 29 percent. By contrast, the death rate at the Union prisoner of war camp in Elmira, New York, was 32.5

---

[1] More than eighty Union chaplains were said to have been residents of Libby Prison during the war. See H. Clay Trumbull, *War Memories of an Army Chaplain* (New York: Charles Scribner's Sons, 1898) 14.

[2] Jefferson Davis, *Rise and Fall of the Confederate Government* (New York: D. Appleton and Co., 1881) 2:607.

percent. Some Northern prisons reported losing 10 percent of their prison population in a single month.[3] However, the death rates alone do not prove that one side was more uncaring or crueler than the other side. Deaths in prisons were related to the relative strength and physical condition of the prisoners when they were admitted to the prison. Half-starved and sick Confederate soldiers did not have a long life expectancy in any prison.

Ministry in prisons was carried out, therefore, by visiting ministers or priests or by inmates themselves. At Andersonville, Father Peter Whalen, a Catholic chaplain for the Confederate soldiers at Fort Pulaski, took on the task of ministering to more than thirty thousand Union prisoners. At times Father Whalen gave his own food rations to starving prisoners which gained him the title of "the Angel of Andersonville." In Libby prison, Union officers had the benefit of several of their own chaplains, some of whom had stayed behind with the wounded on various battlefields and been captured in the process. In other prison camps prayer meetings were held by enlisted soldiers who felt the call to preach or to witness to their fellow inmates.

Hospitals

For every hospital bed occupied by a soldier wounded in battle, there were at least seven others filled by those with diseases such as measles, typhoid fever, malaria, and dysentery.[4] Such a high incidence of disease early in the war caught the Army Medical Department unprepared. For that reason, most Civil War hospitals were initially overcrowded and understaffed.[5] Since no chaplaincy service was available in military hospitals, local ministers and church members ministered to the wounded.

In spring 1862, a number of Washington clergymen petitioned President Lincoln to appoint military chaplains to the city's hospitals that

---

[3] Jim Stockdale, *Thoughts of a Philosophical Fighter Pilot* (Stanford CA: The Hoover Institution Press, 1995) 122. Adm. Stockdale, a former prisoner of war in Vietnam, did a study of Civil War prisons.

[4] Herman A. Norton, *Struggling for Recognition: The United States Army Chaplaincy, 1791–1865* (Washington DC: Office of the Chief of Chaplains, 1977) 114.

[5] In the twelve hospitals of Atlanta, which could accommodate not more than 1,200 patients, doctors treated some 105,000 wounded Confederate and Union soldiers from 1862 to 1865. In addition to the ten thousand Union soldiers buried at the Marietta National Cemetery near Atlanta, there are at least sixteen buried in the Oakland Cemetery on Memorial Drive in Atlanta. Their headstones reveal that most died from 1862 to 1864 probably in the Fair Ground Hospital near the cemetery.

were overflowing with wounded and sick soldiers. Accordingly President Lincoln asked Congress to approve the appointment of US Hospital Chaplains, a request Congress honored on 20 May 1862. Further Congressional legislation followed on 17 July specifying a hospital chaplain's pay at twelve hundred dollars a year with an additional three hundred dollars allowed for quarters.[6]

From 1862 to the end of 1864, President Lincoln appointed many chaplains personally to US Army hospitals.[7] Eventually more than two hundred Union chaplains served in hospital ministries. These did not include the regimental chaplains who were assigned temporary hospital duty while on campaign.[8]

Hospital chaplains made regular reports to the chief surgeon each week or month as required. Many of their reports reveal innovative mini-stries to entertain and educate their patients as well as to offer pastoral support. Some, like Chaplain Amos Billingsley of the 101st Pennsylvania Infantry, saw an opportunity for preaching evangelistic sermons to encourage soldiers to repent and receive God's grace quickly lest their wounds prove fatal.

Several of the stories from the hospital chaplains are pitiful because young soldiers regularly pled with their doctors to let them go home one last time. Unfortunately their pleas often came too late.

---

[6] Norton, *Struggling for Recognition*, 115.

[7] Recently an original handwritten note signed "A. Lincoln" was found in the US Army Chaplain Museum's Civil War collection. It was a presidential appointment of a chaplain to the US Army Hospital in Little Rock AR in 1864.

[8] President Lincoln also appointed the first African-American chaplain in the army, Rev. Henry M. Turner, chaplain of the 1st Regiment, US Colored Troops. Turner's example was followed by thirteen additional black chaplains commissioned in the Union armies in 1863 and 1864. See William A. Gladstone, *United States Colored Troops 1863–1867* (Gettysburg PA: Thomas Publications, 1990) 32.

Memoirs, 1863-1865

Chaplain Charles Cardwell McCabe,

122nd Ohio Volunteer Infantry

By the turn of the century, Charles McCabe was arguably the most famous Methodist in America. Born 11 October 1836 in Athens, Ohio, he became a Methodist on 1 January 1851 during a revival watch-night service at Zion Church in Burlington. During 1860, a few years after he graduated from Ohio Wesleyan University, McCabe was ordained a deacon and married Rebecca Peters.[1]

When mustered 8 October 1862 as chaplain of the 122nd Ohio Volunteers, he had recently been ordained an elder at Zanesville. A gifted preacher with a rich baritone singing voice, Chaplain McCabe liked nothing better than to hold meetings in arbor churches he would manage to build near camp. During one of these meetings, the bugle called for assembly, but Colonel William H. Ball saw only part of the regiment turn out on the parade ground. Learning from his adjutant that "the chaplain has those men in that church he built and he won't let them come out," the colonel sent a runner to request their presence. The messenger returned with Chaplain McCabe's reply that "The meeting is proceeding with such power that I cannot dismiss." His prompt arrest and reprimand brought the chaplain's promise to "hereafter obey orders."[2]

During the Gettysburg Campaign, when Robert E. Lee's Army of Northern Virginia captured most of the garrison at Winchester, Chaplain McCabe was among the "Winchester Eight"—eight regimental chaplains captured 15 June 1863 because they refused to abandon hospitalized members of their units. Many Northern newspapers followed their story. Held in Richmond, Virginia, at Libby

---

[1] "Chaplain McCabe," *Saturday Globe* (Utica NY), 20 April 1895, A3.

[2] Pension Case File of Charles C. McCabe, RG 15, Records of the Veterans Administration, National Archives, Washington DC.

Prison, all were released on 7 October 1863 but for McCabe who was too ill to travel. He left on 31 October.

Only two of the "Winchester Eight" returned to their regiments and served out their terms: Edward C. Ambler, 67th Pennsylvania Volunteers, and Ebenezer Walker Brady, 116th Ohio Volunteers. Chaplain George H. Hammer of the 12th Pennsylvania Cavalry was hospitalized with a prostate problem after his release; he returned to duty after a year in hospital. Chaplains Charles G. Ferris, 123rd Ohio Volunteers, and James Harvey, 110th Ohio Volunteers, were both hospitalized in Richmond and entered army hospitals after release. Both received disability discharges and never returned to their regiments. Chaplain David Christian Eberhart of the 87th Pennsylvania Volunteers fell ill with pneumonia soon after his release but was able to return to his unit after a few months. Chaplain Joseph T. Brown, 6th Maryland Volunteers, the fifty-two-year-old pastor of Cherry Hill Methodist Church near Elkton, went home seriously weakened by chronic diarrhea. He died 8 May 1865. Chaplain McCabe managed to rejoin the 122nd Ohio before the end of 1863, but he resigned 8 January 1864 because he could not fully recover his health.[3]

On 29 March 1864, Reverend McCabe became a delegate of the US Christian Commission. An organization that grew out of the Young Men's Christian Association, the USCC was supported by private donations. It not only provided relief and care to men in hospitals and convalescent camps, but delegates were to assist chaplains or provide religious services in hospitals and regiments without chaplains. With his renown as one of the "Winchester Eight," McCabe was asked to solicit donations as well as political favor in Washington. On 2 February 1864, in Congress for "Christian Commission Day," he impressed President Lincoln with his stirring rendition of the "Battle Hymn." His performance of that song became an oft-requested part of all USCC fund-raising presentations, to the point that it kept him from working in the field. McCabe became so closely linked to the "Battle Hymn" that its author Julia Ward Howe sent him a signed copy of it.[4]

Happily returning to a clergyman's routines after the war, Reverend McCabe became Methodist missions secretary in 1884 and was elected a bishop during 1896. In this capacity, he traveled to Europe, Mexico, and South America. In 1902, he

---

[3] Pension Case Files of Ambler, Walker, Hammer, Ferris, Harvey, Eberhart, Brown, and McCabe, RG 15, Records of the Veterans Administration, National Archives, Washington DC.

[4] Frank M. Bristol, *The Life of Chaplain McCabe, Bishop of the Methodist Episcopal Church* (New York: Fleming H. Revell Co., 1908) 181–203.

became chancellor of the American University in Washington, DC. He died in New York City on 19 December 1906.

Even as a Methodist Bishop, Charles McCabe was usually called "Chaplain," and he was famous for his lecture on the Civil War, which follows.

The Bright Side of Life in Libby Prison.[5]

As I speak, I see the faces of my old comrades, the faces of the noblest men I ever knew, the men of the 122d Ohio Volunteer Infantry. It was a regiment of boys whose average age was twenty-five—nine hundred and seventy-five of them when they marched out of Zanesville in September, 1862, with new and beautiful flags flying in the breeze, all unsoiled and unstained, marching to the front to help save their country. They were with Grant at Petersburg; they followed to Philadelphia; they were under Grant at Richmond. Five hundred and eighty-two of them were shot down and many wounded, bringing down the remainder to twenty-two of the original number. They were with Grant at Appomattox when Lee surrendered. It was a glorious regiment.

Our division was under General Robert Milroy.[6] Robert Milroy! Why, he would attack a force ten times his own number without hesitating a moment! Milroy was at Winchester. They telegraphed him from Washington to fall back to Harper's Ferry. He had six thousand men and six pieces of artillery. Lee had seventy-five thousand men; and yet with that handful of troops Milroy proposed to fight Lee with his grand army. I was down at headquarters one night. We had a good quartette and while we were singing for Milroy, he put his head out of a window and saw a scout who was rapidly approaching. He rode up and said: "General, the enemy is coming, and in my opinion it would be a good thing for us to be getting out of this." "In my opinion!" just think of it! In England a scout would not dare to say that. But in our army scouts had opinions, and they were not backward in expressing them; and I must confess that we all agreed with the scout that we had better get out of there when Lee was coming; but Milroy had no notion of going. Lee, however, scorned to attack our little force. He did not want to lose his men fighting with Milroy. He was on his way to fight the army of the Potomac. He had tested the qualities of that army so often, that there must have come a doubt in his mind whether he could meet

---

[5] Ibid., 120–45.

[6] Maj. Gen. Robert H. Milroy (1816–1890) commanded the Union forces at the second battle of Winchester VA, 14 June 1863.

them upon anything like equal terms. Milroy had one gun which was his especial pride. It would send a three hundred pound shot for five miles. It was called the "baby-waker," and I suppose it must have waked all the babies for miles around. He was a Presbyterian, and when I saw him sighting that gun I thought to myself, "Suppose I should ask him now 'What is the chief end of man?'" I know what the answer would have been. "Just now it is firing this gun." And he blazed away at the rebels with all his might. They went further and further to the right to escape his fire. I saw Milroy go along the lines making little speeches to the boys and these were his very words, "Now, boys, we're in for it; keep cool! keep cool!" It is not always possible to keep cool. Your hair will lift a little, if you have any, on such an occasion as that. "Fire low and fire often." Our boys did it and they fired well. The enemy retired and we held Winchester another day. We saw miles and miles of Lee's men pass by the next day.[7] On the third day, Milroy summoned a council of war. Every way of escape was closed but one, and, as an Irishman would say, that was closed, too! but it was closed four miles out of town.[8] We marched silently along; not a soldier spoke a loud word, not a buckle rattled against a canteen. The camp-fires of the enemy were blazing everywhere. I thought them all asleep, and I wished them sound sleep and pleasant dreams. But they were not asleep. They were waiting for us, and when we got four miles out of town they captured us *en masse*.[9] Our commissary had loaned me a tent to hold my meetings in, for I had three hundred and sixty-two members of Christian churches in my church, and we had meetings every night. There was an everlasting protracted meeting in our regiment. While we were retreating the commissary asked me what I did with his tent. "I folded it up," said I, and was about telling him what I had done with his tent, when the enemy's guns went off on our right and he ran one way and I ran the other. He and I were thrown into confusion, but our regiment was not. They simply cut their way through the enemy's lines. The doctor and I held a council of war behind a tree; it was on the other side of the tree. "Chaplain," said he, "I want you to stay with me and help with the wounded soldiers."[10] So we remained behind. A rebel provost-marshal came

---

[7] Lt. Gen. Richard Ewell's corps, composed of three divisions, surrounded Milroy's 6,900 troops.

[8] Maj. Gen. Edward Johnson's Confederate division blocked the road at Stephenson's Depot north of Winchester.

[9] Confederate Lt. Gen. Ewell captured 3,358 Union soldiers.

[10] Dr. William M. Houston, assistant surgeon, 122nd Ohio Infantry.

up and we were taken into the presence of General J. B. Gordon.[11] We were taken into the presence of General Gordon, and when he found what we were doing, he said, "Let them have fifty soldiers and all the ambulances they want to help get their wounded off the field." When we had finished our work, we went to see General Early, who had by this time assumed command. They made me spokesman of the party, and I addressed him thus, "General Early, we are a company of surgeons and chaplains who have stayed behind to look after the wounded; we have finished our work and would like very much to be sent through to our regiment." He smiled and turning to me said, "You are a preacher, are you?" I answered that I was. "Well," said he, "you preachers have done more to bring on this war than anybody and I'm going to send you to Richmond."

"To Richmond," said I; "that is one hundred and fifty miles away, and it is only thirty to Harper's Ferry, and we would rather go to Harper's Ferry."

"They tell me you have been shouting, 'On to Richmond' for a long time," he said, "and to Richmond you shall go."

Up to this time all captured chaplains had been released, but owing to some dispute that had arisen surgeons and chaplains were now detained. We marched on to Richmond, and in due time stood in the presence of the grim old walls of Libby Prison and waited for somebody to come out and invite us in. We went in. We were invited to register. We registered. Then we were taken into another large room and searched. They took out of our pockets everything that we possessed. If it was not worth anything they gave it back, but if it was worth anything they kept it. I had eighty dollars in greenbacks on my person. Now you will wonder how it was that a preacher ever had eighty dollars in greenbacks in his pocket at one time. It did not belong to me; that was the reason; it belonged to the boys. They had said, "Take this and send it home to my wife or my mother," and I was saving the very bills for the dear ones at home when this fellow was taking them away from me. "Sir," said I, "that is not my money." "I know it," said he, "it is mine now." And he took it away with him. After a while a receipt was given me which pledged that the Confederate government would pay the bearer in Confederate money at the rate of seven to one, and so I got five hundred and sixty dollars in Confederate money when I left the prison. At that time

---

[11] Brig. Gen. John B. Gordon commanded the Georgia Brigade in Maj. Gen. Jubal A. Early's division.

fifty Confederate dollars would buy a pair of boots. It got so bad that a barrel of flour cost eight hundred dollars! I took my five hundred and sixty dollars, but I could not buy a breakfast with the whole of it in the North. My friend General di Cesnola, who has been for many years in charge of the Metropolitan Museum in New York, had seven hundred dollars in greenbacks on his person.[12] "Now," I thought, "they have struck a bonanza." I remember wondering whether he would lie about it, and I fell to wondering whether if he did, under these trying circumstances, it would be laid up against him. "General," said the guard, "have you no money?" "Look and see," said he. They did look, but not a dollar did they find. Oh, how I bless him to this hour! For I borrowed some of it afterwards. If you had plenty of money in Libby Prison you could get along pretty well. One Confederate dollar would buy about six apples, or a quart of milk, and as one greenback would buy twenty-five or fifty Confederate bills we could get along pretty well. That is the best example of fiat money I have ever known. I remember some years ago seeing a five-hundred-dollar Confederate note framed and hanging on the wall of a friend's house, and on the back of it were written these pathetic lines by Major S. A. Jones, subsequent to the great surrender.[13] I thought they were so beautiful that I committed them to memory.

"Representing nothing on God's earth now,
And naught in the water below it;
As a pledge of a nation that's dead and gone,
Keep it, dear Captain, and show it.
Show it to those that will lend an ear
To the tale this paper can tell,
Of liberty born of the patriot's dream,
Of a storm-cradled nation that fell.
"Too poor to possess the precious ore,
And too much of a stranger to borrow,
We issue to-day, our 'Promise to Pay,'
And hope to redeem on the morrow.
Days rolled by, and weeks became years,
But our coffers were empty still;

---

[12] Luigi Palma di Cesnola, American consul to Cyprus, served as a Lt. Col. in the 11th New York Cavalry during the war.

[13] Maj. S. A. Jones, commissary officer in Lt. Gen. S. D. Lee's corps, Army of Tennessee, paroled 26 April 1865.

Coin was so rare that the Treasurers quaked
If a dollar should drop in the till.
"But the faith that was in us was strong, indeed,
And our poverty well we discerned,
And those little checks represented the pay
That our suffering veterans earned.
We knew it had hardly a value in gold,
Yet as gold the soldiers received it;
It gazed in our eyes with a Promise to Pay,
And each patriot soldier believed it.
"But our boys thought little of price or pay,
Or of bills that were over-due;
We knew if it bought our bread to-day,
"Twas the best our country could do.
Keep it! it tells all our history over,
From the birth of the dream to the last;
Modest, and born of the Angel Hope,
Like our hope of success it *passed*."

After we were all searched we were allowed to go upstairs. There a great surprise awaited us. I thought that I should see dead men lying around on the floor and that all would be looking sad and brokenhearted. I saw nothing of the kind. As we newcomers began to come in, some one cried out, "Fresh fish! fresh fish!" And one man whom I had never seen before came up to me and shook me roughly and warmly by the hand and said, "How are you, old fellow? How have you been?" I said that I had been well. "Why didn't you come sooner?" and then, turning to an imaginary porter, he said, "Here, Jim, take the gentleman's baggage and show him to room thirty-six, and see that he does not want for anything while he is with us" Baggage, thought I! I had some baggage once, but it was all gone long ago. Every stitch of clothes I had but those on my back were gone, and I was afraid they would take those too, for that was a way they had. If your clothes were pretty good, they would trade with you; and so it came about that many of our boys in prison had on Confederate grey while the guard outside had on the Union blue. When I first saw them I took them for a company of Union soldiers; but by and by one of them spoke and then I knew that I was mistaken. He said something like this: "Post number foah. All right." When I heard that kind of talk, I knew which side of the line I was on.

"Where shall we three sleep?" said I. There were three of us always together. Dr. Houston, Willie Morgan, and myself.[14] Willie Morgan was a lad of fifteen years of age. His mother consented to his going to the war, providing he would keep near the chaplain and surgeon, and keep out of danger! Willie was our cook. Such a beefsteak as he would toss off the end of a stick on my tin plate, and potatoes cooked in the ashes, and coffee hot as blazes! When I go into the country hotels now, and the girls come in with their arms full of little dishes and set them around my plate, a little dab of this and a little dab of that, I almost wish for another war and that I could again be at the front with the Doctor and Willie. One year after this, at the age of sixteen, Willie was swinging a sabre in the cavalry service.[15] The age-limit for mustering in was eighteen, but the claim of "going on nineteen" admitted many a boy who was several years short of that age. What boys we had in those days! and I think if we should ever have occasion again, we could call as brave boys to the rescue of the country as their fathers were before them.

"Where shall we three sleep to-night?" I asked the officer of the day. "Put your heads up against the door," said he, "and don't obtrude to the right or left, for it's occupied." I laid me down, but not to sleep. After many hours, I was just dozing off when I was awakened by a shout, "Right wheel!" I sat up in bed and looked on. Libby Prison was rolling over on its left side. I asked an old residenter what it meant. He said, "When your bones get sore on one side don't roll over without giving the word of command, or things will get into confusion here." After a while a voice called out, "Left wheel!" and we all rolled back again. I had often seen Hardee's tactics in the perpendicular, never in the horizontal before.

The night passed away and with the morning came a man to count us. I said to Mr. Stark, who was standing by me, "What makes him do that?"[16] "To see if we are all here, to be sure," said he. "Why," said I, "can you get out of here?"

"Have you ten dollars?' said he. "If you have you can bribe the guard, but after you get out you will have to look out for the bloodhounds." It was too true, the guards were always ready to mount their horses and scour the

---

[14] Dr. William M. Houston, assistant surgeon, 122nd Ohio Infantry, who also stayed with the wounded at Winchester.

[15] Four soldiers named William Morgan served respectively in the 2nd, 7th, 8th, and 13th Ohio Cavalry regiments.

[16] Possibly Pvt. Meicher Stark, Co. C, 122nd Ohio Infantry.

country to recapture fugitives. They kept bloodhounds to hunt us. In the books of the Congressional Investigation Committee you can find pictures of these terrible dogs. I confess, I was afraid to meet them. One day an old coloured man came into the prison and I took him aside and said to him, "Uncle, tell me how you coloured people get along with the bloodhounds." He grinned and said, "When I comes in again I'll fotch you a little cayenne peppah, and when you gits out a ways put a little pile of peppah in yo' tracks. By and by, along comes dat dog, sniff! sniff! sniff! and when he sniffs dat cayenne peppah, for a few weeks he's gwine to fergit all about dis war." I knew some of the men who escaped through the famous tunnel. I do not know but that they would all have escaped if it had not been for an accident. A fat man tried to go through. Now, fat men love liberty as well as thin men, and a big fat Dutchman tried to go through. When he got half-way through he stuck fast. He roared for help; he got help from the next man behind him. Imagine yourself in that next man's place—Libby Prison behind you, and liberty before you, and nothing but a fat man in the way! At last they jammed him through, and so the fat man and the lean man escaped, and in all one hundred and nineteen prisoners escaped in one night.[17] Many of them were afterwards recaptured, with the help of the bloodhounds. Among these was Captain Moran, who afterwards lived to write a most interesting account of the escape through the tunnel, which was published by *The Century Magazine* some years ago.[18] The boys dug the tunnel from the cellar of Libby Prison to an old shed some distance away across the street. They had no tools except an old broken case-knife. They would go down to the cellar two at a time at night and one would dig while the other would gather up the dirt in his hands and pile it up in another corner of the cellar. The hole was made from an old fireplace. When morning came they would cover up their dirt with some straw that was down there, and so clever were they at their work that the discovery was not made by the guards until a tunnel large enough for a man to crawl through had been completed. It was gruesome work. They dared not have a light, and the place was infested with rats, so much so that they had to fight the hungry creatures off while they worked. After Libby Prison was transported to Chicago, I went to see it one day, and

---

[17] A total of 109 prisoners escaped on 9 February 1864 through a fifty-three-foot tunnel dug from a fireplace to a vacant lot on the east side of the prison. Forty-eight were recaptured, two drowned, and fifty-nine reached the Union lines.

[18] Capt. Frank E. Moran, "Colonel Rose's Tunnel at Libby Prison," *Century Illustrated Monthly Magazine* (March 1888): n.p.

there it was, true as life, every brick and timber in its old familiar place.[19] The guide took me down into the cellar and showed me the hole where the prisoners escaped. "Wonderful enterprise," said I, "to transport a hole all the way from Richmond to Chicago." One day Captain Warner, a commissary, entered Libby Prison and enquired for me.[20] When I presented myself, he said that he had gone to school to my mother in Marietta, Ohio, and that she was the best friend he ever had. I told him I would like a bath-tub. I could have one. Three bath-tubs were provided, and then we had three tubs to six hundred men, two hundred men to a tub. We took turns, and after a while all got clean once more. I asked him if he could get me a book, which he very kindly did. When the men saw me with a book they said, "Why cannot we have books, too?" To be sure they could. I made a long list of the books the men wanted, which list I still have. The men gave him the money and he procured as many of them as he could. We had a notable company of men in Libby Prison. There were doctors, and teachers, and editors, and merchants, and lawyers. There were forty lawyers there. Now some of you will wonder how we could have a good time at all with forty lawyers in prison at once. I do not say that there ought not to be forty lawyers in jail at once, but, I do say, it is an unusual thing to get so many of them there at one time. One of these was Benjamin F. Blair, of New York.[21] Then there were editors, including Junius Brown, of the *New York Herald*, and Richardson, of the *Tribune*.[22] They got up a paper which was published weekly and called the "Chronicle of Libby Prison," and the guards used to listen eagerly to the reading of these journals. We established a university, called the University of Libby Prison. We had classes in German, French, Spanish, and Italian, and natives to teach all these languages. We bought books when we needed bread. I was cook for twenty men. What I had to do was to make soup out of a quart of wormy beans and put in enough water to go around for twenty men. We made it a rule that no one should have anything to eat at all until he could ask for it in French, and so we would sit at our table empty as Mother Hubbard's cupboard and say Avez-vous this

---

[19] Libby Prison was moved to Chicago in 1888 and was there during the Columbian Exposition of 1893, which was also known as the Chicago World's Fair.

[20] Capt. Jackson Warner, Confederate commissary in Richmond.

[21] Capt. Benjamin F. Blair, Co. B, 123rd Ohio Infantry, captured at Winchester VA, 15 June 1863.

[22] Junius Henri Browne (1833–1902), Civil War correspondent for the *New York Tribune*.

Ministry in Prisons and Hospitals 195

and Avez-vous that and Voulez-vous this and Voulez-vous that. There was more of the "Voulez" than of the "Avez," I assure you.

One of the grand events of our captivity was the celebration of the Fourth of July. A committee was appointed on programme and one on decorations. Some of the men were appointed to speak and others to sing. We had great rehearsals. The audience was present at every rehearsal. Everything was going well except that we had no flag. A bright idea dawned on some one. We found a man with a blue shirt and then we found one with a red shirt; then came the tug of war. It was harder to find a white shirt. But finally one was found that had been white, and the three were given into the hands of a tailor, who in due time produced a tolerably good flag. I saw the committee examining his work and heard one man remark, "Tis distance lends enchantment to the view." And another, "I can see the stitches four feet away." But the flag would do. It was rolled up and put away in a crack in the wall, and on the morning of the Fourth of July Captain Reed climbed up and fastened it to the rafters.

When you think of Libby Prison you must not think of it as one great room, but as a large warehouse divided into several large rooms. When we had our concerts and celebrations we would crowd into one room. On the morning of the Fourth of July we all crowded into Colonel Straight's room, where our flag was suspended.[23] The Colonel made us a speech. He said, "Gentlemen, if there is anything said here today that pleases you do not cheer, for if you do they will know what is going on. Keep still and cheer in your hearts." I know it was bad advice, for we had never been still before and they would think it was a conspiracy. They would think we were going to break out and capture the guards and march north with the whole Confederacy. We often talked of it, but never did it. Sure enough, the guard soon came up to see what we were about. He stood looking at our flag. "Who put that thing up there?" he said. Oh, how mad the tailor was when he called his flag a thing! "Take it down," commanded the guard. Did not General Dix say, "If any man tears down the American flag, shoot him on

---

[23] Col. Abel D. Streight, 51st Indiana Infantry, was a native New Yorker who led a force of 1700 on an April 1863 raid to destroy enemy arsenals at Rome GA and then cut the Western & Atlantic Railroad. Mounting half of his men on sure-footed and intelligent mules, Streight ran afoul of Nathan Bedford Forrest, who captured nearly all the raiders on 3 May 1863 outside of Rome.

the spot?"[24] We didn't want to be shot, so we did not take down our flag; but the guard climbed up and took it down himself and disappeared with it downstairs and we never saw our beautiful banner any more; but we celebrated just the same. It must have required a good deal of patience for the rebels to hear us singing, "We're Coming, Father Abraham, Six Hundred Thousand More," and "Rally Round the Flag, Boys." They liked to hear us sing, and frequently crowds of people would gather outside the prison windows and occasionally some one would shout out, "Sing us that song about Old Abe!" They stood it all very well till we came to "Yankee Doodle," but that always made them mad.

Bad news began to come into Libby Prison thick and fast. We heard one day that there had been a great battle at Gettysburg and that forty thousand men had been captured on their way to Richmond. On the morning of the sixth of July, old Ben, a negro who had permission to sell us papers, came in as usual. He looked around upon the prostrate host and then cried, "Great news in de papers!" If you have never seen a resurrection, you could not tell what happened. We sprang to our feet and snatched the papers from his hands. Some one struck a light and held aloft a dim candle, and by its light we read these headlines, "Lee is defeated! His pontoons are swept away! The Potomac is over its banks! The whole North is up in arms, and sweeping down upon him!" We sang all our national airs from "Yankee Doodle" to "Old Hundred." Every voice rang out with the words of the Doxology; it was sung on the key of "Q," as I remember it. Some time before, I had cut out of *The Atlantic Monthly* Julia Ward Howe's "Battle Hymn of the Republic," and committed it to memory; discovering that it would go well to the tune of "John Brown's Body," we learned to sing it in Libby Prison, and we made the welkin ring with its chorus of "Glory, Glory, Hallelujah!" The rebel guard came up and compelled us to stop, but the song was out and it still echoes over the city. A few days afterwards, we got the sequel of our celebration. There was in the prison a coloured man whom they called General Jackson, a member of a Pittsburg regiment, that had been captured. They made him the janitor of the prison, and he came up every morning to smoke us with a pine-knot by way of fumigating the prison. Every morning he would shout, "Here's your good Union smoke, without money and without price!" On the morning of the eighth of July he

---

[24] Maj. Gen. John A. Dix (1798–1879). As secretary of the Treasury in the Buchanan Administration, Dix sent a telegram to a Treasury agent in New Orleans to this effect.

came up and shouted, "Here's your good Union smoke all the way from Vicksburg!" "What do you know about Vicksburg?" asked a hundred voices. "Grant is in Vicksburg." We went to the window and looked out and saw the newsboys selling extras. The people in the street read them and looked gloomy and sad. Somebody brought us a copy, and the man who got it stood on a table and read aloud these words: "Adjutant-General Cooper: Compelled by circumstances, I surrendered the post of Vicksburg on the Fourth of July to Major-General U. S. Grant of the Federal Army." And it was signed "Pemberton."[25] When we heard this, we sang all our national songs over again. A guard put his head in at the door and shouted, "You Yanks up there, you'll be singing out of the other side of your mouths in a few days!" In a few days Port Hudson fell, and then we sang them all over again. At the risk of being shot, I saw a man put his head out of the window and call out, "We're a-singing out of both sides now!" Vicksburg captured? Some one asked what day it was and what time of day. It occurred to us that it was the same day and the same time of day when that fellow was pulling down our little old shirt flag, General Grant was pulling down the Rebel flag at Vicksburg. Gentlemen, that was the finest coincidence of the war.

One day seventy-three captains were sent for to come downstairs and two chaplains, of whom I was one. We were formed into a hollow square and the officer in charge addressed us thus, "Gentlemen, I have an unpleasant duty to perform. I am ordered to select two of you for execution; and as the fairest way to do this I have written your names on slips of paper and put them in this hat. One of the chaplains will take out two names and the other captains can go back upstairs." The other chaplain, Father Brown, as we called him, nearly eighty years of age, picked the names from the hat.[26] They were Captains Sawyer and Flynn and they were put into the dungeon and were to have been executed the next day, but owing to some disagreement among the authorities the execution was delayed. A letter to Mr. Lincoln was written by the prisoners and I saw one of them, by the name of MacDonald, who had just been exchanged, pry open the sole of his boot and hide the letter therein. As soon as he reached Washington he took

---

[25] Gen. Samuel Cooper (1798–1876), New Jersey-born adjutant general of the Confederate States, and Lt. Gen. John C. Pemberton (1814–1881), Pennsylvania-born commander of Confederate forces in the Department of Mississippi and East Louisiana.

[26] Chaplain Thomas G. Brown of the 21st Connecticut Infantry was born in 1799.

it to Mr. Lincoln. It so happened that Captain Fitzhugh Lee and Captain Winder,[27] a son of General Winder who had ordered this execution, had just been captured. Mr. Lincoln sent this message, "If you execute Sawyer and Flynn, I will execute Lee and Winder. A Lincoln." They never were executed. That was a way the President had, and I think it was a pretty good way.[28]

I never thought I should cry "Fresh fish!" to a man I had never seen before and had never been introduced to, but one day the cry of "Fresh fish!" rang through the prison and we ran to see who had come. There was Brigadier-General Neal Dow, of Maine.[29] He was that grand old dreamer who was the first to conceive that it is possible to have one State free from the curse of rum. We made him make us a temperance speech and then the rebels laughed. I had never seen them laugh before, and I remember I used to wonder whether their faces would crack if they smiled, they looked so solemn. But they laughed at our temperance meetings. They said, "Why, you couldn't get a pint of whiskey in Libby Prison to save your life. What's the use of holding temperance meetings?" The newspaper reporters got hold of it, and they would come and report his speeches and print them in the papers of Richmond. One day an invitation came for him to make a tour of the South. He was the guest of the most distinguished citizens of Georgia. He was gone six weeks and came back to the prison merry as a lark. One day he told us what a fine time he had had. He said that the Confederacy was nothing but a shell. That there was nothing left but old men and boys for them to recruit from. Just then the sergeant came in. I supposed he would stop talking at once, but he went right on as though nothing had happened and said with great emphasis and a forcible gesture of his right fist, "As I was remarking, gentlemen, intemperance is the *greatest evil* in the world!" We all looked as though we thought so too, and the sergeant went off downstairs saying, "That old crank is delivering another temperance lecture."

---

[27] William Henry Fitzhugh "Rooney" Lee, second son of Gen. Robert E. Lee, was captured at Brandy Station in June of 1863 and exchanged in March of 1864; Adj. I. P. S. Winder was captured 20 June 1864 at Dallas GA by soldiers from Maj. Gen. George H. Thomas's Army of the Cumberland.

[28] President Lincoln did approve General Order No. 252, dated 31 July 1863, which ordered that "For every soldier of the US killed in violation of the laws of war, a rebel soldier shall be executed."

[29] Brig. Gen. Neal Dow (1804–1897), captured at Port Hudson on 27 May 1863 and exchanged for W. H. F. "Rooney" Lee in March 1864.

We got up a singing society and had a concert. It was a grand success. Everybody was present. We had solos, duets, and trios, and a grand chorus. We had Irish songs, French songs, Hungarian songs, Scotch songs, German songs. Sometimes we would wind up our concerts by singing, "There's no Place like Home." One day an Irishman was very much depressed and he sat dejectedly crooning to himself:

"Backward, turn backward, O Time in your flight,
Make me a child again just for to-night,"

when another Irishman heard him and exclaimed, "Yis, and a girrul child at that that!"

One night when we were giving a concert, the guard outside shouted, "Lights out up there!" The lights went out, but the concerts went on. We had only one tallow-dip, which we fastened to the table by its own grease, and it was so dim that it only served to make the darkness visible. We were a noisy company and it was hard to sleep. I moved that hereafter at nine o'clock everybody should get quiet. I was voted down unanimously. By and by, another fellow got up and said: "With the privilege of this association I have a conundrum to propound. Why is Libby Prison like a church?" His answer was, "Because we have fasting and prayer." Up sprang another fellow and said, "Why is Libby Prison like a literary institution?" Nobody could guess. His answer was, "Because it is a *lyceum*." "Put him out! Put him out! they cried. We didn't want anybody to know that, and here's a fellow who blurts it right out in meeting. There was one man there who could never see a joke for five hours, and after that he would laugh. How many of us have laughed at John B. Gough's story of the man who said to another man, "A fine day for the race, isn't it?" "What race?" "The human race."[30] That was a fine joke, and he thought he would get it off on the next man he met. Meeting a friend soon after, he said, "Fine day for the trot, isn't it?" "What trot?" "Well, I thought I had a joke, but somehow it is gone from me." So this man who could not see a joke for five hours kept saying to himself, "See 'em! See 'em!" "You can't see 'em, but you can feel 'em all the time." And so we could. Vermin dropped down on us from the ceiling and crawled out on us from the walls. We were covered with vermin from head to foot. This was not one of the least of our troubles in Libby Prison. Men, the peers of any who listen to me to-night, intellectual, refined, sensitive, were forced to endure daily and hourly torture of this kind, and there was no release night

---

[30] John B. Gough (1817–1886) English-born writer and humorist.

or day. But if you could have seen that company, what would you have thought if you had heard the laugh that greeted this joke! We had seven Irishmen with us who were the delight of my heart. Such wit as they had! If you were dying of starvation and an Irishman would get off a joke, such as I have heard them relate in Libby Prison, it would make you laugh. Dr. Buckley told a joke once which reminded me of these Irishmen.[31] He said, "There was an Irish tax assessor in New York whose friend had a pet goat. He sent him a tax bill for eight dollars. The man came into his office very much incensed and asked why he had made such a tax as that on his goat. The Irishman took down his book of instructions and showed him the page which said, 'All property abounding and abutting on the front street must be taxed four dollars a front foot.'" Two Irishmen were going along the road and they saw a gallows. One of them said to the other, "Pat, if those gallows had their just dues where would you be?" "Sure, I would be walking along here alone." Such wit we were accustomed to all the time in Libby Prison. I think it kept us alive.

One day Dr. Sebal, the Confederate surgeon, who still lives in Jacksonville, Florida, and whom I love, came to me and said, "Chaplain, I will have to ask you to go to the hospital." The fact was, I was coming down with typhoid fever. When I was last in Richmond I saw the canal that flowed by the prison and remembered how we used to get our water to drink from it, and how our sewer pipe emptied into it, and I wondered that we did not all die. I was taken to the hospital to wrestle for six weeks with the dread fever. As they took me downstairs, I heard footsteps behind me and as I looked around there came Willie Morgan. "Where are you going, Willie?" I asked. "I'm going with you, sir." "You had better go back and stay with the doctor." "No," he said, "I'm going to take care of you." I saw him prepare my bed of straw with a dirty blanket laid over it. I saw him brush off the vermin with his hand. He folded up my old overcoat and it was the only pillow I had. I went down to the gates of death. One day I awakened to consciousness and they were holding a consultation about me. I knew by their faces that they thought I could not get well. The doctor said something to Willie in low tones and then I heard him say, "You're a good boy. Just give him this medicine every hour." One day soon after Major-General

---

[31] Dr. William C. Buckley, assistant surgeon, 10th Pennsylvania Reserve Infantry.

Powell, a dear friend, came in and sat down beside me.[32] He took out his pocket scissors and cut off my long beard and unkempt hair and gave me a bath with his own hands. He afterwards told my wife that the condition in which he found me as he turned back the soiled blanket and saw me lying covered with vermin was a sight he could not well endure. After he had made me as comfortable as possible, he said, "Chaplain, there is a letter for you; would you like to hear it?" The letter was from Dr. Isaac Crook, a member from my own Conference. He told me that they had just had a session of Conference and that when my name was called they had said, "He is in Libby Prison." The bishop who was presiding spoke of the time when Paul and Barnabas were prayed out of prison and suggested that they pray for me. Two hundred and fifty Methodist preachers got down on their knees and asked for my release. I was used to suffering; I could endure loneliness without tears, but I was not used to tenderness, and that tender letter broke me down. The tears rolled down my cheeks like rain. As soon as I could control myself, I began to sing. I broke out into a profuse perspiration and the tide was turned. In the evening the doctor came in and felt my pulse and started back in surprise. "Why," said he, "there's a big change in you. That last medicine has helped you wonderfully," and he rolled up a big blue-mass pill and gave it to me with a drink of water; but I got well all the same!

In twelve days Willie Morgan stood by my side, his face all aglow, and said, "Chaplain, we're exchanged! We are going home this morning and the ambulance is standing at the door. They have sent me to wash and dress you." Then they picked me up and carried me down to the ambulance. I weighed less than one hundred pounds.

We went to Petersburg by water and there took the train. A man came into the car with a basket and walked right up to me and gave me a piece of fried chicken and some bread, and also gave some to Willie Morgan; and I said to him, "Sir, what is your name?" "I am Captain Hatch," he said.[33] I asked him how he knew me, and he answered, "Ask your father when you get home." When I reached home I asked my father how Captain Hatch

---

[32] Maj. Gen. William Henry Powell (1825–1904) was captured at Wytheville VA on 18 July 1863 and exchanged in February 1864. After the war, Gen. Powell was awarded the Congressional Medal of Honor for bravery in an attack he led at Sinking Creek VA on 26 November 1862. With twenty men of the 2nd West Virginia Cavalry, Powell captured a Confederate force of 500 soldiers in their own camp.

[33] Capt. W. H. Hatch, Confederate adjutant general's corps and an assistant agent of exchange.

happened to know me, and he said, "My son, I went clear down to Fortress Monroe after you and, when I could get no further, I sent word along the line; and if you were a *Mason* you would understand." So I never knew how Captain Hatch happened to know me; but somehow I have always associated Masonry and fried chicken; and if any one asks me what Masonry is, I answer, "It is a thing that gives a fellow fried chicken when he is hungry."

Oh, friends, not a word of exaggeration shall pass my lips, when I tell you of the voyage home. What was it just to be going home! They laid me down on the deck of the vessel under the flag that was floating above me. Willie was by my side, his blue eyes out on the James River down which we were steaming. By and by, a Union soldier stepped in front of me and called out, "Hello, don't you want something to eat?" Then he put a tin plate down on my breast and on it was a piece of beefsteak and a baked potato. Friends, I have seen Niagara, I have walked amid the grandeur of Yosemite Valley, but I never saw anything that moved my soul like that beefsteak and baked potato! Then they brought me coffee and it was hot, and in half an hour I was able to walk. I took Willie's arm and we strolled about the boat. There were four hundred men on it. I saw that two of them were dying. The doctor was leaning over one to catch his words. He was saying, "Doctor, couldn't you give me something to strengthen me a little so I could just get home? I want to get home once more." But the doctor could not. They placed the men in rude coffins and nailed them up and sent them home to their loved ones.

Down the James we went and up the Potomac, and landed at Washington. As soon as I put my foot on land I enquired for a telegraph office and sent this message, "We are safe and coming," and a few hours afterwards the despatch [sic] was thrown into the lap of a blue-eyed lady out in Ohio, and she and our little boy went aside to give thanks. I cannot forget that many a wife and mother in this audience had a different message from that. When we went away, the regiment turned the corner of the road and the band was playing and the flags flying and your boy turned and lifted his cap and swung it over his head and sent back a cheerful smile, which meant that he would come back again; but he never came back. He sleeps in a soldier's honoured grave.

God bless you who have lost your loved ones, and God bless you, old soldiers, whom I see before me tonight! You are the men who saved your country! If it had not been for you and men like you, the Republic would have been lost and we would have had no flag flying over our homes tonight. God bless you! and when Death beats his low tattoo for you, I hope that the next sound you hear will be the *reveille* of angels, and that you will hear God's voice saying, "Well done, old soldier, the war is over. Come unto me and rest," and may I be there to greet you!

"Inside the Stockade"

Chaplain John Scouller McCulloch,

77th Illinois Volunteer Infantry

John S. McCulloch was born 5 September 1829 near Pittsburgh, Pennsylvania. He graduated from Jefferson College in Washington, Pennsylvania, in 1854 and from the Associated Reformed Theological Seminary at Allegheny, Pennsylvania, in 1858. He was ordained by the Associated Reformed Presbytery of Big Spring on 23 August 1857 and accepted a call from the Associated Reformed Presbyterian Church in Peoria, Illinois, the same year.

In 1864, Reverend McCulloch accepted a commission as chaplain of the 77th Illinois Volunteer Infantry Regiment, a regiment in which his brother also served. He reported for duty on 5 April 1864, three days before the Battle of Sabine Crossroads, which took place near Mansfield, Louisiana.

The 77th Illinois Infantry left New Orleans as part of Major General Nathaniel P. Banks's Red River Expedition, which meant to locate and defeat Confederate forces in Louisiana and Texas under Major General Richard Taylor, son of former President Zachary Taylor. At Sabine Cross Roads, Taylor's 5,300 Confederate infantrymen overwhelmed the Union vanguard. Approximately 1,100 Union soldiers were taken prisoner, among them Chaplain John S. McCulloch of the 77th Illinois.

Chaplain McCulloch recalled that the Confederate guards marched the prisoners about 140 miles to Camp Ford near Tyler, Texas. The march lasted for seven days. Rations consisted of corn meal and salt beef, but without cooking vessels. At length someone borrowed a pot from a farmhouse so that the men could eat mush with wooden paddles around their campfires. The soldiers took turns eating through the night, sharing their few implements.

The seven-acre prison stockade at Camp Ford had no buildings or tents to house the 4,700 Union prisoners that arrived there over the course of thirteen months. The men gathered brush to make dugouts to serve as shelter from the sun or rain. Nevertheless, the chaplains there provided what religious support they could. Chaplain McCulloch's account, written in longhand, includes his reflections on the prison, on war, and on his ministry in the army.[1]

---

[1] A copy of Chaplain McCulloch's account is in the Norton Papers, US Army Chaplain Corps Archives, US Army Chaplain School, Ft. Jackson SC.

Inside the Stockade

We had to take turns with the tools, and sometimes wait for hours and days to get a chance to bore a hole, or split a shingle or clapboard. I belonged to a mess of sixteen, and in about two weeks, we had a shanty sixteen feet square, with a clap-board roof and a wooden chimney, plastered inside with mud. Here, we ate, slept and cooked. It was a rough place; and yet it was one of the best in the stockade. I have seen thirty-five men on several occasions, when it rained, spend the night in that shanty, and they were very thankful for the accommodations.

We made a table of clapboards, and our service of plate and china was not extensive. I made myself a wooden spoon, and with this, and my pocket knife, and my fingers, I got along. I was peculiarly fortunate in getting hold of a small empty tomato can, and with this I made a small plate, and left enough for another plate, and then we were just so much better off than some others of our mess. Trained as we were in these lessons of household economy, we feel ourselves quite competent to advise the ladies how to furnish a table in hard times.

There was a vast amount of trading done among the prisoners. I was very much surprised at this. Soon after we arrived in prison, a man came in one day with cornmeal and he sold out in a very short time at a dollar a pint, in greenbacks. The same day our mess bought twenty pounds of flour at a dollar a pound. There were men among the prisoners, who lived by their wits, just the same as anywhere else. They tried to keep up the price of provisions, and bring down the price of watches, pens, pencils, rings, and other things that were much sought after in the South. I knew one man who made not less than $200 in a month in this way. Of course it came off his fellow prisoners, and some of them imagined he was doing them a great favor. Some bakers and barbers and potters no doubt made considerable money honestly, but there was much swindling and gambling too.

The Texans, also, were great traders. One of the guards soon traded me out of my hat, and they tried over and over again to trade me out of my boots.

The first two weeks we received full rations—a pound of cornmeal unsifted and about a pound of beef. In the following winter, however, the ration of beef was reduced to three or four ounces. Several times the rations were stopped for a short time, and threats were often made to do so, when some mischief had been done. Another way of punishing us was to allow no one to go out for wood. This was frequently done, but the importunity of the prisoners generally prevailed very soon to have the punishment removed.

A trivial offense was often made the pretext for punishing forty-five hundred men for one or two days.

Escapes were frequent, and they were a constant source of annoyance to the authorities. These escapes were effected in various ways—sometimes by loosening a post in the stockade, and sometimes climbing over it, and sometimes by bribing the guard. There was very little difficulty in getting out. The main object was to keep the officers from finding it out, that any were missing, and many were the expedients at roll call, to escape detection. Sometimes a week would elapse before an escape was discovered.

A dark rainy night was the time to escape. This was to prevent the bloodhounds from getting the scent. As soon as it was known that a prisoner was gone, the horn was sounded for the dogs, and in a little while we could hear them howling after their game. To escape these faithful dogs was next to an impossibility. A good bloodhound was worth several men for guarding prisoners; and hence I have heard more curses and dreadful threats of vengeance against these poor innocent dogs, than against their guilty, inhuman masters.

Scores of men were caught, and brought back, and punished, for doing what they felt was duty—that is trying to escape. Some would be caught in a day or two, and others were brought back for two or three weeks.

The punishments were various, and some of them barbarous and cruel. Usually they were kept a few days in the guard-house, but in some cases they were required to stand bare-headed in the sun for hours, or to stand in some peculiar position under penalty of being shot.

One of the best men we had, a most devoted and consistent Christian, escaped, and was caught, brought back, and cruelly punished. Colonel Borders tried to make him promise that he would never try to escape again, and that he would also use his influence to induce the other prisoners not to escape. He was a noble fellow, and he seemed never to fear the face of man. And he replied, "Colonel you know you would not consent to such a thing if you were a prisoner. Our government makes it our duty to escape if we can, and as I have sworn to defend that government, I cannot conscientiously comply with your demand." This was the substance of his reply. He was respectful but very firey. So the Colonel determined to make him feel his power. He ordered him to be placed on a stump about seven or eight inches in diameter for several hours a day. The stump was cut as you have often seen with one side sloping down, and the other up so that one toe was inclined downward and the other up—a most painful position, and yet the sentence was ordered, if he should not stand on both feet all the time, or if he should step off, or fall off, to shoot him on the spot.

But no sooner had John Edwards got off than he commenced singing hymns, and patriotic Union songs, in spite of the guards.[2]

When at length the time came for exchange, Colonel Borders came up to him, and said, "Well, Edwards, you're going now. I have had a good deal of trouble with you and you may think I have treated you harshly sometimes, but you must remember, that when you took sick at Camp Groce, I sent two men, and had a straw bed made for you." "I know it, Colonel," said Edwards, "and I thank you for it." "And," said the Colonel, "you must remember that I sent you some food from my own table when you were getting better." "I know it Colonel, and I thank you for it." Quite a crowd, by this time, had gathered round, both of his own men and prisoners. "Now," said the colonel, "I may be sent to the front, and some day fall into your hands, and I have just one request to make of you—that if ever I fall into your hands as a prisoner, you will treat me as I have treated you."

"No, Sir!" said Edwards. "Why?" said the Colonel. "What do you mean?" And every man stretched his neck to hear better. "Why Colonel," said Edwards, "If ever you became a prisoner in my hands, I'll treat you so well that you'll be ashamed of yourself." The Colonel dropped his head, and shot through the crowd, while they enjoyed a hearty laugh at his expense.

Another man for trying to escape was compelled to stand, with his bare heels on two sharp pins driven into the ground, for eight hours a day without his hat in a southern sun.

There is a long list of cruelties in connection with Camp Ford. Several of them resulting in death, which their inhuman perpetrators may well wish forgotten.

Robbing Prisoners

The robbing of prisoners was generally done on the battlefields or very soon after surrender. Some eleven hundred, captured when I was, were not robbed at all, except a very small number, while twelve hundred captured a few days after were nearly all robbed. Watches, knives, pocket books and

---

[2] Pvt. John L. Edwards, Co. I, 77th Illinois Infantry Regiment.

money, combs, pencils and pens, and black cases, and when these men came in, they were in a very destitute condition.

Amusements
The amusements of the prisoners were very much like those of a regular army camp. Men could be seen every hour in groups playing chess and checkers, and cards. Others played baseball until the place became too crowded for this. The few books that could be found were read over times, and many spent their time whittling and carving wood, but a large proportion of the time was spent in idle talk, and in sleep. There was one violin but there was no promiscuous dancing though there were many a hoe-down. I have no recollection of seeing either a quadrille or a round dance, and I conclude that men don't like to dance with their arms around each other, and their chins over each others' shoulders.

Religious Meetings
The religious privileges were all we could expect, and indeed, I believe the religious element of our camp made a good impression in Texas.[3]

Mr. Robb and myself were the only chaplains at first, but two others came in afterwards.[4] We applied at once for the privilege of holding meetings, and we were permitted to hold three meetings on Sabbath, and one every night till nine o'clock. We felt very little restraint, and prayed as fervently for the success of our arms and the downfall of slavery and the rebellion. The post commander, with his wife and a number of ladies came in one Sabbath, and listened with great apparent respect while I preached. But he afterwards told two of our Captains, that I was a black-hearted Abolitionist. Those meetings were not often dry and cold and lifeless. The men who made up the audience were the very pith of the religious element of that large camp of 4500 men. The current of religious feeling, I may say religious enthusiasm was strong, and I have no doubt that many men, and perhaps some of the rebel guards, date their first deep conviction of sin, and sense of pardon, from those meetings.

---

[3] At Camp Ford, the Union prisoner of war camp near Tyler TX in April of 1864.

[4] Chaplain Hamilton Robb (1800–1881), Baptist, 46th Indiana Infantry, age sixty-four.

Sanitary Condition

The health of the prison was remarkable, and disappointed many apparently well grounded fears. Had anyone told me that I could live six weeks, when we were turned into that pen, I would have thought him a fool. But out of a hundred and thirty men of our regiment, we lost only two in fourteen months. Others lost half their men, mainly because they allowed themselves to lose heart, and had such poor facilities for cooking their food. Many precious lives could, no doubt, have been saved, if the sick could have been removed to a hospital. Without any of the conveniences of a sick room, you may see that the sick man's comrades would be almost glad when he died, because it left them a little more room in their miserable hut, and relieved them of care.

Prison life, long continued, develops some of the worst traits of human nature, and never perhaps was selfishness more gross and intense then in the prisoner's hut where one was sick or dying.

Rumors of Exchange

It was all important to the prisoners to keep up their spirits. If they once gave way to despondency, they were almost sure to die, and hence rumors of exchange had a good sanitary effect. Every few days a report came, that several hundred men had been exchanged. When I came away I carried more than two hundred letters with me, and in nearly every one of them, the hope of speedy exchange was expressed. I have seen sober sensible men, almost beside themselves with temporary joy, when these plausible reports came in. There was not a time, perhaps, when every man did not hope to be exchanged in three weeks. Their hopes of speedy release, too, prevented many men from attempting escape. They kept thinking it would be only a few days longer and hence nothing would be gained by escape. For my own part, I was constantly, while able to keep my feet, planning and scheming how we could get away without being caught, or overpowered and brought back.

After enjoying good health for six weeks, I was suddenly taken sick and for some time I familiarized my mind with the thought of burial in the adjoining sandhill more than two thousand miles from home. In about two weeks the fever was broken and in three weeks more I was able to preach a short sermon at one of the most solemn meetings I ever attended. I had obtained my parole that day, and I bid them farewell, intending to start in the morning to report at Kirby Smith's head quarters at Shreveport.⁵ There were about twenty in all, of us released. Poor Chaplain Lamb was sent back because they found out that he belonged to a colored regiment. Colonel Borders insulted him in the grossest manner and said, "We don't recognize nigger officers.⁶ You can go back into the stockade. Go off!"

When we reached Shreveport we found that we would have to wait two weeks for a boat. We drew our rations for two weeks, and turned them in to a boarding house, and strolled about the city. Here we became familiar with southern prices. In the market, small cups of coffee were freely sold at $2.50, in Confederate money, water melons at from ten to twenty dollars. Milk was one dollar a quart. Each boarder could have any extra dish by paying for it.

Ordinarily the prices were about from ten to fifteen times as high as in New Orleans. The principal dining room in the city had a large run of custom, and the regular charge was $15 a meal. I visited the stores. There were fine, large store-rooms, but many of them were closed, and of the others the array of empty shelves proved that our fleet maintained something more than a "paper blockade." At length about a thousand prisoners came on and overtook us, and we embarked for our lives. Our hearts thrilled, when our boat pushed off, floating the white flag. But it was a timid joy. So often had we been disappointed, that we had learned not to be too confident. Four months had now elapsed since I left home, and I had never heard a word, or seen a line from my family. As we came nearer and nearer to the Mississippi the suspense became painful. Some had heard no word from home for nearly a year—some more. What changes had come. Many of us revealed our secret fears, and hopes to each other, as we steamed along. When, therefore, we, at last, reached our lines, and were once more under the stars and stripes, now dearer than ever, and when a most unexpected letter, direct from home, was found on the cabin table, and when the first few lines revealed that wife and daughter and son were all alive and well, you must not think me weak if I wept for joy as I sought a secret place and gave God thanks. That capture and imprisonment, is an epoch in my life, and I only speak the experience of thousands of others when I say that nothing of a merely worldly nature ever impressed me half so much.

---

⁵ Confederate Gen. E. Kirby Smith (1824–1893), commanding the Trans-Mississippi Department.

⁶ Col. John P. Border, commander of Border's Texas Cavalry. There was no commissioned chaplain in the Union army by the name of Lamb.

After that, whenever we went out to meet the enemy, my greatest dread was not so much wounds and death, but capture. Distressing dreams, even to this day, have almost invariably some unwelcome connection with being flanked and surrounded. And the most awful nightmare is when I think I am trying to escape, and I hear the sound of the horn, and the bloodhounds coming nearer and nearer, and yet I can neither run, nor swim, nor climb a tree.

I am satisfied—satiated with war. It originates in wickedness, and it develops wickedness at almost every step. The soldier, above all things, needs the truth of God, and the grace of God in his heart, that he may resist temptation, and honor his Christian profession; but when war becomes a necessity to resist encroachments, and drive back the invader, let the Christian Church do everything possible to mitigate its evils; for it is true that nowhere is Christian effort more fruitful in blessing than in the army.

After the war, McCulloch accepted a call to be pastor of the Harlem Church on 116th Street in New York City from 1865 to 1877. From 1877 to 1899, he was president of Knoxville College in Tennessee, one of the first colleges established for freed slaves. In 1879, he received an honorary DD degree from Monmouth College in Illinois. From 1900 until his death in 1910, Dr. McCulloch resided in Omaha, Nebraska. In his History of the 77th Illinois Volunteer Infantry *published during 1883, William H. Bentley called McCulloch "a conscientious, God-fearing, faithful chaplain, regarded by saint and sinner alike, as a great acquisition to any regiment."*[7]

---

[7] William H. Bentley, *History of the 77th Illinois Volunteer Infantry* (Peoria: Edward Hine, Printer, 1883).

Chaplain Amos Stevens Billingsley,

101st Pennsylvania Infantry and Hospital Chaplain of US Volunteers

Amos Stevens Billingsley was born 14 October 1818 in East Palestine, Ohio. At age twenty-three, he completed a course of studies at Franklin College in Athens, Ohio, and another at Jefferson College, Canonsburg, Pennsylvania, during 1845. He was licensed to preach in 1851 after graduating from Western Seminary, Alleghany, Pennsylvania, and ordained as a Presbyterian minister the following year. He immediately took up responsibilities as a pastor in the town where he was born, serving there until 1854 when he accepted the call from a church in Slippery Rock, Pennsylvania. From 1857 until mustered as chaplain of the 101st Pennsylvania Volunteer Infantry, the Reverend Billingsley was a home missionary in the Territories of Nebraska (1857–1861) and Utah (1861–1863.) He heard about Fort Sumter as he was leaving Omaha for Denver. "Seeing the mighty struggle for our national existence waxing hotter and hotter, and feeling deeply anxious to aid in quelling the rebellion," he "pulled up stakes and hastened to lend our assistance as chaplain of the 101st Pennsylvania Volunteers." Having taken the field in early 1862, the regiment lost Chaplain John D. Glenn when he resigned on 29 August 1862, so the Keystoners of the 101st gave their new chaplain a warm reception on 19 December 1863 when he arrived in their camp at Plymouth, North Carolina. Even before he was mustered into the regiment on 9 January 1864, Chaplain Billingsley preached a Christmas sermon in the town's large Methodist church, which "was crowded to overflowing: hundreds...had to go away for want of room."

Situated on the south shore of Albemarle Sound near the mouth of the Roanoke River, Plymouth was a fortified supply depot with a garrison of nearly 3,000 under Brigadier General Henry W. Wessells. None of its land or water defenses mattered very much, however, in an attack launched on 17 April 1864 by Confederate Brigadier General Robert F. Hoke. After three days of fighting, Wessells found himself and his remaining men inside an earthwork fort at the center of his defensive network. "On April 20, I had the mortification of surrendering my post to the enemy with all it contained." [1] *Chaplain Billingsley was among Hoke's 2,500 prisoners. Shipped to Libby Prison in Richmond, Virginia, he was soon released with a group of other chaplains and surgeons. Back in 1862, War*

---

[1] Wayne Mahood, *The Plymouth Pilgrims: A History of the Eighty-Fifth New York Infantry in the Civil War* (Highstown: Longstreet House, 1989) 182–184.

Departments of both sides had ordered that, as non-combatants, surgeons and chaplains would not be held as prisoners of war. The 101st Pennsylvania carried on, her ranks restored by eight companies of new recruits, and the regiment was mustered out in 1865. Chaplain Billingsley was considered as "detached to hospital service" and never returned to his unit.[2] Effective 13 February 1865, Billingsley was commissioned as a hospital chaplain of US Volunteers and served another five months with this rank. In From the Flag to the Cross *published in 1872, Billingsley describes his work at an army hospital in New York City Harbor as well as the Chesapeake and Hampton US General Hospitals in Virginia.*

Reverend Billingsley was a pastor in Iberia, Ohio, for a few years before embarking on "missionary work in South for many years." In addition to From the Flag to the Cross, *he authored* The Life of George Whitfield, Pulpit Power, *and* The Life of Saint Paul. *He died 11 October 1897 in Statesville, North Carolina.*

The following descriptions come from From the Flag to the Cross *and describe some events during Chaplain Billingsley's time at the Hampton General Hospital, Fort Monroe, Virginia.*

A Prayer Meeting In The Bushes[3]

When God's Spirit is powerfully poured out, it always draws men to their knees; and when man, just converted, gets a glimpse of the great things God has done for him in "pulling him out of the fire," with a heart overflowing with gratitude and burning with desire for the salvation of souls, he cannot help but pray. Such was the feeling of the small squad of soldiers in Hampton Hospital. And wooed by the Spirit, and desiring a more retired place than the crowded, suffering ward afforded, they retired to the leafy copse daily for prayer and supplication. Armed with the sword of the Spirit, and the little Army and Navy Hymn-book, thither this little band of suppliants would daily resort to pour out their hearts unto God for the preservation of the country, and for the salvation of the sick and wounded. There, secluded from the world, and shut in with God, with no covering but the canopy of heaven, and no altar but the cross of Christ, they read, sung, and prayed; and while the earth was drinking the blood of our brave veterans

---

[2] Military Service File of Amos S. Billingsley, Record Group 94, Records of the Veterans Administration, National Archives, Washington DC.

[3] Amos S. Billingsley, *From the Flag to the Cross* (Burlington IA: R. T. Root, 1872) 102–107.

at the front, dying for the salvation of their country, their prayers ascended to God for the salvation of their souls.

And so eager were they in this blessed work, that sometimes a few of them would collect and go out to pray, after the regular weekly prayer-meeting, late at night. And there, overshadowed by the darkness of the night, yet with their souls lit up by the light of God's Spirit, they found the way to the throne of grace and got so nigh unto God that one says, "We all felt very happy." Another active spirit in these bush prayer-meetings says, "We always come back much refreshed." "What a blessing! how encouraging! Always come back much refreshed!" "Yes!" "Why, George?" "Well, I don't know, chaplain; but so it is. We go out into the bushes. God meets with us; and, by singing and praying, we endeavor to get very near to God, and always come back much refreshed." What the cooling brook is to the thirsty heart, or the thirsty soldier on a long march on a warm day, prayer is to a thirsty soul—*always refreshing*. "And doubtless, George, it is your drinking so deeply of the wells of salvation that proves so refreshing to your longing hearts." "Yes, I suppose, chaplain, that is so. We always find the nearer we get to God, and the more earnestly we pray, the more refreshed we feel." "Yes, God is an inexhaustible 'fountain of life;' and the oftener you draw, and the deeper you drink, the more refreshed you will be.

"Then, George, let me entreat you, go on with your prayer-meetings. As you have got the fire burning in the bushes, fan it, and keep it burning until it spreads all over the camp, and burns upon the altar of every sinner's heart, so that when the patients go back to the front, they may go armed with weapons not carnal, that they may be mighty through God to the pulling down of the strongholds of the rebellion. Oh, then, George, *pray on*. Gather up the forces, and lead them on in the battles of the Lord! You have every encouragement. It was in answer to the prayers of eleven apostles that the Holy Spirit was poured out on the day of Pentecost, when three thousand souls were converted in a day. In answer to the prayers of the church, the chains fell off of Peter, and he was released from prison.[4] Thus you see what great things God has wrought in answer to the prayers of his people. How very encouraging to pray on, George! Then go on with unfaltering determination."

---

[4] Acts 2 and 12:7–9.

Preaching To Men On Their Death-Beds
Overburdened with labor, and surrounded with so many critical cases of sick and wounded men requiring prompt attention, our ingenuity was sometimes taxed to know how to meet them to the best advantage. Hence, on entering a ward, and seeing so many brave heroes lying upon the verge of eternity, and others, perhaps, just passing the crisis of the soul, and all anxiously inquiring what to do to be saved, and not being able to reach them all in due time in *personal* conversation, we were led to adopt the plan of preaching in the wards, where we could at the same time instruct, beseech, and implore all in the whole ward to come to the Saviour at once. This plan seemed to work very well. A word of prayer and praise, accompanied with a plain, pointed, brief sermon, was a relief to the patients, tired of the dull monotony of the hospital. After entering a ward, and securing the approbation of the ward-master, we usually commenced the solemn service by singing some appropriate hymn *full of Christ*, the soldiers joining in, followed by reading a short passage of Scripture, such as the parable of the prodigal son, the case of the Philippian jailer, or the story of blind Bartimeus, etc.[5] Then followed the sermon, which we always endeavored to make searching, powerful, and practical; always endeavoring to convince the sinner of his sins, the imminent *danger* of his course, and the great importance of *immediate* repentance; urging them by the love of Christ, by the pain of hell, and by the eternal glories of heaven, "to flee the wrath to come," and fly to the cross at once. With the sick, the dead, and the dying around us, and with the stern realities of eternity rising before us, and God's Spirit stirring within us, the services were usually very solemn and interesting. Preaching to men lying upon their death-beds, who had laid down their lives for their country, and feeling that it was "*the last time*," and the *last* warning to some of them, and that their salvation under God, hung suspended upon the decision of the hour, seemed to add much to the solemnity of the occasion, to heighten our responsibility, and to help and strengthen us for the arduous, important work. This work, though very laborious to the chaplain, was to me very pleasant and delightful. To point out the way of eternal life to him who had sacrificed his life for his country, though a sad, was no melancholy, duty. The patients enjoyed it much. And very often would they express their gratification, as I passed their couches, in

---

[5] Luke 15, Acts 16, Mark 10:46.

such words as these. "You don't know, chaplain, how much good that sermon did me. Please come in and give us another as soon as you can."

A colored soldier said to me, "*I liked to jumpt out of bed while you was preaching, last night, I felt so happy; my very heart seemed to leap with joy.*"

I preached on this way, averaging more than a sermon a day, for several months. Very often I preached two or three times a day, besides writing letters for the patients, burying the dead, and canvassing the hearts of the most dangerous cases, noting down their religious experience and prospects for the future.

There, standing between the living and the dead, we endeavored to hold forth the cross of Christ as the only way of salvation; endeavoring to comfort and console the suffering patient by the meek submission of Him who died upon Calvary that guilty sinners might enjoy eternal life.

The following extract will give the reader an idea of our manner of addressing the patients in the wards.

The Last Warning
An Appeal To Wounded Soldiers In Hospital

Having spoken to the Christian soldier and to the backslider, we come now, my impenitent friends, to give you a word of warning and encouragement. You have had many warnings. The thrilling, heart-rending scenes of battle—dear comrades falling; bleeding, dying at your side, beseeching you with their last breath, "*Be ye also ready*"—the departed spirits of half a million slain in this war, whose tongues are now mute in death, bid you "*Prepare to meet thy God*." The daily funeral notes of the death march of the escort bearing a cart-load of dead soldiers to the grave is but the voice of God warning you "to flee the wrath to come." The gushing tears and earnest prayers of a tender mother, an affectionate wife, and anxious sister, warn you; trust in God and fly to Jesus. And yet, withal, here you are to-night, still impenitent, lying prostrate upon your couches, and, doubtless, many of you upon your death-beds, dying for your country, and yet rejecting Him who died for you. You kill men for rebelling against the government, and yet you still live in rebellion against God. Your sufferings for your country have been terribly severe, but they are *nothing* compared with the sufferings that await you if you die impenitent. You have felt the raking fire of long lines of rebel heavy artillery, but that is nothing to the "unquenchable fire," artillery, and torments of hell. And here you are still careless and insensible to your danger. Careless! insensible! with the grave yawning, the devil seeking, and hell moving to destroy you! Insensible! with God smiling, the Spirit striving, and heaven stooping to save you! Oh, then, we beseech you, by the mercies of God, by the love of Christ, and by the joys of heavens, bestir yourselves; repent, and come to Jesus. This is, without doubt, the *last* warning to some of you. It is now or never; tomorrow, doubtless, will be too late. "Now is the accepted time." I heard a dying soldier say, last night, with his life-blood flowing from him, "It is too late! Too late!" And so it will be with you, unless you soon repent. Oh, then, let this be the day of your salvation! May God bless you! And yet the Lord *waits* to be gracious. Jesus is here waiting to forgive your sins, and wash your souls in his own blood. Jesus is here earnestly crying, "Turn ye! *turn ye*! for why will you die!" And *will* you die, patriot soldier? Will you die with Jesus, "the Prince of Life," at your hand, waiting to give you eternal life? You may die, die here in the hospital, covered with glory and honor defending your country—that is glorious—but, oh, if you die to save your country and lose your own soul, is not that lamentable? Die for your country! Die beside the Prince of Life, and to enter "the second death," which never dies! Die for Him who died for you, and yet die and be lost! Oh, how lamentable! Oh, my dear friend, stop, think, consider, turn, look, and come to Jesus, and come *now*! May God have mercy on you, and bless you! May the love of Christ constrain you! Jesus is *here*—*here* in this ward—*here* in all the plenitude of his power, readiness, and willingness, to give you life, pardon, peace, and salvation—

"Jesus ready stands to save you,
Full of pity, love, and power."

As the compassionate Saviour cried to the anxious throng around the lovely heights of Jerusalem, "Come unto me, and I will give you rest," so he still cries to you, my impenitent friends, in tones of love and mercy, with the same gushing heart and encouraging promise, "*How often would I have gathered you!*" Yes, *you*, my dear soldier; and *must* it, *shall* it, be said of *you*, as of them, "*ye would not!*" Oh, remember, I pray you, only think of the Saviour's "I would, " and your own, "*ye would not!*" And are you not *willing* to be saved? Are you willing to *die* for the salvation of your country, and not willing to be saved "without money and without price?" And *will* you, *can* you, reject such a Saviour, who has suffered, bled, and died to redeem you? "Who of God is ready to be made unto you wisdom, righteousness, sanctification, and redemption." Oh, then, come unto him! "Come, for all things are now ready." Come, for yet there is room. Yes, room for every patriot soldier; room in the church below; room in the church above; and room in the Saviour's bleeding heart. See how he pleads! hear how he entreats! by the thrilling scenes of Bethlehem, Gethsemane, and Calvary he cries, Come! by his bleeding hands and dying groans, he cries, Come unto me, and I will give you rest—rest from sin—rest from error and doubt—rest from sorrow and suffering—rest in heaven, where there will be no more sorrow, pain, nor death; for God himself shall wipe away all tears. Oh, then come! Come *where*? Come *here*! Come *when*? Come *now*! Come *how*? Come just as you are! But, oh, come! May God bless and enable you to come!

Chaplain Reports

Among the first army regulations to address Union chaplains during the Civil War was Congressional Act Number 28 dated 22 July 1861, which ordered chaplains to submit quarterly reports to immediate commanders regarding the moral and religious condition of their regiments. Nothing more was said about reporting until 9 April 1864, when another Act of Congress discontinued the quarterly reports of 1861 and instead directed both regimental and hospital chaplains to report monthly to the Adjutant General's Office.

One of the best commentaries on chaplains' reports came from Charles Alfred Humphreys, age twenty-five, who was ordained a Unitarian minister on 14 July 1863 at Harvard Divinity School. He also received his commission as chaplain of the 2nd Massachusetts Cavalry. Humphreys caught up with his unit on 21 August 1863 and remained until 12 April 1865. Throughout that time, the 2nd Cavalry's mission was to operate against John Singleton Mosby; nothing could have been so simply stated yet so difficult to accomplish. During the latter half of the war, "Mosby's Confederacy" was an area of Virginia marked by overwhelming Union presence but no Union control because of nighttime assaults and daytime surprises staged by Confederate partisans under Mosby.[1] With its heart in Fauquier County, Mosby's domain stretched northerly to Leesburg, southerly to Fredericksburg, to Strasburg in the west, and Fairfax Court House in the east. Chaplain Humphreys found his regiment at Centreville, Virginia. The 2nd Massachusetts Cavalry was then a link in a defensive chain forged from cavalry posts set at half-mile intervals which ran from Dranesville on the upper Potomac to Alexandria on the lower, with Centreville at its midpoint.[2]

Guerilla warfare was uncomfortable. Anything could happen, and probably would. Ambush preoccupied the mind, woods and vegetation looked sinister. While in the open, a rider's shoulder blades itched in anticipation of the thud of a bullet between them. Humphreys was captured 6 July 1864 near Aldie, Virginia. When Confederate Jubal Early slipped away from Lee's army to make his raid into Maryland, the 2nd Massachusetts Cavalry was ordered to observe the passes of the Blue Ridge Mountains. The chaplain rode out with a 150-man detail which was overwhelmed by Partisan Rangers, and he eventually found himself in a prison pen

---

[1] Kevin H. Siepel, *Rebel: The Life and Times of John Singleton Mosby* (New York: St. Martin's Press, 1983) 123.

[2] Ibid., 71.

at Macon, Georgia. Though a non-combatant, he was held for a few months because, as one rebel put it, "You're a damned abolitionist preacher, and you've got to suffer for it."[3]

After he had been in his role for five months, Chaplain Humphreys reported on the moral and religious condition of the 2nd Massachusetts Cavalry to Major Casper Crowninshield, then commanding the regiment. He stated that "true religion is never demonstrative." The regiment's religious condition lay in the extent that the troopers recognized their relations to God, and their obligations to obey God's law, which "cannot be measured by words or tabulated by figures." [4] Feeling that he could minimally "expose habits and practices that must inevitably, if unchecked, undermine all religious feeling and weaken all religious principle" the chaplain then went into "the profanity of trifling with God's name" and "with God's judgments by curses and execrations."[5] He also pointed to the slight attendance at church service. "As to the moral condition of the regiment, it is good while the temptations to immorality are withdrawn. Men cannot gamble after they have exhausted their own money...nor will they get intoxicated when the whiskey is out of their reach."[6]

Examples of reports to regimental commanders turn up in unit histories and officers' personal collections of documents, but they never had a final repository. Reports from Minnesota regimental chaplains represent an unusual case because many are preserved in Minnesota in the Civil and Indian Wars, 1861–1865, which was published in separate volumes from 1890 through 1893. Many of the reports by hospital chaplains can be found in "Returns, Station Books, and Related Records" of the Adjutant General's Office, Record Group 94, National Archives.

Chaplain Chauncey Hobart, 3rd Minnesota Volunteers, was a Methodist minister mustered at Redwing, age fifty-one. He was the first of four chaplains who served with the 3rd Minnesota, being with the unit while it guarded the Louisville & Nashville Railroad. He resigned on 13 April 1862.

---

[3] Charles A. Humphreys, *Field, Camp, Hospital and Prison in the Civil War, 1863–1865* (Boston: Press of Geo. H. Ellis Co., 1918) 113.
[4] Ibid., 385–389
[5] Ibid., 387.
[6] Ibid., 388.

Belmont, Ky., Feb. 15, 1862.
To Col. H.C. Lester,
Commanding,
SIR: According to the act of Congress of July, 1861, it becomes my duty to report quarterly to you "the moral and religious conditions of the regiment," and to make "such suggestions as may conduce to the social happiness and moral improvement of the troops," which report and suggestions for the first quarter, Nov. 15, 1861, to Feb. 15, 1862, I herein submit:

The moral condition of the regiment, as a whole, is highly gratifying and encouraging. A decided majority are men of high-toned moral principles, whose lives and conduct are governed by the acknowledged rules of sound morality.

The decidedly religious portion of the regiment is not large. Those, however, who are thus recognized are manifesting commendable zeal in maintaining a consistent christian [sic] and religious deportment, so far as I know. A little advancement has been made in this direction during the quarter.

As to such suggestions as may conduce to the social happiness and moral improvement of the troops, but little need be said, as under the circumstances but few things are practicable.

If a few dollars could be placed in the hands of a proper committee, to be used by them in securing for the use of the regiment some tea or more copies each of the leading literary and religious periodicals now being published, much, it is thought, would be done to advance the social happiness of the troops. The subscriptions might commence for one or two months, with the right to renew if occasion required.

My labors in part in the regiment embrace the following items:

Preaching once or twice each Sabbath (save one, which was rainy), excepting those when the regiment was on the march, since we left Minnesota.

Prayer meetings on Sabbath and Thursday or Friday afternoons or evenings, when circumstances would permit.

Prayer at dress parade, up to February 3d, when relieved from that duty, except on Sabbath evenings, forty-three times.

Visited the hospitals some 154 times up to this date.

Held religious service with the sick, consisting of reading the Scriptures and prayer, eighty-one times.

Attended the funeral and burial of the four following named persons:

Joseph Abel, Company E, Jan. 8, 1862; C. M. Wood, Company B, Jan. 29, '62; O. C. Shurtleff, Company G, Feb. 3, '62; J. W. Goodwin, Company C, Feb. 8, '62.

Superintended the erection of proper headboards (two-inch white oak plank) at the graves of the dead.

Purchased and distributed several hundred pages of tracts.

Distributed several thousand pages of books and pamphlets to the sick and others.

All of which is respectfully submitted.

Chauncey Hobart,

Chaplain Third Regiment Minnesota Volunteers.[7]

---

[7] Chaplain Hobart returned to the Minnesota Conference of the Methodist Episcopal Church after his resignation. He ministered in the conference for many years, at one time serving as conference secretary to the bishop. He died in Redwing in 1904.

Rev. Charles Spear

Reverend Charles Spear was sixty-one when commissioned 23 June 1862 as a hospital chaplain of US Volunteers. Where regimental chaplains were members of a unit and moved with it, hospital chaplains were assigned to a medical facility and subject to its director. They held different commissions. Where regimental chaplains were state volunteers, hospital chaplains were "United States Volunteers." Through the war, there were 181 men commissioned as hospital chaplains and another 60 also commissioned as regimental chaplains. There were 2,154 regimental chaplains.

Since hospital chaplains were not required to file reports in 1862 and because he wrote to the surgeon general and not the director of a particular hospital, Chaplain Spear seems to be searching for support in the continuance of his commission. In addition, he states that he visited a number of hospitals, which was not the usual assignment for a hospital chaplain. The only other facts known about Chaplain Spear include the revocation of his appointment effective 11 December 1862 and his death on 13 April 1863.

Spear's particular capitalizations and spellings have been retained.

Chaplain Charles Spear,
Military Hospital for Massachusetts Soldiers, Washington, DC
November 9, 1862
Report of Labors in the United States Military Hospital in Washington,
District of Columbia by Rev. Charles Spear, Chaplain MS. Hospital
To The Surgeon General.

Sir,
In the discharge of my official duties as Chaplain of United States Hospital, I have the honor to present my Report for the month of October 1862.

My labors have been very extensive during the month. No day has passed without taxing my energies to the utmost and contributed in some way to relieving the Sick and Wounded Soldier brought here from the Camp to this District, which now may be called the City of Hospitals. A new population has been suddenly thrown into the Capital of the Republic. Daily, thousands arrive, strong and healthy from every profession and employment, ready for the general contest. At the same moment there is entering the Sick and the Wounded from the war & camp life. Both need a great Will and generous temperament; one for the camp; the other to be returned either to the camp or to the quiet home to resume once more the peaceful duties of domestic life.

Among the hospitals to which I have given more attention than to others, have been the Capitol, the St. Aloysius and the Branch General Hospital.

In addition, at each returning Sabbath I have added to my labors the Old Capitol Prison and the Jail; places of extreme religious destitution.

It would be difficult to sum up very briefly the labors of any faithful chaplain. He is called on to perform every variety of duty. The Soldier in his weakness, becomes a child in his dependence on his attendants and on the labors of the Philanthropist. The following will approximate to the truth:

Number of visits—78

Books, papers distributed—5000

Patients visited—4000

In addition to other labors I have been preparing some amusements including instruction for the patients. They need not only physical but mental and moral helps.

I brought from Boston, my native place, a very valuable collection of paintings fitted for the Magic Lantern—lectures on a variety of subjects.

I humbly trust with the longer experience of over thirty years in visiting hospitals, prisons and other institutions that I may be enabled to add something to relieve the sick soldier as he returns from the battlefield.

Yours truly,
Charles Spear

Oliver P. Light
7th Minnesota Volunteers

Chaplain Oliver P. Light of the 7th Minnesota Volunteers was a Methodist minister who initially entered the army as a soldier in the 6th Minnesota Infantry. An item which appeared on 24 March 1863 in the Saint Paul Pioneer *reported "Rev. O. P. Light, Fourth Sergeant in Company H, Sixth Minnesota Volunteers, has been appointed Chaplain of the Seventh."[1] He is among the few chaplains named in the* Official Records.[2] *In his report on the 7th's participation in General Sibley's campaign against the Sioux in Minnesota, the regiment's commander stated that Light "remained at Camp Atchison and was faithful in his ministrations."*

Chaplain Light's report is actually his resignation sent to the governor while the regiment was stationed for a month in the Department of the Tennessee. They would soon be assigned to the 16th Army Corps and sent to Memphis, from where they would take part in an expedition to Tupelo, Mississippi. Elijah Evan Edwards, an Episcopal cleric, assumed the 7th's chaplaincy and served to the unit's discharge 16 August 1865 and eventually became a rather famous landscape artist. Reverend Light died 28 March 1904 in Wymore, Nebraska.

Paducah, Ky., May 14, 1864.
Governor S. Miller,
St. Paul, Minn.,

Dear Sir: Your kind favor last written was received at a time when I was unable by sickness to reply, and since then I have been on leave to my father's in Illinois. Having but recently joined the regiment I have at my earliest opportunity—as I desired first to acquaint myself somewhat with the condition of the command—seated myself to address you a reply.

My own health is improving slowly, yet, as my disease has rendered it a rather precarious matter for me to remain in the field, I have, upon advice of the surgeons, sent forward my resignation as chaplain of the Seventh Minnesota, and will in a few days be a citizen again. I regret very much to be

---

[1] Anonymous news item, *Saint Paul* (MN) *Pioneer*, 24 March 1863, 4.

[2] US War Department, *The War of the Rebellion: A Compilation of the Official Records of the Union and Confederate Armies*, 70 vols. (Washington DC: US Government Printing Office, 1880–1901) Vol. 22, pt. 1, p. 369.

compelled to this course, as I had become very much attached to the men of the regiment and desired to remain with them to the end of our enlistment, but an overruling Providence has directed otherwise. I shall return again to Minnesota immediately. My warmest regards will ever remain with the regiment and I shall always deem it an honor to have been associated with so fine a body of men. As soldiers the gallant Seventh has no superiors and, as far as I have seen, but few equals, both as regards soldierly bearing and gentlemanly conduct. Both here and in St. Louis it has earned for itself a very enviable reputation for good morals and orderly conduct, and the inhabitants and military commanders of the two cities vie with each other as to which shall have the benefit of its services. I do not intend or desire to use flattery in speaking of the regiment which, by your kindly offices, I have had the honor to serve for the last twelve months, but you will allow me to add that Minnesota may well feel proud of the Seventh Regiment.

Religiously the regiment is doing about as well as at any previous time, I believe, but its social privileges and opportunities for mental improvement are not as good as they were in St. Louis. This may be called emphatically a reading regiment, and hence to be placed where they cannot obtain books and papers is to them a deprivation deeply felt, and the necessity of having another chaplain, one who will feel, appreciate and labor to meet the necessities of the regiment, is pressingly demanded at once. The regiment has already been too long deprived of chaplain's services by my protracted illness and I hope that the authorities will at once see to it that the place is supplied with a good man, one full of faith and zealous of good works. As far as possible, will you please encourage them to this end!

The general health of the regiment is good, but few reported in hospital—three with varioloid.[3]

I have the honor, Governor, to subscribe myself,
Most respectfully, your obedient servant,
O. P. Light,
Chaplain, Seventh Regiment Minnesota Infantry

---

[3] A mild form of smallpox.

Simon Putnam

Chaplain, Third Regiment Minnesota Volunteer Infantry

Simon Putnam did not follow Chauncey Hobert in the chaplaincy of the 3rd Minnesota, but was the regiment's third of four chaplains. He enlisted in Afton, Minnesota, and was mustered 20 September 1863. This chaplain's report is one made to the adjutant general as ordered by the War Department. Putnam died of disease on 11 September 1864 at his home in Afton. Chaplain Anthony Wilford was mustered in December and served with the regiment until it was discharged.

Pine Bluff, Ark., May 31, 1864
Gen. L. Thomas, Adjutant General, U.S.A.,[1]
General: The following report of the general history and moral condition of the Third Regiment Minnesota Volunteer Infantry, is submitted in accordance with section 3 of General Orders, No. 158, dated "War Department, Adjutant General's Office, Washington, April 13, 1864."

I entered upon my duties as chaplain at Little Rock, Ark., Oct. 20, 1863. The regiment had formed a part of the "Arkansas Expedition," and immediately on entering the city on the 10th day of September it was selected by General Steele, on account of its "efficiency and good discipline," as one of the regiments to be employed as provost guard, in which service it was continued until leaving for this place.[2]

Colonel Andrews having been selected as commander of the post, the command of the regiment devolved upon Lieutenant Colonel Mattson.[3] He, early in December, with three other commissioned officers, six sergeants and four corporals, visited Minnesota as a recruiting party, and during the winter the regiment was under the command of Maj. E. W. Foster.

The men were in excellent health, and diligent efforts were made by the officers to perfect them in military discipline and drill. A large proportion of the men having re-enlisted as veterans, four of the companies

---

[1] Maj. Gen. Lorenzo Thomas was the US Army adjutant general.
[2] The 3rd Minnesota saw previous service during the campaign to capture Little Rock in August of 1863. Maj. Gen. Frederick Steele was the commander of the US Army's Department of Arkansas and the VII Army Corps.
[3] Col. Christopher C. Andrews, Lt. Col. Hans Mattson, and Maj. Everett W. Foster led the regiment to Augusta AR, midway between Jonesboro and Little Rock.

were furloughed and absent during the latter part of the winter and early part of spring.

On the evening of March 30, the remaining six companies, B, C, E, G, H and I, under the command of Major Foster, took the cars for Devall's Bluff, and on the morning of the 31st they were joined by a company of cavalry, and the entire force, under command of Colonel Andrews, embarked on board the steamer Dove and, accompanied by a gunboat, moved from the bluff up White river to Augusta to reconnoiter the rebel forces in that vicinity.[4] The next day, April 1st, after having marched into the country twelve miles or more, without discovering the enemy in force, it was decided to return to the boats. About five miles from the landing a force of cavalry under General McRae made a fierce attack upon our rear and this was soon followed by another upon our left flank.[5] A most spirited engagement ensued in Fitzhugh's woods, continuing for three hours or more, during which time our men handsomely repelled each attack of the foe and persistently held the ground against more than twice their number, retiring only when their failing ammunition and the approaching night made it absolutely necessary to seek the protection of the boats.[6] The fact that we were not molested after leaving the field, although we marched as infantry, while the rebels had good horses, shows that they were severely punished and thoroughly satisfied. The conduct of the regiment is worthy of record. Although pressed by a superior force for nearly three hours, in front and on both flanks, so that it seemed as if the enemy would soon surround and close in upon us, the officers evinced the most intrepid courage, rallying the men and directing their movements, or leading them in person with the utmost fearlessness in the face of imminent peril, and the men fought as if inspired with the valor of true veterans, driving the enemy once and again to the shelter of the heavy timber, and leaving the field with great reluctance when ordered to retire. Colonel Andrews' horse was shot under him; the clothing of several of the officers was pieced by the enemy's bullets and

---

[4] Devall's Bluff is on the White River. On 31 March 1864, the 3rd Minnesota Infantry, consisting of 186 soldiers, was joined by 45 troopers from the 8th Missouri Cavalry.

[5] Brig. Gen. Dandridge McRae's Confederate brigade.

[6] Fitzhugh's Woods was about six miles from Augusta. After a fight of two and a half hours, Col. Andrews withdrew the Union troops. They sustained thirty-one casualties, or 24 percent of those engaged on the Union side.

among the men were numerous hair-breadth escapes. The loss of the regiment was eight killed and nineteen wounded.

Returning to Little Rock we were soon rejoined by Lieutenant Colonel Mattson and his recruiting party, accompanied by the four furloughed companies and upwards of 200 recruits.

On the 19th of April the regiment was again in motion for Augusta, to cooperate in a more extensive movement against the force of General McRae, who, on our arrival there, fled across the Cache river and was out of our reach.[7] But the expedition was not altogether fruitless on our part. We captured several prisoners, took off about eighty contrabands, fifty horses and mules and a considerable quantity of hams and cotton, besides which the cavalry that accompanied us captured a rebel colonel from General Price's army.[8]

We again returned to Little Rock and had been in camp but a few days when we were ordered to this place to accompany a supply train to Camden. On arriving here it was reported that General Steele was falling back to Little Rock, and in a day or two we formed our camp in the rear of the town, where we still remain. The men are employed in constructing fortifications and details are also made for grand guard duty each day.

The daily average of sickness for the month of May is eight in hospital and thirty-seven in camp, the recruits furnishing much the greater proportion. It is reported that four of our men have died in hospital at Little Rock since we left, but no death has occurred here.

It is a pleasure to be able to report favorably concerning the moral condition of the regiment. The best of feeling prevails among the officers and their bearing toward each other is gentlemanly and courteous. In this way, adding to a strict military rule the force of a commendable example, they are both respected and esteemed by the men, whose deportment on their part is such as becomes at once the soldier and the man. Brawls are unknown, the best of discipline prevails and the camp is a model of neatness. I could write morality too, but we are not entirely free from the vices that infest all our cities, towns and villages and tempt the young to their ruin. But the camp collects the social vices of whole communities and the force of evil habits is greatly augmented and intensified, so that the restraints and influences which, at home, almost unconsciously held many a young man to

---

[7] The Cache River is about seven miles east of Augusta AR.

[8] Maj. Gen. Sterling Price superseded Lt. Gen. Theophilus Holmes in command of the Confederate District of Arkansas on 16 March 1864.

a virtuous life, are but as tow in the focus of a burning lens. To remove these vices, or to counteract their influence, infringing as they do alike upon the welfare of the individual and society, must ever be objects of earnest desire, both to the patriot and the christian. These objects have been kept in view, and by the distribution of good reading, both among the sick and well; by friendly conversation and appropriate counsels; by occasional religious services in the hospital and regular Sabbath services in camp or church, together with social christian [sic] gatherings for prayer and conference during the week, it has been sought to strengthen those convictions that form the basis of a correct moral life, and to develop and cultivate those principles and affections which pertain to a devout christian character.

An attempt has also been made to interest the men in vocal music, both sacred and secular. Whenever it has been necessary to call upon the officers for aid in carrying forward these plans it has been promptly given, and, although the results attained are far below my wishes, they are sufficient to afford encouragement to renewed efforts for the future.

Very respectfully, your obedient servant,
Simon Putnam,
Chaplain, Third Regiment Minnesota Volunteer Infantry.

Chaplain Chauncey B. Thomas,
USA, 3d Division, General Hospital, Alexandria, Va.

Chauncey Boardman Thomas, a Congregationalist minister from Massachusetts, was commissioned as a chaplain in 1862 at the age of twenty-eight. He served as a hospital chaplain for four years: at Alexandria, Virginia, from 1862 to 1863, and at New Orleans, Louisiana, from 1863 to 1866. For some reason, Chaplain Thomas was required to make weekly reports to the division surgeon, Dr. Edward Beaty, rather than monthly reports as required by the Army surgeon general. It is evident from the abbreviated style of Thomas's report for 7 March 1863 that he did not find much pleasure in meeting this requirement. Army paperwork was never fun, especially when the chaplain had to justify his absences.

Thomas's original spelling and capitalization has been retained.

Saturday P.M.
March 7, 1863
Chaplain's Weekly Report
To Dr. Edwin Beaty. Surgeon, U. S. V. in chge 3d Div.[1]

Sir.

In response to your order of March 3d to furnish for your office every Sunday morning a written report of my labors and observations with the sick & wounded in this Division setting forth the wants & complaints of the Soldiers in detail, giving as far as possible the condition and state of mind of the Soldiers previous to death & such other information as I may deem of importance to the office or of interest to friends, giving also the no. of funerals attended & if not attended by me the reason why;

I have the honor to make the following report for the week ending March 7th, 1863.

March 1st—Sabbath.
On Sunday I preached in Washinton St Hospl Old Building at 10 _ A.M. at Queen St. at 3 P.M. at Grovenor House at 7 P.M. My Services at each place were about one hour in length. My sermon in each case was about 25

---

[1] Original in RG 94, E-679, Monthly Reports of Civil War Chaplains, National Archives, Washington DC.

minutes. There were at each place about 25 patients present. I went through all the Wards of Washington St Hospl & Grovenor House & invited the patients to attend excepting in the 3 upper Wards of New Hallowel House. I did not invite them here because I found in the lower ward of New Hallowel a young man quite sick. (Pvt Henry D. Pierce 19th Conn) who desired to converse with me on the subject of Religion & who delayed me so long that I could invite no more.[2] At his request I read the Bible and conversed with him.

March 3d. 4th. 5th. 6th. 7th.
Visited the San. Comm'n Christian commn & Pay Dept. at Washington for & with soldiers.[3] Conversed and counseled & prayer with the men in the Wards and made preparation for Sabbath. Also devised and executed plans for procuring Reading for the Hospls.

I have the honor to report that there are no complaints which I have heard from the Soldiers against the officers connected with the Hospls.

The only complaint deserving attention is the one so universal among soldiers that they are not promptly paid. But the blame is with the Pay Dept which is managed in a most wretched manner truly.

With much respect,
I am y'rs truly
C.B. Thomas.
Chaplain in 3d Division
Genl Hospl
Alxa, Va

---

[2] Pvt. Henry D. Pierce, Co. C, 2nd Connecticut Heavy Artillery.
[3] The US Sanitary Commission and the Christian Commission offices.

"Disclosures of the Soldier's Heart"

Chaplain Henry Clay Trumbull,

10th Connecticut Volunteers

Trumbull smiled for many of his wartime cartes de visite.[1] In those days, photography was regarded as a novelty because it had been around for only twenty-five years. Subjects were told to look at cameras with the same sort of flat emotionless faces seen in formal portraits done by painters. It was the sort of tradition which Reverend Trumbull ignored. His unconventional approach to life was obvious to Southern Brigadier General Thomas Jordan, who encountered the chaplain when he was a Confederate prisoner. "He is a tricky fellow," wrote Jordan, "and has little the air of a chaplain." Colonel Harris M. Plaisted, 11th Maine Infantry, recorded a different opinion in his 7 October 1864 report about action at Petersburg, Virginia:

> *I cannot fail to mention Chaplain Trumbull, Tenth Connecticut, who was constantly at the front with his regiment, as is his wont at all times. He was conspicuous on this occasion, with revolver in hand, in his effort to stay the crumbling regiment. An hour later he officiated at the burial of our dead, while the skirmish line was still engaged and every moment a renewal of the attack was expected. The sound of prayer mingled with the echoes of artillery and musketry and the crash of falling pines for hastily constructed breast-works. His services to the brigade, not only on this but on so many other like occasions, are gratefully acknowledged.[2]*

Mustered 10 September 1862 as an army chaplain, Henry Clay Trumbull had already done quite a bit with his thirty-two years of life. From 1850 through 1857, he and Alice Gallaudet had started a family while Henry earned a livelihood in "the railroad business" at Hartford. Trumbull left his secular job when appointed Sunday school missionary for Connecticut, and he also became active in what would

---

[1] The carte de visite was a photograph printed on paper and mounted on a card measuring approximately 2.5 x 4 inches.

[2] US War Department, *The War of the Rebellion: A Compilation of the Official Records of the Union and Confederate Armies*, 70 vols. (Washington DC: US Government Printing Office, 1880–1901) Vol. 42, pt. 1, p. 732.

become the Republican party. Commissioned and ordained the same day as a Congregational minister and chaplain of the 10th Connecticut, he replaced another of that denomination, young Henry L. Hall, whose kidneys failed after eight months with the regiment. The 10th saw action in North Carolina during 1862, South Carolina in 1863, and fought through 1864 in Virginia, first at Bermuda Hundred and then Petersburg. In the trenches before Richmond during 1865, they were at Appomattox Court House when the Army of Northern Virginia surrendered.

On 19 July 1863, Chaplain Trumbull strayed into enemy hands on Morris Island, near the entrance of Charleston harbor, while searching for members of his regiment who fell in the fight for Battery Wagner. He was confined at Richmond in Libby Prison until 24 November 1863.

H. Clay Trumbull gained fame in his time as an author, and many of his books drew on his Civil War experiences: Some Army Sermons *(1864)*; The Knightly Soldier *(1865)*; and The Captured Scout of the Army of the James *(1869)*.

Trumbull's War Memories of a Chaplain, *published during 1898, is an eloquent and detailed account of what befell a regimental chaplain.*

Disclosures of the Soldier Heart[3]

The soldiers in our Civil War were hardly more than boys, as a rule. A battery boy shot in the wrist was given chloroform in the field hospital at Whitehall, North Carolina. While he was unconscious, his hand was amputated and the stump bound up. I was kneeling by his side as he came again to his senses. Looking vacantly about him at first, his eyes slowly turned to the bandaged stump, and he realized the truth. Tears stood in his eyes as he exclaimed unselfishly, "What will my mother do now?" It was for her sake that he grieved over his lost right hand; but he did not grudge his gift to his country.

"There goes a hand for the Union," said another brave soldier, as his forearm was shot away.

More than once a wounded soldier called out to me after a battle, as he saw I was taking the names of the dead and wounded to report them in a home paper: "Say 'slightly wounded,' Chaplain."

---

[3] Henry Clay Trumbull, *War Memories of an Army Chaplain* (New York: Charles Scribner's Sons, 1898) 46–47.

He wanted to spare anxiety to his home dear ones, true soldier that he was.

Tenderness and courage went together always. As I was going from shelter-tent to shelter-tent, visiting the men of my regiment, one hot Sunday afternoon in the summer of 1864, at Deep Bottom, Virginia, I found a little fellow crying bitterly with homesickness. As I talked with him tenderly, I found he was disappointed, and so almost heartbroken, because of his lack of home letters which he had looked for. I spoke words of sympathy and cheer, and as I left him I thought he was still too much of a boy to be away from home in the army.

A few weeks later my regiment stood in battle line, repelling one of the fiercest attacks of the enemy we had met in our three years of service. As I stood by my colonel and my brigade commander, just back of the line of battle, I saw that homesick boy hurrying into his place in the ranks. He had been out all night on picket duty, and, coming into the camp in the morning, he had learned of the regiment's new move, and had hurried to be with his comrades in their peril. Hardly had he taken his place and fired his first shot when he fell with a bullet through his lungs. Tearing open his coat, and gasping for breath, as his lifeblood rushed out through his death-wound, with never a whimper or a groan, he looked along the unwavering line, and called out cheerily with his failing breath, "Fire away, boys; fire away!" And the homesick boy, who was the heroic soldier, found his final rest.

Seeing Slavery and Emancipation

The Emancipation Proclamation bore date of January 1, 1863; it was "sealed and delivered" at Appomattox Court House, April 9, 1865. What had before been a glad promise, then became an accomplished fact. Only those who witnessed the scenes following that event can have any apprehension of the mighty outburst of rejoicing that went up from a race of four millions of slaves enfranchised in a moment.

My regiment was in the victorious column of the Twenty-fourth Army Corps, that turned back from the scene of Lee's surrender to find rest and quarters in evacuated Richmond. At every point along the route the negroes swarmed out to welcome and honor the army which had won them freedom. They shouted their thanks to them; they called down blessings on their heads; they threw themselves on the ground before them, as the column passed along, hailing them as their deliverers. Yet, under and back of all this outburst of rejoicing and of welcome and thanks to the Union soldiers, there was manifest the feeling, on the part of the enfranchised race, that it was God's work, and that to him was the praise due. They had long prayed, as they waited, for this day, and at last it had come in response to their prayers. Of this they had no doubt.

As a comrade told me, at one point an old negro mammy, waving her bony arms, shouted to the passing soldiers, above the welcoming cry of the younger blacks:

"Dun' yer t'ink *yer* did it. De Lord dun't all. He jus' use *yer*, dat's all. Bress de Lord, ebery one o'yer!"

And that it *was* God's work, who can doubt?[4]

Harriet Beecher Stowe's graphic delineation of slavery as it was, in the story of "Uncle Tom's Cabin," was at the time of its writing much discussed and bitterly denounced both North and South. But when slavery had become the occasion of a war which united all the North, that story was dramatized and became popular in the theaters of New York. The "stage," which never attempts to lead public sentiment in an unpopular direction, can always be depended on to follow at a paying distance behind the average public sentiment in a question of morals; and so that story became familiar to many who now wanted to believe the worst that it told of a representative institution of the South.

After the war many Southerners who came North went to see that play of "Uncle Tom's Cabin," although they had never read the book. Two of my acquaintances, the one from Missouri and the other from South Carolina, went together, in this way, to see it performed in a popular New York theater. As they left the theater at the close of the evening, as my Missouri friend informed me, the South-Carolinian walked along for some time without saying a word, and then laconically expressed himself:

"Will, *that's* what licked us."

And it was not strange that he thought so.[5]

After he was mustered out of the army 25 August 1865 along with the 10th Connecticut, Trumbull was appointed missionary secretary of the American Sunday School Union for New England. Yale conferred an honorary master's degree on him in 1866. He moved to Philadelphia during 1875 and established his religious newspaper, The Sunday-School Times. *Reverend Trumbull spent 1881 on an*

---

[4] Ibid., 404–405.
[5] Ibid., 411.

archeological expedition through Egypt, Arabia, and Syria, returning to receive DD degrees from Lafayette and the University of the City of New York. He was an active member of veterans' organizations as well as the Freemasons. Death came 8 December 1903, and his remains were interred at Spring Grove Cemetery, Hartford.

Chapter 5

The Measure of Ministry

"His truth is marching on..." Julia Ward Howe

How would one measure the ministries of more than twenty-three hundred Union chaplains during the great ordeal of the Civil War? That the majority of them performed pastoral ministries of presence, encouragement and evangelism for thousands of soldiers is evident from their written records and published memoirs. Official reports of battles, from commanders of regiments and brigades and from those of higher rank bear ample testimony to the courage, efficiency, and faithfulness of regimental chaplains who fell in battle, or who wore out their lives in ministry to soldiers. Perhaps it should be noted that the greatest number were not professional military men. They had no careers in the army. Like the soldiers they served, they were volunteers, and after the war they returned to their parishes, seminaries and mission fields.[1] As Chaplain Henry Clay

---

[1] Chaplain Clay Trumbull listed thirty-eight former regimental chaplains who made significant contributions to churches, colleges, publications, and government agencies after the war. For example,

Chaplain John Ireland of the 5th Minnesota became the first Roman Catholic archbishop of St Paul MN; Chaplain Gilbert Haven of the 8th Massachusetts, Chaplain Samuel Fallows of the 32nd Wisconsin, Charles C. McCabe of the 122nd Ohio, and William A. Spencer of the 8th Illinois Cavalry were consecrated as Methodist bishops. Henry M. Turner, 1st USCT, was consecrated an AME bishop in Georgia; and Baptist chaplain Norman Fox of the 77th New York became an editor, pastor, and professor at William Jewell College. See H. Clay Trumbull, *War Memories of an Army Chaplain* (New York: Scribner's Sons, 1898) 11–13.

Trumbull of the 10th Connecticut Volunteers believed, "Their names are written on high, and ought to be borne in mind below as competent and worthy, bearing well their part as chaplains and as citizens, faithfully serving their God and their country."[2]

In 1892 James H. Bradford of the 12th Connecticut Volunteers, Clay Trumbull's colleague in the Military Order of the Loyal Legion, presented the reasons he was glad to have served as a chaplain during the war. His remarks to an audience of veterans in Washington were analytical, humorous, and poignant. They serve as a fitting conclusion to his reminiscences of being present at a signal revolution in the nation's history.

---

[2] Ibid., 14.

Chaplain James Henry Bradford,

12th Connecticut Volunteers

Born 24 August 1836 in Grafton, Vermont, to a Congregational minister who claimed an ancestor had been chaplain to the Queen of England, Bradford was himself ordained in that denomination. He left Yale to join the army on 4 February 1862, serving with the 12th Regiment until his term of service expired on 2 December 1864. He is one of few chaplains whose names appear in the 128-volume War of the Rebellion: A Compilation of the Official Records of the Union and Confederate Armies. *In volume fifteen, he is cited by his colonel "for the fearless activity with which he ministered to the suffering during the April 1863 battle of Fort Bisland, Louisiana." He married when he got home from the war and raised four children. After a few years of holding the post of pastor in Hudson, Wisconsin, Bradford assumed the chaplaincy of a Massachusetts reform school. He then returned to Connecticut where he became chaplain of the Middletown Industrial School for Girls. After 1881, he held a number of bureaucratic posts in Washington, DC. He died 22 December 1913.*[1]

On 6 April 1892, Bradford read his masterful description of Civil War army chaplains at a meeting of the Washington chapter of the Military Order of the Loyal Legion of the United States, a veterans organization composed of men who served as commissioned officers in the Civil War.

The Chaplains in the Volunteer Army

One or two things should be remembered in our judgment of chaplains in the army during the rebellion.

1st. Their duties were not very definitely stated in the Regulations of the Army. In fact, only the few following lines which I quote bear upon that subject in a book of more than 500 pages, going into the minutest detail regarding every other person, from a major-general to a private:

"And shall be required to report to the colonel commanding the regiment to which he is attached, at the end of each quarter, the moral and religious condition of the regiment, and such suggestions as may conduce to the social

---

[1] Service and Pension Case Files of James Henry Bradford, RGs 94 and 15, Records of the Veterans Administration, National Archives, Washington DC.

happiness and moral improvement of the troops."—Army Regulations, page 507, Act July 22, 1861.

2d. The chaplain was only one in a thousand; yes, more than that, for some regiments had none. One authority says there were 2,047 regiments in the Union army during the war. I have not been able to find out how many chaplains there were in the whole army.[2] But from Connecticut there were 49 chaplains, whose average term of service was 1 year 1 month and 20 days; 3 were with 3-months' troops and 8 with 9-months.[3] The chaplain-in-chief of this order, Rev. Henry C. Trumbull, served 2 years 11 months 15 days—the longest from that State; Chaplain Samuel F. Jarvis, of the 1st Connecticut Heavy Artillery, came next—2 years 10 months 11 days; but both of these chaplains were the second chaplains in their regiments, and the writer came third in term of service—2 years 9 months 20 days, and had the honor of being the only chaplain who went through with a 3-years' regiment from the Nutmeg State. Of these 49 chaplains *12* were mustered out of service by expiration of term, *9* were honorably discharged, *27* resigned, *1* died, *2* were wounded, *1* was captured by the enemy. Possibly these figures may give a fair average with those of other States.[4]

A very high standard of character and duty was expected of the chaplain, as his principal business was to promote a high standard in the character of others. Hence he was closely watched. Every failure in duty was commented upon and noised abroad through the camp.

3d. The Regulations required that a man must be a regularly ordained minister of the Gospel, and in order to that he must have spent several years in the quiet life of a student, and in most instances added years of residence in his own home, among the most favored people, seeing almost nothing of such scenes and life as he would meet with in camp; so that army life was to him a total change. He was not accustomed to life among people the majority of whom were strangers to him, and probably not inclined to his way of life or mode of

---

[2] There were 2,399 commissioned chaplains who served in the US Army Volunteer Force, as hospital chaplains of US Volunteers, as US Army chaplains, and US Navy chaplains.

[3] Records actually indicate there were fifty-two commissioned chaplains who served Connecticut regiments; their average length of service was fourteen months.

[4] Chaplain Jacob Eaton, 7th Connecticut, died of typhoid fever at Wilmington NC on 20 March 1865. Chaplains Trumbull, 10th Connecticut, and Charles Dixon, 8th Connecticut, were held as prisoners of war. Three Connecticut chaplains were wounded in action: Thomas G. Brown, 21st Connecticut; John W. Leek, 27th Connecticut; Franciscan Brother Leo Rizzo da Saracena, 9th Connecticut.

thinking. The rough of camp life, exposure to storms and hunger, his delicate constitution, housed so long, fed on the best prepared food regularly, was hardly prepared for, and after the first few months, sick at heart because he could not hold his services regularly, and sick in body because of exposure, he resigned and returned to post up his former flock on the terrible hardships of army life. This statement does not apply to all army chaplains, however.

My own army life, spent in a comparatively small department—that of the Gulf, and later with the 19th Army Corps, under Gen. Phil. Sheridan, in the Shenandoah valley—did not afford so great an opportunity to observe the doings of army chaplains as others had; but even in these small bodies of troops I found many stalwart men who took life as it came; who, not expecting much, were not disappointed in getting little; men who knew enough of human nature to know that camp life was not expected to be conducive to sainthood, as it passes in the quiet of peaceful villages and towns; who knew, also, that noble traits of character might lie hidden under rough exterior, to be revealed by the stern discipline of the camp; whose aim was to be of some use day by day—not ambitious for great deeds, but hoping for opportunity to do a great many small ones that would on the whole weigh well. These men knew that in camp life the props of ordinary society were all knocked a way, and that each man stood on his own foundation if he had any, and they were not unprepared to find some marvelous transformations of character both ways. To see men who passed for very respectable people at home unable to breast the storm, and others who had not attracted much attention in civil life show great self-control and poise, gaining steadily in the respect of all their companions while drilling, and shining out with brilliant lustre in the fierce conflict of battle, in courage, endurance, brotherhood, risking life for comrades, helping the wounded, shielding the weak, and proving themselves true heroes by a hundred unlooked-for acts.

Chaplains had great opportunities. At first there was much sickness. Most of the men had been cared for by mothers, sisters, or wives at home, who cautioned them against exposure and nursed them back to health when attacked by disease. They were not used to caring for themselves. Some had never been sick, did not know what they wanted then, found it hard to submit to keeping quiet or controlling their hunger. Here the chaplain found his field. He nursed the sick, cautioned them; advised, comforted, encouraged them; helped to get them proper food for returning convalescence after a run of fever; wrote letters home or read those received; looked after the mail and express matter; sent money home for the boys; appeared always as their friend; kept them cheerful with bright stories, and by little gifts from friends kept up their connection with home life. He was the servant of everybody, and was found as willing to give aid to the private as to the field and staff. So in the course of time the chaplain came to be greatly respected and a man of influence. If boys got tight and in the guard-house, they sent for the chaplain to present their case to the colonel. If they were wounded, it was his pleasure and duty to hunt them up, get a surgeon, improvise a hospital, and help them to as many comforts as possible. If they died from disease or were killed on the field of battle, it was his duty to see them decently buried, and so to mark their resting-place that it could be identified "when the cruel war was over" and friends sought to transfer the sacred dust to the home and family lot on the old hillside or near the old church.

I happened to find among my books recently a little vest-pocket memorandum with a page inscribed to each of the one hundred men of my regiment who laid down their lives in the first 18 months of our campaigning. I find quite a variety of history in these brief statements. The first one was an assistant surgeon who left home full of high hopes and in perfect health, but who died of fever on shipboard eight days out from New York, and his body was returned by the same steamer to his sorrowing friends on Berkshire hills. His sudden demise seemed to have been foreseen by a lady who entered our state-room just before we sailed, and, startled at seeing a third bunk improvised in that narrow place, exclaimed, "Why, I thought that was a coffin!" It became the coffin of this assistant surgeon. I find recorded the death of the first man killed in battle in our ranks. With that strange premonition of something serious to happen he came to me to write a long letter to his home just before the battle, and seemed unable to rally from a certain sadness that had taken possession of him. He was noticed to fall back just a little out of line when under fire, and the lieutenant, putting his hand upon his shoulder, said, "Keep up there, man," but while the words were yet in his mouth a piece of a shell made a rent in the man's breast over the heart as large as one's fist, and he was stone-dead before he could step. That lieutenant has been for twenty years in yonder insane asylum. Here is a page to a captain whose body was packed in a cask of whisky and shipped home; to a private who went into the Mississippi to bathe at Camp Parapet and drowned; to another who fell off a bridge and breathed his last in the water 40 feet below, loaded as he was with a gun and 30 rounds; to one out of eight killed by a stroke of lightning in the guard-tent at midnight; to a lieutenant who was such a gentleman everybody liked him, but fever cut him down; to a private who was struck fairly in the back and side by a wild Texas steer coursing full tilt across our camp-ground—pitched 20 feet and killed instantly by an animal he did not see at all, as the steer hardly slacked his speed.

And so there is history and incident in every case, sometimes pathetic, as where six men, awakened suddenly by the cry of fire on a steamer anchored off New Orleans, in the turbid waters of the Mississippi, jumped overboard and floated away in darkness to death; or when one died in captivity out of thirty captured men, who were returned from Texas, after fifteen months' confinement, with the same clothes they wore away, and who exclaimed: "Oh, give us water for a bath; we are eaten alive with vermin." It has been my pleasure to look upon the faces of some of these men within a few months, at a reunion.

But why linger on these sad details? Into the ears of the chaplain were poured the private ills of nearly the whole command. The colonel or lieutenant-colonel commanding would tell him in the twilight talk what to do with his belongings in case of accident. And when the same man was brought back bleeding to death from a shell wound in the knee, he was tenderly watched over through the night and kept from bleeding to death, until 7 o'clock the next morning, when his soul went back to his God. It became the chaplain's duty to make his coffin of boards from a fence, wrap his blanket about him, and lay away what remained of one of the most gentlemanly officers of the corps; and only within a week have I discovered that he was twice brevetted from that day, to be colonel and also brigadier-general. His instructions were carried out. His horse, sword, field-glass, and saddle were delivered to his mother, and the little boy who had been his servant for months was left in her care for education by his dying request.

The chaplain's tent was the great resort; men came there from all the ten companies—came for books to read, for paper to write on; to bring letters to frank, having no stamps; for the mail once in a week or two, when it could be obtained; and, if sad news came from home or glad news, came back for him to read their letters and share their joy or sorrow. No other officer stood in any such relation to the men as the chaplain. He did not have to command. There was rivalry among the men to find out his wishes and gratify them. If he was about to go for the mail to the city, there were hosts of things wanted, from a whole suit of officer's clothes by a recently promoted sergeant who was to wear the straps, to a fresh tobacco pouch or new jack-knife for one who missed his old one from its accustomed place. So he came in contact with the soldiers on their warm side, so to speak; and even if they had little respect for his religion, they paid him an outward deference that was very gratifying. In the course of years, as he had opportunity to serve each one in some trivial fashion, there grew up a strong attachment, a little different from that felt for any other officer. A good chaplain must necessarily be a broad man. No chance for successful

The Measure of Ministry

narrowness in any direction, either in theology or conduct. While sympathizing deeply with the men, he must not lose caste with the officers. His tent, if he had one, was in line with theirs. He constantly mingled with them, messed with them, and was one among them. Others might be sick; he must be well. No one could take his place—there was only one of him! Others might be discouraged; he must keep up good heart. Others might be promoted; there was no promotion for him, though Chaplain Trumbull was recommended for promotion to the rank of major for signal service and bravery. Others might be tempted and drawn away in devious paths; he must keep to the straight line all the while. An officer or private, when angry, might swear—once in awhile men did that in the army! The chaplain must not swear; he should be a pattern of obedience, for that principle lay at the foundation of all he taught and believed. He must possess a strong constitution, for all these drafts on his nerves must be unable to stampede him. No officer had opportunity to do more for the real welfare of the regiment than the chaplain. Not to speak of his life and daily example, he was the medium to connect each man with his home, by means of mail coming and going through his hands, and money sent home every pay-day. If Adams Express did not follow up the paymaster he must be an express, and whether carrying $30,000 on his person on an ocean voyage, or $10,000 in his boot-leg on horseback on a solitary ride for 27 miles through the enemy's country, the men expected what they delivered him to be safely landed at home—and it was. At Christmas and Thanksgiving time he must pilot to their owners the scores of boxes from home, containing books, papers, clothing, or fried and baked chicken, that had been on the way three weeks, much of the time in the hold of a vessel around by the Gulf. If the camp was of long continuance he must inaugurate games and gymnastic exercises to enliven the routine. On the march his horse must be loaded with blankets, etc., thrown away by the tired men, for he knew they would need them in the cool of night. In fact, to maintain his position he must stay with the boys. Other officers might desert the camp for a cooler place in some house; he must stick to his tent, and, above all, he must have courage—no skulking in the hour of battle. If he fled to a safe distance then, it was all up with him, so far as his influence for good with that regiment was concerned. He might as well resign and go home. Dress parade chaplains were not wanted in the army. I find the names of eleven chaplains who were killed in battle.

Probably the most fortunate thing that happened to me in the army was to miss my way in a cane field, pass between two regiments that had parted, and ride up on horseback in front of the picket line. Perhaps I should have been going yet if I had not seen a sergeant mount a stump and peer around, and so found from him where I was. Of course he told everybody that night where he found the chaplain, and thus through a blunder in this first engagement my reputation for courage was established. I look back with very great pleasure on nearly three years of army life. No man in my command ever gave me an unkind word, and I think there were scores of them who would have saved my life at the expense of their own. My regiment had no other chaplain. I was never sick or wounded or captured, though having very close calls on several occasions, both in Louisiana and in the Valley. I was able to procure a library and keep it until the enemy wanted it and took it. I found some of the books afterwards in a Sabbath-school library and concluded that they needed them more than we did. I raised money for a band and bought the instruments; generally got something to eat every day, but sometimes missed; dined with rebel officers in Port Hudson, on the last mule tongue, with corn-cob cake; and was able to see more queer, laughable things from day to day than any other officer. I could sleep almost anywhere and at almost any time on the ground, on horseback, on a pile of rails, in a snow-storm, in the mud. I made quite a successful fight against mosquitoes, dor-bugs, and other vermin, though they outnumbered the regiment ten to one. The night I slept in a powder car it did not explode, and when one did tear up half a dozen cars and men and sink the track three feet I was some rods away. I never doubted but I was to come out alive, for I believed in God and my father's prayers, and thought it was my destiny, as it proved.

No more ludicrous scene was enacted in the Louisiana campaign than when, after a march of 25 miles, we halted quite near Bayou Teche, on a very large plantation. The bayou was about 100 feet wide. It was a sultry afternoon, and as soon as the line was dismissed along the bank hundreds of men went for a bath. It happened that in a large field on the other side the stream was a herd of swine feeding, and before long the men were running them down a steep place into the water. Two would have a big porker, who did not relish a bath, and when half-way over he would slip out of the men's hands and travel back, only to be pursued and recaptured. The shouts of the men in the water; the squealing of the swine of all sizes; the cheers of the crowds along the shore for about two miles; the scampering of hundreds of naked men over the field on the other side the bayou; chasing, catching, dragging, and losing the pigs, made up a scene seldom equaled, never repeated, and never forgotten. It was a lively time in camp that night, and long after midnight the laughter of the boys standing around camp-fires, eating fresh pork and hard bread, could be heard along the bayou as they recounted their experiences. The fresh pork tendered the chaplain that night would have lasted him during the remainder of his service. The chaplain was not a fighting man, but he did somewhat enjoy seeing a stout fellow in Company A rush into a crowd of men of the company next in line and scatter them like a flock of sheep because they had trespassed on Company A's rails for cooking supper. About the time he lighted down among them, some five or six men lay sprawled on the ground on four sides of a square. They found it convenient to let those rails alone.

It seems a strange thing to say, in view of sickness, suffering, death, always staring one in the face, but nevertheless it is true—I never saw so much merriment in any other three years of my life as in the army. I am sure I am not heartless, and certainly deeply sympathize with those in trouble of any sort. Perhaps it was necessary to relax one from the stern realities of hospitals, wounds, hardship, and exposure, and to maintain a cheerful spirit. When my horse in jumping a ditch on the way to a funeral slipped and threw me headlong into the soft mud, I could only laugh at the ludicrous figure I presented. When coming up the Mississippi river in the first passenger steamer after the river was opened, when the cry of "Fire!" rang through the boat and a lieutenant on furlough seized his handbag and, pale with fright, rushed through the cabin shouting, "Run her ashore," I could only laugh at him and ask if "he proposed to foot it"! When our captured mule balked in the middle of a crossing, upset the cart and we saw our blackberries floating down the stream with sundry belongings of the hospital equipment, the frightened face of that contraband driver was worth a journey to see. And so it was day by day. How indifferent one got to danger; how hardened to exposure! How impossible in the midst of shot and shell, wounded men, and confusion incident to a battle to impress oneself with its importance any more than with daily life now! Even after the carnage was passed and one went over the field, seeing dead horses and men in every direction, no night-dreams disturbed slumber under the stars; for one was so tired, sleep would quench all visions of misery and hush the sounds of suffering which had been companions all the day.

Oh, the helplessness of man in battle! Just as at sea when the storm roars, if the ship goes down it would seem useless to try to get anywhere, so the very absurdity of trying to find safety in battle no doubt prevented many scared men from running away.

After the fight, when the full moon looked down upon the stillness, to go along the lines of wounded men who suffered in silence, saying a cheering word here and there, securing messages for home and loved ones, and last words of patient heroic souls when the life was ebbing away; to stand over the long trench where, enshrouded in coffinless blankets, lay those who had died that their country might live, and say the well-known words: "I am the resurrection and the life. He that believeth in me, though he were dead, yet shall he live"—the chaplain's message, not to the dead, but to the living—how like a dream all this history appears now! There was no monotony in a chaplain's life. No one could tell what a day might bring forth. When the weather permitted dress parade, he was present, and for a few brief moments the sound of command was hushed, while the voice of prayer for protection, for loved ones at home, for country, for sick and dying comrades, rose on the evening air.

When the dusky servants became eager to imitate the white man in the new-found liberty in founding a home, the chaplain was sent for, and in the captain's tent, in the dim candle-light, when the camp was hushed to rest, with the adjutant and a few lieutenants as witnesses, in the most grave and solemn manner the holy knot was tied—and the usual ceremony of kissing the bride was dispensed with. It was stated that one chaplain in Louisiana spent a part of one Sabbath in digging sweet potatoes, and another one a Sabbath evening in butchering sheep. It is not known whether they had lost their calendar or considered that a work of necessity and mercy. At times a chaplain was called upon to minister to dying Confederates, captured or wounded in battle; at others to follow his own or the men of other regiments who had no chaplain to be deposited in a grave nearly filled with water, and to hear among the dismal swaying gray moss on the trees an owl set up his most plaintive note during the solemn service. He listened to the zip of the bullets and was spattered with mud from an exploding shell during the day, and at night rode for miles to hunt up the lost cooks and get coffee and hard bread for the hungry, growling men at the front. He washed in a retired pool his only red shirt, and while it dried in the sunshine tried with the same water to discover his own skin. He volunteered to bring up the paymaster, who had not been seen for months, starting down the railroad on a platform car in the night, pushed by an engine with only one side in working order, and in the darkness ran into the approaching paymaster on a hand-car, scattering his greenbacks for rods along the track, but fortunately, by the aid of lanterns, recovering enough to balance his cash minus a few cents. He rode captured horses in the night to try their mettle, because the major was a little timid. He bought eggs for the boys by the barrel, and the tub of oranges in his tent-door was free to all while they lasted. When his horse was captured he could go on foot, meanwhile admiring those laws in some Western States that hang men for stealing horses. He could scout around a deserted colored camp to find four bodies left behind unburied, and spend the closing hours of a beautiful Sabbath in placing them decently beneath the sod, or spend the same holy hours in planting a hedge of evergreens about the mound where were laid more than twenty fallen comrades, representatives of ten companies, who fell in a few moments along the pike in that sharp morning fight. A fitting spot for a soldier's monument! He could speak to the men, formed into a hollow square, of the land of perfect peace, the abode where hunger and thirst are unknown, and "where God shall wipe away the tears from every eye;" or, standing on a box, address swarms of the dusky race, who had taken refuge in camp, fleeing, some of them, with shot in their backs or iron collars about their necks or ankles, from the only place they had known as home, to go they knew not where—speak to them of a life of freedom and a home from which they should go no more out forever. So, with varied duties, always busy, the days and weeks, summer and winter, flew by until the end came, the term of service closed, and friendships were welded in that strange life never to be forgotten. Like all our army life, these scenes seem unreal, like tales of adventure we have sometimes read in a book long ago; and it requires an effort to believe that this great prosperous country of ours was ever so enshrouded in gloom.

Stories of what the chaplain did, and what the army mule did, have passed together into history. How the former prayed and the latter brayed have sometimes pointed a story; but if all the work and influence and life of the chaplains of the volunteer army could be blotted out of history, there would be left a blank not less conspicuous than that of the same number of officers of equal rank in any part of the service. The form of the chaplain is not represented in bronze, or marble, or stone, but he will live in the hearts of some who knew him in the dark days of war, and if stories are sometimes told to his discredit—which doubtless have some foundation—until the last comrade is laid away and the last word of peace chanted over his grave the chaplain's work will not be done, or his deeds forgotten. In so far as the chaplains, with all their failures and frailties—for they are very human—helped on the cause represented by the dear old flag, they rejoice, if still alive; and if they have followed the long line of their fellow-soldiers into the realms of the unknown, I may safely affirm that they never saw the day they were sorry to have had the experience of a few months or a few years in the volunteer army of '61 to '65.

Appendix

Biographical Anecdotes of Chaplain P. G. Cook, Presbyterian,

94th New York Volunteer Infantry

The Burial of a Hero
Before the train had completely halted at the Exchange Street station, Chaplain Cook alighted on the platform to oversee removal of a metal coffin from the baggage car. The remains of Major Henry H. Fish had returned home over the Erie railroad, filling the depot with sad scenes that were all too familiar after four years of war. His black wools rumpled from days on trains, he nevertheless managed an erect military posture as the escort—a detachment from Buffalo's 74th New York National Guard—took charge of the casket. The company's flag was wrapped closely around its staff and draped in mourning, and as the soldiers took up their line of march with reversed arms and solemn step, Cook could not but feel sick of the rebellion.

Yet Chaplain Philos G. Cook also felt great joy. It was a most wonderful thing to stand before his wife and children in April 1865. Having gone off to the army in 1862 at the age of fifty-five, it was a tribute to his durability and his faith that he had lasted this long. His regiment—the 94th New York—was with the 5th Corps, under General Griffin. The boys were likely marching over miserable roads somewhere west of Petersburg, moving to a place where, God willing, Lee's army would soon be defeated.

The mission which granted the chaplain a brief visit with his family was one which brought untold grief for two others because he brought them the bodies of two young members of the 94th who had fallen during the 1 April 1865 battle of Five

Forks. Major Henry Fish was a Buffalo boy and Captain George French was a Canadian who had settled in Rochester.[1] *The major was twenty-two and the captain twenty-three.*

In August 1862, before Cook had signed on, Henry Fish joined western New York's 105th regiment as a private. He was scarcely nineteen and his father had to sign a consent for his enlistment, but the boy was cited for gallantry at South Mountain, became a captain after Gettysburg, and soon rose to the unit's majority.[2]

On 31 March, in the fighting at Gravelly Run, Major Fish was knocked from his horse and stunned by a ball that grazed his head. Although such a wound could have excused him, he stayed with his men. Chaplain Cook finally convinced him to go to a hospital in the rear, where his wound was dressed and he was able to get some sleep. Henry wrote a letter to his friends that evening, in which he stated that his wound was slight and that he planned to go into the field the next morning. "Our old flag is to be given to the ladies of Jefferson County this week," he told them, "and we are already hard at work getting holes made in the new one."

At ten o'clock the following morning, Major Fish rode back to the front, and again his aged chaplain protested earnestly against going into battle. Chaplain Cook wrote, "But the brave young soldier refused to consider my advice. He could not waive the opportunity to lead the 94th in action. He had hungered and thirsted for that privilege, and nothing would deter him. The order for the Fifth Corps to advance was finally given, and away went the brave boys to charge the enemy's breastworks in front of the Southside Railroad, six miles distant." Major Fish rode ahead of his men and his colors. At one point, the 94th's national banner was torn in two by enemy fire. Their major wound the loose half around his neck and rode

---

[1] George French was a farmer born in Canada who joined the 105th New York Infantry at Rochester NY on 12 November 1861 at the age of nineteen. He rose in the ranks, was elected first sergeant of Company H in December 1861, and mustered as second lieutenant 22 September 1862. During March 1863, the 105th was consolidated with the 94th New York Volunteers, and Lt. French was assigned to Company G. He was mustered 10 May 1864 as first lieutenant. Captured 19 August at the Weldon Railroad, he was paroled in October "due to belief he was near death with constant fevers." Military Service File of George French, RG 94, Records of the Veterans Administration, National Archives, Washington DC. Promoted to captain while on leave after his release by the Confederates, he rejoined the 94th New York later that month.

[2] "How He Fell. Major Henry H. Fish of the 94th N. Y. V. at Five Forks," *Buffalo* (NY) *Commercial Advertiser*, 13 April 1865, 3. All subsequent details about Fish are from this article unless otherwise noted.

on. *Emerging from a wood, he encountered a breastwork manned by the enemy. A bullet struck him square in the head, and he was dead on the ground before his regiment came up.*

Cook reported, *"It was quite dark by the time that our advance halted. I listened for the voices calling units to rally. 'This way, 91st!' 'This way, 56th!' 'Come here, 39th Massachusetts!' But there was no voice calling for the 94th. I eventually encountered Lieutenant J. D. Holley, who told me that Major Fish had fallen and that he was probably buried.[3] But I could not let that be. I made the Lieutenant lead me back to where the Major fell and we pulled his body from a fresh and shallow grave. I carried it back on my horse." "By the afternoon of April 2, I was at Humphrey Station, from where the wounded and dead are transported to City Point. I fashioned coffins using wood stripped from a barn. Major Fish and Captain French were good fellows and brave officers—I could not bear to leave their mortal remains in the rebel dust of Virginia. My intentions were supported by Medical Officer Parker at City Point, and he obtained my pass from Lieutenant General Grant."[4] The bodies were embalmed at City Point and "placed in proper coffins." It took nearly three days and four trains to get back to Buffalo.*

Chaplain Cook buried Major Fish in the city's Forest Lawn Cemetery one week from the hour that he had led the 94th into action. A newspaper account recalled some of the chaplain's graveside words: "I will never forget the boy major, with the colors wound above his heart, leading his men to the charge. 'Died in battle for the Union at Five Forks.' No prouder epitaph need any man desire."

A Pastor and Social Worker

The following entry, from a history of Buffalo and Niagara Falls churches, provides an accurate summary of P. G. Cook's postwar activities. It is difficult to imagine that this description starts when Cook is nearly sixty.

---

[3] Born at Pierrepont Manor, Jefferson County NY, Holley was a twenty-four-year-old farmer who joined the 94th New York Volunteers at Sackets Harbor on 30 November 1861 as a corporal in Co. B. Promoted to sergeant when he re-enlisted 4 January 1864, he was promoted 19 March 1865 to second lieutenant of Co. C and first lieutenant of Co. B on 13 June 1865.

[4] Surgeon George B. Parker, US Volunteers, acting chief medical officer, Army of the Potomac, had started his army career 4 September 1862 as assistant regimental surgeon of the 42nd New York Volunteers. Promoted 4 August 1863 to assistant surgeon USV and surgeon USV on 30 June 1864, he was given the brevet rank of lieutenant-colonel USV effective 28 October 1865 in recognition of his service. He was mustered out 3 November 1865.

Until the death of this Christian philanthropist, there were doubtless few men in Buffalo more widely known, and none more favorably, than Philos G. Cook, familiarly known for many years as "Chaplain Cook," who for half a century labored in this part of the Lord's vineyard and accomplished grand work among the poor and lowly of the city…Like John Alden of the pilgrim fathers' days, he excelled as a writer of letters, and his communications from the front to the Buffalo newspapers were eagerly looked for by those who had friends in the field. His army experience made him a host of friends who were steadfast through life.

From 1865 to 1870, Chaplain Cook served as missionary for the Y. M. C. A., and while thus engaged he established the Wells Street Sunday-school, which grew rapidly and soon became the largest and most widely-known mission of the city. The Wells Street church was subsequently organized with Chaplain Cook as pastor, and to this charge he gave the best efforts of his life, receiving in return the love and devotion of its members.

His chief characteristics were love for his fellow-men, a cheerful disposition, and great physical endurance, and he possessed a clear voice which was of great value in his mission work. At 8:30 A.M., he started every Sunday with his faithful horse "Billy" for a service at the penitentiary, where he was both chorister and preacher, at the age of seventy years. At 10:30 A.M., he preached in his own church, afterwards distributing religious papers in the streets and saloons. At 2:30 P.M., he conducted a large Sunday-school, in which the singing was a most prominent feature, and from there he went to Canal Street, where, mounted on a store box, he sang, prayed, and preached to the crowds in the open air. After a short rest at home he again held service in his church, which often consisted of three parts: singing, a sermon, and 'after-meeting.' His Saturdays were devoted to his pulpit preparation, and the other five days he was busily engaged in pastoral work.

For years he went, accompanied by ladies, to Buffalo General Hospital, where many weary invalids were cheered by a song-service, and no Sabbath-school convention or gathering in the city, county, or State was considered complete without his presence.

During 1881, Buffalo's Camp Number 233 of the Sons of Union Veterans of the Civil War was named in honor of Chaplain P. G. Cook. Rev. Cook organized several missions and homes for the friendless, and his knowledge and good judgment in charitable work gave him the confidence of the substantial business men of the city, who entrusted him with large sums of money to carry on his noble work among the poor and afflicted. He was constantly engaged in visiting families in need, supplying the wants of the poor, his special care being children, and, as one writer has said, "he was the only minister of the Gospel known to an immense section of Buffalo's population." By the gentlest and kindliest methods and the sincerity of his life he overcame opposition, and it was impossible to doubt Chaplain Cook's honesty of purpose. He died in 1895.

Bibliography

Primary Sources

Manuscripts and Record Collections

Bradford, James Henry. Service and Pension Case Files, Record Groups 94 and 15, Records of the Veterans Administration, National Archives, Washington DC.

Collins, Gamaliel. Service and Pension Case Files, Record Groups 94 and 15, Records of the Veterans Administration, National Archives, Washington DC.

Gregg, John Chandler. Pension Case File, Record Group 15, Records of the Veterans Administration, National Archives, Washington DC.

Military History Institute Library. Civil War Documents and Photographic Archives, Carlisle PA.

Norton, Levi W. Pension Case Files, Record Groups 94 and 15, Records of the Veterans Administration, National Archives, Washington DC.

Ross, Randall. Service File, Record Groups 94, Records of the Veterans Administration, National Archives, Washington DC.

Books and Articles

Abbott, Chaplain Stephen G. *The First Regiment New Hampshire Volunteers in the Great Rebellion.* Keene: Sentinel Print Co., 1890.

Adams, John M. and Albert E. Adams. *Memorial and Letters of Rev. John Ripley Adams, Chaplain of the Fifth Maine and the One hundred and Twenty-First New York Regiments.* Cambridge: University Press, 1890.

Beaudry, Richard E., ed. *War Journal of Louis N. Beaudry, Fifth New York Cavalry.* Jefferson NC: McFarland & Company, Inc., Publishers, 1996.

Bentley, William H. *History of the 77th Illinois Volunteer Infantry.* Peoria: Edward Hine, Printer, 1883.

Boudrye, Chaplain Louis N. *Historic Records of the Fifth New York Cavalry.* Albany: S. R. Gray, 1865.

Chidlaw Family. *Sunset & Morning Star: Rev. Benjamin Williams Chidlaw, D.D.* Utica NY: Press of T. J. Griffiths, 1894.

Craft, Chaplain David. *History of the One Hundred Forty-First Regiment, Pennsylvania Volunteers.* Towanda: Reporter-Journal Print Co., 1885.

Cudworth, Chaplain Warren Handel. *History of the First Regiment Massachusetts Infantry.* Boston: Walker, Fuller and Co., 1866.

Eastman, Chaplain William Reed. "The Army Chaplain of 1863." M.O.L.L.U.S. talk, New York, 13 December 1911.

Eaton, Chaplain John. *Grant, Lincoln and the Freedmen: Reminiscences of the Civil War.* New York: Longmans, Green, and Co., 1907.

Eddy, Chaplain Richard. *History of the Sixtieth Regiment, New York State Volunteers.* Philadelphia: Crissy & Markley, Printers, 1864.

Fisher, Chaplain Hugh Dunn. *The Gun and the Gospel: Early Kansas and Chaplain Fisher.* Kansas City: Hudson-Kimberly Publishing Co., 1902.

Fuller, Richard B. *Chaplain Fuller: Being A Life Sketch of a New England Clergyman and Army Chaplain.* Boston: Walker, Wise and Co., 1864.

Gage, Chaplain Moses D. *From Vicksburg to Raleigh; or, A Complete History of the Twelfth Regiment Indiana Volunteer Infantry.* Chicago: Clarke & Co., 1865.

Germain, Dom Aidan Henry. "Catholic Military & Naval Chaplains: 1776–1917." Ph.D. dissertation, Catholic University of America, 1929.

Gracey, Chaplain Samuel Levis. *Annals of the Sixth Pennsylvania Cavalry.* Philadelphia: E. H. Butler & Co., 1868.

Gregg, John Chandler. *Life in the Army, in the Departments of Virginia, and the Gulf, Including Observations in New Orleans, with an Account of the Author's Life and Experience in the Ministry.* Philadelphia: Perkinpine & Higgins, 1866.

Haines, Chaplain Alanson Austin. *History of the Fifteenth Regiment New Jersey Volunteers.* New York: Jenkins & Thomas, Printers, 1883.

Hamilton, Edward J. "A Union Chaplain's Diary." *Proceedings of The New Jersey Historical Society* (January 1957): 1–17.

Hammond, Rev. Jonathan Pinkney, MA. *Army Chaplain's Manual: Designed as a Help to Chaplains in the Discharge of Their Various Duties.* Philadelphia: n.p., 1863.

Harwell, Richard and Philip N. Racine, eds. *The Fiery Trial: A Union Officer's Account of Sherman's Last Campaigns.* Knoxville: University of Tennessee Press, 1986.

Haynes, Chaplain Edwin Mortimer. *A History of the Tenth Regiment, Vermont Volunteers.* Lewiston ME: Journal Steam Press, 1870.

Hepworth, George H. *The Whip, Hoe, and Sword; or the Gulf Department in '63.* Boston: Walker, Wise and Company, 1864.

Hincks, Elizabeth Eaton. *Undismayed: The Story Of A Yankee Chaplain's Family In The Civil War.* Privately printed, 1952.

Hudson, Chaplain Henry Norman. *A Chaplain's Campaign with General Butler.* New York: n.p., 1865.

Hudson, Chaplain Henry Norman. *General Butler's Campaign on the Hudson.* Boston: J. S. Cushing & Co., 1883.

Johnston, Marianne C. *The Young Chaplain.* New York: N. Tribbals, 1876.

Locke, Chaplain William Henry. *The Story of the Regiment.* Philadelphia: J.B. Lippincott & Co., 1868.

Lucas, Chaplain Daniel R. *History of the 99th Indiana Infantry.* Lafayette: Rosser & Spring, Printers, 1865.

Mann, Albert W. *The History Of The Forty-Fifth Regiment, Massachusetts Volunteer Militia.* Boston: Wallace Spooner, 1908.

Marks, Chaplain Junius J. *The Peninsular Campaign in Virginia.* Philadelphia: J. B. Lippincott & Co., 1864.

Merrill, Chaplain Samuel Hill. *The Campaigns of the First Maine and First District of Columbia Cavalry.* Portland: Bailey & Noyes, 1866.

Mickley, Chaplain Jeremiah Marion. *The Forty-Third Regiment USCT.* Gettysburg: Wible, 1866.

Moors, Chaplain John Farwell. *History of the Fifty-Second Regiment Massachusetts Volunteers.* Boston: Press of George H. Ellis, 1893.

Morrison, Chaplain Marion. *A History of the Ninth Regiment Illinois Volunteer Infantry.* Monmouth: John S. Clark, Printer, 1864.

Muffly, Joseph W. *The Story of Our Regiment: A History of the 148th Pennsylvania Volunteers.* Des Moines IA: Kenyon Print & Mfg. Co., 1904.

Murphey, Chaplain Thomas Grier. *Four Years in the War, The History of the First Regiment of Delaware Veteran Volunteers.* Philadelphia: James S. Claxton, 1866.

Pepper, Chaplain George Whitefield. *Personal Recollections of Sherman's Campaigns in Georgia and Carolinas.* Zanesville OH: Hugh Dunne, 1866.

Phelps, Ethel Lowerre. *A Chaplain's Life in the Civil War.* Privately printed, 1945.
Pyne, Chaplain Henry Rogers. *The History of the First New Jersey Cavalry.* Trenton: J. A. Beecher, 1871.
Raup, Hallock F., ed. *Letters of a Pennsylvania Chaplain at the Siege of Petersburg.* London: The Eden Press, 1961.
Redkey, Edwin S. "Black Chaplains in the Union Army." *Civil War History* 33/4 (December 1987): 331–51.
Sherman, William T. *Memoirs of General William T. Sherman.* New York: Da Capo Press, 1984.
Simmons, Chaplain John T. *History of the Twenty-Eighth Iowa Volunteer Infantry.* Washington: William H. Moore, 1865.
Smith, George W. *Memoir of John Visger Van Ingen.* Rochester: Scrantom, Wetmore & Co., 1878.
Stevenson, Chaplain Thomas M. *History of the 78th Regiment Ohio Veteran Volunteer Infantry.* Zanesville OH: Hugh Dunne, 1865.
Stormont, Gilbert R. *History of the Fifty-Eighth Regiment of Indiana Volunteer Infantry.* Princeton: Press of the Clarion, 1895.
Taffe, Thomas G., ed. "A Year With The Army Of The Potomac—Reverend Peter Tissot, S.J." *U. S. Catholic Historical Society Records & Studies.* (January1903): 3.
U.S. House of Representatives. *Journal of the U.S. House of Representatives,* 37th Congress, 2nd Session. Washington: Government Printing Office, 1863.
Walker, Chaplain William Carey. *History of the 18th Regiment Connecticut Volunteers in the War for the Union.* Norwich: Gordon Wilcox, 1885.
War Department. *Revised United States Army Regulations of 1861.* Washington: Government Printing Office, 1863.
Windsor, Chaplain Anthony H. *History of the Ninety-First Regiment, Ohio Volunteers.* Cincinnati: Gazette Printing House, 1865.
Woodbury, Chaplain Augustus. *A Narrative of the Campaign of the First Rhode Island Regt in the Spring and Summer of 1861.* Providence: Sidney S. Rider, 1862.
Wright, Chaplain J.E.M. "From Petersburg to Appomattox Court House." *Maine Bugle* (1894): 115–23.
Wyatt, Chaplain William. *The Life and Sermons of Reverend William Wyatt.* Albany: Chas. Van Benthuysen and Sons, 1878.

Secondary Materials

Appleton's Cyclopedia of American Biography, 6 vols. New York: The Press Association Compilers, Inc., 1915.

Armstrong, Warren Bruce. "The Organization, Function, and Contribution of the Chaplaincy in the United States Army, 1861–1865." Ph.D. dissertation, University of Michigan, 1964.

Brinsfield, John W. "In the Pulpit and in the Trenches," *Civil War Times Illustrated* (September/October 1992).

Coulter, E. Merton. *The Confederate States of America*. Baton Rouge: Louisiana State University Press, 1950.

Daniel, Larry J. *Shiloh: The Battle That Changed the Civil War*. New York: Simon and Schuster, 1997.

Davis, Burke. *Sherman's March*. New York: Random House, 1980.

Davis, William C. et al. *Faith in the Fight: Civil War Chaplains*. Mechanicsburg PA: Stackpole Books, 2003.

Gladstone, William A. *United States Colored Troops 1863–1867*. Gettysburg PA: Thomas Publications, 1990.

Glatthaar, Joseph T. *The March to the Sea and Beyond*. New York: New York University Press, 1986.

Hankinson, Alan. *Vicksburg, 1863*. London: Osprey Publishing Ltd., 1993.

Hicks, Roger W. and Frances E. Schultz. *Battlefields of the Civil War*. Topsfield MA: Salem House, 1989.

Luvaas, Jay and Harold W. Nelson. *Guide to the Battle of Gettysburg*. Lawrence: University Press of Kansas, 1994.

Maryniak, Benedict. "Their Faith Brings Them." *Civil War Times Illustrated* (March/April 1991).

Piston, William Garrett and Richard W. Hatcher III. *Wilson's Creek: The Second Battle of the Civil War*. Chapel Hill: University of North Carolina Press, 2000.

Shanahan, Edward P. *Chickamauga Staff Ride Briefing Book*. Atlanta GA: Office of the Command Historian, US Army Reserve Command, 1995.

———. *Atlanta Campaign Staff Ride Briefing Book*. Atlanta GA: Office Of the Command Historian, US Army Reserve Command, 1995.

The Declaration of Independence and the Constitution of the United States with an introduction by Pauline Maier. New York: Bantam Books, 1998.

Yale University. *Obituary Record of Graduates*. New Haven: Yale University, p. 430.

Index

Abercrombie, Brigadier General John J., 102
Allen, Chaplain Michael Meir, 2
Ambler, Chaplain Edward C., 186
American Sunday School Union, 236
Ames, Chaplain Lyman Daniel, 39
Andrews, Colonel Christopher C., 227-228
Arnold, Major General Olney, 105
Ashby, Colonel Turner, 55
Augustine, Lieutenant Colonel Jacob M., 161, 164

Ball, Colonel William H., 185
Ballou, Major Sullivan, 105
Banks, Major General Nathaniel P., 56, 102, 108
Barber, Chaplain Lorenzo D., 104
Barritt, Frederick, 81
Battle Hymn of the Republic, 186
Battle of Atlanta, 165-166
Battle of Ball's Bluff, 35
Battle of Chickamauga, 138-143
Battle of Cold Harbor, 25
Battle of Five Forks, 252-253
Battle of Fredericksburg, 126-129
Battle of Groveton, 109
Battle of Kernstown, 55
Battle of Roanoke Island, 59
Battle of Second Bull Run, 109
Battle of Shiloh, 146-150
Beauregard, General Pierre Gustave Toutant, 146
Beecher, Catharine, 75
Beecher, Chaplain James Chaplin, 75

Beecher, Chaplain Thomas Kinnicut, 75-85
Beecher, Edward, 76
Beecher, Isabella, 75
Beecher, Rev. George, 75
Beecher, Rev. Henry Ward, 27, 75
Beecher, Rev. Lyman, 75
Benton, Chaplain Orlando Newell, 99
Bermuda Hundred, 47, 58
Billingsley, Chaplain Amos, 39, 212-218
Black, Chaplain William H., 97
Border, Colonel John P., 210
Bradford, Chaplain James Henry, 239, 240-249
Brady, Chaplain Ebenezer Walker, 186
Bragg, General Braxton, 146
Brayton, Colonel Charles R., 102
Breckinridge, Major General John Cabell, 146
Brown, Chaplain Joseph T., 186
Brown, Chaplain Thomas Gibson, 197, 241
Browne, Junius Henri, 194
Buchanan, President James, 67
Buckingham, Brigadier General Catharinus Putnam, 49
Buckley, Assistant Surgeon William C., 200
Buell, Major General Don Carlos, 148
Burstenbinder, Colonel Otto, 47, 52
Bushnell, Rev. Horace, 76

Butler, Major General Benjamin Franklin, 25, 58

Camp calls, 38, 39
Camp Chase, 48
Camp Dennison, 48
chaplain casualties, xvi
Chaplain School, U.S. Army, 58
Chaplin, Lieutenant Commander James Crossan, 115
Chase, Bishop Philander, 17
Chase, Salmon Portland, 17
Cherry Hill Methodist Church, 186
Chevaux de fries, 69
Christian Commission, 33, 83, 97, 186, 232
Clark, Chaplain Edward W., 27
Clark, Chaplain Orson B., 6
Cobb, Brigadier General Howell, 67
Collins, Chaplain Gamaliel, 34-36
Colporteurs, 19
Colt, Colonel Samuel, xiii
Commutation, 22
Conscription, 22
Cook, Chaplain Philos Gunikos, 251-255
Cooney, Chaplain Peter Paul, 86-92, 97
Cooper, General Samuel, 197
Corby, Chaplain William, 134-137
Crabbs, Chaplain John, 39, 47-58
Crouch, Chaplain Lewis P., 145
Crowninshield, Major Casper, 220
Curtiss, Rev. Smith, 47

da Saracena, Brother Leo Rizzo, 241
Denison, Chaplain Frederic, 101-121
Denominations of Civil War chaplains, xv
Devall's Bluff, 228
Di Cesnola, Lieutenant Colonel Luigi Palma, 190
Dix, Major General John Adams, 196
Dixon, Chaplain Charles, 241
Dodd, Chaplain Stephen Grover, 59

Dow, Brigadier General Neal, 196
Duffie, Colonel Alfred Nattie, 102, 107, 108

Early, Major General Jubal Anderson, 189, 219
Eaton, Chaplain Jacob, 241
Eberhart, Chaplain David Christian, 186
Edwards, Chaplain Elijah Evan, 225
Eighth Connecticut Infantry Regiment, 13, 241
Eighth Illinois Cavalry Regiment, 238
Eighth Kentucky Cavalry Regiment, 2
Eighth Massachusetts Infantry Regiment, 238
Eighty-Eighth Illinois Infantry Regiment, 96
Eighty-Eighth New York Infantry Regiment, 134
Eighty-First Indiana Infantry Regiment, 97
Eighty-Seventh Pennsylvania Infantry Regiment, 186
Eighty-Sixth New York Infantry Regiment, 179
Eighty-Third Pennsylvania Infantry Regiment, 6
Eleventh New Jersey Infantry Regiment, 40, 179
Eleventh New York Cavalry Regiment, 190
Eleventh Ohio Infantry Regiment, 138, 140, 141
Ellett, Colonel Charles, Jr., 70
Ellsworth, Colonel Ephraim Elmer, 69
Ewell, Lieutenant General Richard Stoddert, 186

Fallows, Chaplain Samuel, 238
Fearing, Colonel Benjamin D., 138
Ferris, Chaplain Charles G., 186

Field confessional, 89
Fifteenth Indiana Infantry Regiment, xvi
Fifteenth Ohio Infantry Regiment, 172
Fifth Minnesota Infantry Regiment, 238
Fifth Pennsylvania Cavalry Regiment, 2
Fifth Rhode Island Heavy Artillery Regiment, 117
Fifty-Fifth Illinois Infantry Regiment, 39, 99, 145-171
Fifty-First Indiana Infantry Regiment, 195
Fifty-First New York Infantry Regiment, 99
Fifty-Second Massachusetts Infantry Regiment, 12
First New York Engineer Regiment, 114
First Regiment U.S.C.T., 184
First Rhode Island Cavalry Regiment, 101-121
First Rhode Island Light Artillery Regiment, 3
First Wisconsin Heavy Artillery Regiment, xvi
Fish, Major Henry H., 251
Floyd, Brigadier General John Buchanan, 67
Ford, Captain Hyatt G., 52
Fort Stedman, 179
Fortieth Infantry Regiment U.S.C.T., 97
Forty-Fourth Massachusetts Infantry Regiment, 8
Forty-Seventh Massachusetts Infantry Regiment, 27
Forty-Sixth Indiana Infantry Regiment, 208
Foster, Major Everett W., 227
Foster, Major General John Gray, 102

Fourteenth Wisconsin Infantry Regiment, 1
Fox, Captain William, 128
Fox, Chaplain Norman, 238
Frankel, Chaplain Jacob, 2
Franklin, Major General William Buel, 128
French, Captain George, 252
Fuller, Chaplain Arthur Buckminster, xiii, 128

Gallaudet, Alice, 233
Garnett, Brigadier General Richard Brooke, 55
Geneva Convention, 118
Gillmore, Major General Quincy Adams, 102
Glenn, Chaplain John D., 212
Gordon, Major General John Brown, 179, 189
Gore, Surgeon Joel R., 156
Gough, John B. 199
Grant, General U. S., 151-154
Greble, Lieutenant Colonel John Trout, 69
Gregg, Chaplain John Chandler, 126-133
Grosvenor, Assistant Surgeon Joseph W., 114

Hall, Chaplain Edward Henry, 8, 10
Hall, Chaplain Francis Bloodgood, xvi
Hall, Chaplain Henry L., 234
Halpine, Charles Graham, 112
Hammer, Chaplain George H., 186
Haney, Chaplain Milton Lorenzo, xvi, 39, 99, 145-171
Haney, Chaplain Richard, 145
Haney, Sergeant Richard, 156
Hardee, Lieutenant General William Joseph, 146
Harvey, Chaplain James, 186
Haven, Chaplain Gilbert Haven, 238

Hepworth, Chaplain George
  Hughes, xiii, 26, 27, 28
Hill, Chaplain James Hill, xvi
Hobart, Chaplain Chauncey, 220-222
Hobart, Ella (*aka* Ellen Elvira
  Gibson), xvi
Hoke, Brigadier General Robert
  Frederick, 212
Holley, Second Lieutenant J. D., 253
Hood, Lieutenant General John Bell,
  165
Hooker, Major General Joseph, 102
Hospital chaplains of U. S.
  Volunteers, 182-183, 220
Houston, Assistant Surgeon William
  M., 188, 192
Howard, Major General Oliver Otis,
  131
Howe, Julia Ward, xi, 1, 98, 182, 186,
  238
Howell, Chaplain Horatio Stockton,
  99, 109
Hudson, Chaplain Henry Norman,
  113
Humphreys, Chaplain Charles
  Alfred, 5, 8, 10, 12, 219-220
Hutcherson, Chaplain Francis A., 97

Immortal Six Hundred, 118
Ireland, Chaplain John, 238

Jamaica ginger, 32
James, Chaplain Horace. 39, 59-74
Jaquess, Colonel James Frazier, 99
Jennings, Colonel William W., 128
Johnson, Major General Edward, 186
Johnston, General Albert Sidney, 146
Jones, Colonel William G., 138
Jordan, Brigadier General Thomas,
  233
Keith, Chaplain William K., 53
Kimball, Brigadier General Nathan,
  55, 86
Klinck, Captain John G., 48

Lander, Brigadier General Frederick
  West, 54, 69
Lane, Chaplain Andrew J., 53
Lane, Colonel Philander P., 138
Lawton, Colonel Robert B., 102
Leek, Chaplain John Wickliffe, 241
Libby Prison, 185-198, 234
Light, Chaplain Oliver P., 225-226
Lightburn, Brigadier General Joseph
  Andrew Jackson, 150
Lincoln, President Abraham, xii – xiv,
  xvi, 184, 197
Livermore, Mary Ashton, 34
Lyle, Chaplain William W., 138-144
Lyon, Brigadier General Nathaniel,
  69

Malmborg, Colonel Oscar, 161
McCabe, Chaplain Charles Cardwell,
  185-203, 238
McClellan, Major General George
  Brinton, 47, 102
McClernand, Major General John
  Alexander, 151
McCulloch, Chaplain John Scouller,
  204-211
McDowell, Major General Irvin, xiv,
  102, 107,
McPherson, Major General James
  Birdseye, 165, 166
McRae, Brigadier General
  Dandridge, 228
Medal of Honor, xvi, 99, 145, 168,
  198
Melville, Herman, 4
Metcalf, Colonel Edwin, 102
Military Order of the Loyal Legion
  of the United States (MOLLUS),
  239-240
Milroy, Major General Robert
  Huston, 187-188
Mitchel, Major General Ormsby
  McKnight, 113
Moon, Private S. Dallas, 52
Moore, Governor Thomas, xi

Moors, Chaplain John Farwell, 12
Moreau, Rev. Basil, 86
Morris, Chaplain John Moses., 13
Morrow, Chaplain James M., 95
Mosby's Confederacy, 219
Mullen, Colonel Bernard F., 86
Murray, Sculptor Samuel Aloysius, 134

Ninetieth Pennsylvania Infantry Regiment, 99, 109
Ninety-Fourth New York Infantry Regiment, 251-253
Ninth Connecticut Infantry Regiment, 241
Norton, Chaplain Levi Warren, 43-46

One Hundred and Fifth New York Infantry, 252
One Hundred and First Pennsylvania Infantry Regiment, 39, 212
One Hundred and Forty-Fifth Pennsylvania Infantry Regiment, 99
One Hundred and Forty-First New York Infantry Regiment, 75, 76
One Hundred and Sixteenth Ohio Infantry Regiment, 186
One Hundred and Tenth Ohio Infantry Regiment, 186
One Hundred and Twenty-Second Ohio Infantry Regiment, 185
One Hundred and Twenty-Seventh Illinois Infantry Regiment, 156
One Hundred and Twenty-Seventh Pennsylvania Infantry Regiment, 126
One Hundred and Twenty-Third Ohio Infantry Regiment, 186

Parker, Surgeon George B., 253
Pay of chaplain, xv, 31, 49, 83
Pemberton, Lieutenant General John Clifford, 197

Pentecost, Chaplain George F., 2
Pierpont, Chaplain John, 2
Plaisted, Colonel Harris M., 233
Polk, Lieutenant General Leonidas, 145
Pond, Colonel Francis B., 53
Pope, Major General John, 102, 110
Porter, Harriet, 75
Poucher, Chaplain John, 97
Powell, Major General William Henry, 198
Preacher's Regiment, 99
Prentiss, Major General Benjamin Mayberry, 146
Presson, Quartermaster Sergeant Joseph H., 161
Price, Major General Sterling, 229
Putnam, Chaplain Simeon, 227-230

Quinn, Chaplain Thomas, 3
Quint, Chaplain Alonzo Hall, 39, 122-125

Rations, 51
Reports by chaplains, 219-232
Reynolds, Major General Joseph Jones, 138
Rinker, Chaplain Henry, 40, 179-181
Robb, Chaplain Hamilton, 208
Robie, Chaplain John E., 28-33
Rogers, Chaplain James B., 1, 257
Roller, Surgeon Edward O. F., 147
Rosecrans, Major General William Starke, 87
Ross, Chaplain Randall, 172-178
Rothrock, Sergeant John M., 48

Saint Patrick's Day celebration, 130
Sanitary Commission, 83, 232
Saxton, Major General Rufus, 113
Sayles, Lieutenant Colonel Willard, 102
Second Massachusetts Cavalry Regiment, 5, 10, 219-220

Second Massachusetts Infantry Regiment, 39
Second Rhode Island Infantry Regiment, 105
Second U. S. V. Sharpshooter Regiment, 104
Second West Virginia Cavalry Regiment, 198
Seventh Connecticut Infantry Regiment, 119, 241
Seventh Maryland Infantry Regiment, 53
Seventh Minnesota Infantry Regiment, 225
Seventy-Fourth New York National Guard, 251
Seventy-Second New York Infantry Regiment, 43
Seventy-Second Pennsylvania Infantry Regiment, 34
Seventy-Seventh Illinois Infantry Regiment, 204
Seventy-Seventh New York Infantry Regiment, 238
Seventy-Sixth Infantry Regiment U.S.C.T., 27
Seventy-Third Illinois Infantry Regiment, 99
Sherman, General William Tecumseh, xi, xii, xiii, 151-157, 172
Shields, Brigadier General James, 47, 55
Sickles, Major General Daniel, 43
Siege of Petersburg, 25
Sisters of the Holy Cross, 88
Sixteenth Illinois Infantry Regiment, 145
Sixteenth Massachusetts Infantry Regiment, 128
Sixteenth New York Infantry Regiment, xvi
Sixth Maryland Infantry Regiment, 186

Sixty-Eighth Regiment of New York State Militia, 43
Sixty-Ninth New York Infantry Regiment, 130
Sixty-Second Ohio Infantry Regiment, 53
Sixty-Seventh New York Infantry Regiment, 75
Sixty-Seventh Ohio Infantry Regiment, 39
Sixty-Seventh Pennsylvania Infantry Regiment, 186
Smith, Chaplain Moses, 13
Smith, General Edmund Kirby, 212
Sons of Union Veterans of the Civil War, 254
Sorin, Rev. Edward, 86
Spear, Chaplain Charles, 223-224
Spencer, Chaplain William A., 238
Sprague, Governor William, 105
Stanley, Major General David Sloan, 90, 91
Stanton, Secretary of War Edwin M., 4, 98, 171
Stoughton, Chaplain Jonathan C., 156
Stowe, Harriet Beecher, 75
Streight, Colonel Abel D., 195
Stuckenberg, Chaplain John Henry Wilbrandt, 99
Substitutes, 22

Taylor, Benjamin Franklin, 93-97
Taylor, Lieutenant James P., 108
Taylor, Major General Richard, 204
Tenth Connecticut Infantry Regiment, 120, 233, 239, 241
Tenth Pennsylvania Reserves, 200
Third Minnesota Infantry Regiment, 220, 227
Third Rhode Island Heavy Artillery, 101, 114
Thirteenth Ohio Infantry Regiment, 97

Thirty-Eighth Ohio Infantry Regiment, 97
Thirty-Fifth Indiana Infantry Regiment, 86
Thirty-Fifth Infantry Regiment U.S.C.T., 75
Thirty-Second Wisconsin Infantry Regiment, 238
Thomas, Chaplain Joseph Conable, 96
Thomas, Major General George Henry, 138
Thomas, Major General Lorenzo, 227
Thomas. Chaplain Chauncey Boardman, 231-232
Tod, Governor David, 49
Toucey, Isaac, 67
Trumbull, Chaplain Henry Clay, xiii, 120, 133-135, 233-237, 238, 242
Turchin, Brigadier General John Basil, 138
Turner, Chaplain Henry McNeal, xvi, 184, 238
Twelfth Connecticut Infantry Regiment, 239
Twelfth Michigan Infantry Regiment, 145
Twelfth Pennsylvania Cavalry Regiment, 186
Twenty-Fifth Massachusetts Infantry Regiment, 39, 59, 60
Twenty-First Connecticut Infantry Regiment, 197, 241
Twenty-First Iowa Infantry Regiment, xvi
Twenty-First New York Infantry Regiment, 28
Twenty-Ninth Ohio Infantry Regiment, 39
Twenty-Second Massachusetts Infantry Regiment, 2
Twenty-Seventh Connecticut Infantry Regiment, 241

Twenty-Third Kentucky Infantry Regiment, 97
Twenty-Third New York Infantry Regiment, 81
Tyler, Brigadier General Erastus Barnard, 55

Uniform of chaplain, xv, 32, 88, 103

Van Horne, Chaplain Thomas Budd, 97
Veteran volunteers, 162
Vincent, Brigadier General Strong, 136

Ware, Rev. John Fothergill Waterhouse, 5, 8
Wayland, Chaplain Heman Lincoln, 119
Weed, Brigadier General Stephen Hinsdale, 136
Wessells, Brigadier General Henry Walton, 212
White, Chaplain Henry Sumner, 117
Whitehead, Chaplain John Milton, xvi
Wiley, Private Joseph, 52
Winchester Eight, 185-186
Winthrop, Private Theodore, 69
Wooley, Chaplain Joseph J., 13

Yates, Governor Richard, 151
Young, Corporal Friend, 52